What Th

"These frightenin   big
ideas. In the beautifully *used Supercommunities*, Keith Harrison-Broninski explains how very contemporary digital tools can be used to reinforce old and important ideas about community and common interest. Our politics and economics of 'me' must return to being about 'we', and this book shows us how."
Martin Parker, Professor & Lead, the Bristol Inclusive Economy initiative

"Keith draws on rich, eclectic sources to steer readers artfully through humanity's stumbling efforts to approximate the 'summum bonum', the good life of meaning and connectedness we almost universally aspire to, asking a simple question: are we now able to meld what we learned in psychology, micro-economics and organizational behavior with the new possibilities offered by technology and the information age to (re-)create a shared living which is spiritually nourishing and paradoxically natural? Supercommunities is timely and compelling as we look to build back better following the COVID-19 pandemic with resilience 'baked in' to our social and economic order."
David Hayward Evans, Senior Advisor, UNICEF

"Yes, Supercommunities is a handbook for the 21st century; more importantly, however, this is a handy book on how to fix our increasingly complex and troubling future. Handy and timely. An essential read."
Andrew Keen, Author, entrepreneur, and host of KEEN ON podcast

"A truly important piece by Keith Harrison-Broninski on how small communities can thrive under stress. As we ponder what we can do in our own enclaves to make a positive impact under truly daunting stressors, this is the kind of book we need right now."

Phaedra Boinodiris, FRSA, Author & Trust in AI Business Transformation Leader, IBM

"Systems theory has told us for decades that optimizing a subsystem always results in the suboptimization of the system it resides in, always. Yet our system of society has insisted on focusing on optimizing its many subsystems of government, business, education, healthcare, media, science, even art and sport. The consequences have been increasing inequity and balkanization of society across all its dimensions, along with increased fragility of all its parts. Systems theory also tells us that optimization of the system requires a dynamic network of interactions among all the subsystems and elements that make up the subsystems, where the efficacy of the relationships self-organize and trump the efficiency of the subsystems. Keith Harrison-Broninski has synthesized and distilled the many elements of this into *Supercommunities*, the ultimate self-help book for society and a handbook for those who want to understand how to change it."

Jim Stikeleather, Author & Fmr. Chief Innovation Officer at Dell

"Collaboration alone buys better outcomes for individuals, but the real big deal is applying collaboration to communities. This book describes the nature of communities and gives a significant prescription for creating and maintaining healthy communities. Digital technologies can accelerate results for all kinds of communities in the dynamic world we live in today."

Jim Sinur, Digital Business Analyst and Fmr. Vice President, Gartner

"The current Digital Transition of society is also a shift from 'command-and-Control to a 'connect-and-collaborate' society where the norm is 'What do we have in common?' rather than 'What sets us apart?' - i.e., the community model will become the norm. This book explains where it comes from and how you can keep on going."

Frits Bussemaker, Business Community Builder & D1G1T4L C0NN3CT0R

"In *Supercommunities*, Keith succinctly targets the escalating challenges and risks facing communities today and well into the future. His perspective on communities needing to independently organize and become self-sustaining entities is prophetic. He raises issues that communities should begin to consider now because the future is closer than we think."

William Ulrich, Author & President of the Business Architect Guild

"In these difficult times, when many process people are focused on automation and AI, it's important to maintain our sense of balance. Processes work because people make them work. While many process gurus focus on IT, Keith Harrison-Broninski has maintained a steady focus on the human side of making organizations productive and effective. Supercommunities is a thought-provoking contribution to the process literature."

Paul Harmon, Author and Executive Editor of BPTrends

Supercommunities

A handbook for the 21st century

Keith Harrison-Broninski

Meghan-Kiffer Press
Tampa, Florida, USA
www.mkpress.com
Innovation at the Intersection of Business and Technology

Supercommunities

A handbook for the 21st century

Keith Harrison-Broninski

Meghan-Kiffer Press
Tampa, Florida, USA
www.mkpress.com
Innovation at the Intersection of Business and Technology

Publisher's Cataloging-in-Publication Data
Harrison-Broninski, Keith.
Supercommunities – A handbook for the 21st century — 1st ed.
p. cm.
Includes bibliographic references, appendices and index.

1. Wellbeing. 2. Well-being. 3. Welfare (Personal well-being). 4. Community development. 5. Community organization. 6. Community property. 7. Collaborative economy. 8. Public ownership. 9. Municipal ownership. 10. Capital market. 11. Strategic planning. 12. Measurement. 13. Social change. 14. Change, Social. 15. Cultural change. 16. Cultural transformation. 17. Societal change. 18. Socio-cultural change. 19. Technological innovation. 20. Sustainability 21. Sustainable development. 22. Development, Sustainable. 23. Ecologically sustainable development. 24. Economic development, Sustainable. 25. Economic sustainability. 26. Smart growth. 27. Sustainable economic development. 28. Sustainable development reporting. I. Harrison-Broninski, Keith. II. Title.

Published by Meghan-Kiffer Press
310 East Fern Street — Suite G
Tampa, FL 33604 USA

Any product mentioned in this book may be a trademark of its company.

Meghan-Kiffer books are available at special quantity discounts for corporate education and training use. For more information write Special Sales, Meghan-Kiffer Press, Suite G, 310 East Fern Street, Tampa, Florida 33604 or email mkpress@tampabay.rr.com

Meghan-Kiffer Press
Tampa, Florida, USA
www.mkpress.com
Innovation at the Intersection of Business and Technology

To Ann, Bertie, and Daisy
for giving me many of the books referenced here, and discussing them at innumerable mealtimes both helpfully and patiently.

Me. We.
— Muhammad Ali, 1975 (the shortest poem ever written in the English language)

Table of Contents

Table of Figures

All the images in this book are available for download as a single zip file, from the following link:

www.supercommunities.info

Acknowledgements

Before I thought of writing a book, PETER FINGAR commissioned one and set me on the road as a keynote speaker.

DR NICK GAUNT of the NHS Institute of Innovation and Improvement saw how the ideas could underpin a systemic solution to innovation in the NHS.

ROB CHESTERS of the NHS England Innovation Team helped make NHS GATHER a reality.

TOO MANY NHS STAFF TO LIST HERE contributed innovations, many of which proved the power of community to enable wellness.

PETER MACFADYEN of Frome Town Council, LOU MATTER of the RSA, DR PAUL TURNER, DR EWAN HAMNETT, and DR RICHARD KIMBERLEE saw the potential of Town Digital Hub to release this power.

CLEO LAKE, JIM COOK, DAVE WHITE, and TED FOWLER helped turn a vision for Stakeitback into a simple, concrete way to fund good things, see the impact, and get a return.

Heartfelt thanks to them all.

Foreword by Vint Cerf and Matthew Taylor

Matthew Taylor, Chief Executive, The RSA

Reflecting his own many talents and interests, Keith Harrison-Broninski's 'Supercommunities' is a fascinating, eclectic and powerful call for us to rebuild society from the bottom up. As we move into a post Covid period still facing the many challenges that existed before the pandemic there is a need for us to rethink our ideas of human and social flourishing and to respond to the palpable public appetite for new ways of thinking.

Ranging from ancient history to economics to psychology to public policy 'Supercommunities' is both authoritative and highly readable. It puts our current challenges in context, shows why change is necessary and provides a trove of practical ideas for change makers.

Figure 1: Matthew Taylor, Chief Executive, The RSA

Vint Cerf, Co-Inventor of the Internet

There are trends, forces and formulas that are driving social and economic conditions onto a precarious knife's edge. On the one side, dramatic growth in wealth and well-being and on the other a precipitate decline in both. Worse, some of those forces foretell serious and hazardous conditions brought about by centuries of environmental neglect. Failure to appreciate the power of these phenomena can only result in catastrophic consequences for most of the population of the planet. But it is not too late to recognize and set into motion processes to counter the worst-case potential outcomes. Supercommunities offers a path away from social and economic meltdown, but following that path will require cooperation and consensus on a scale unprecedented in human history.

Every tool at our disposal will be needed to accumulate data, formulate and test theories, and willingness to cast aside old nostrums in favor of new remedies. Old economic theories of ownership and wealth distribution will need revision if all the world's population is to thrive in the remainder of the 21st Century. The power of computation and access to it through the global Internet offers us one collaborative means by which to tackle the complex problems now facing our modern world. It is very late but perhaps not too late to adopt new directions, recognizing the common threat posed by our present, inequitable and ultimately disastrous practices.

We will need to replace short-term thinking with long term planning and execution if we are to regain upward motion towards common benefit for everyone on Spaceship Earth. To begin, read this book!

Figure 2: Vint Cerf, Co-Inventor of the Internet

Preface

By 2050, almost half the world's population, in both developed and developing economies, will be living on some form of knife edge. To address this, we must create more cohesive and caring communities.

Experts tell us that the world is not only a better place than it was two hundred years ago, but continues to improve. Charts from researchers at the University of Oxford show how many of each hundred people worldwide were in extreme poverty, had basic education, could read, lived in a democracy, had been vaccinated, or died before the age of five from 1820 to 2015:

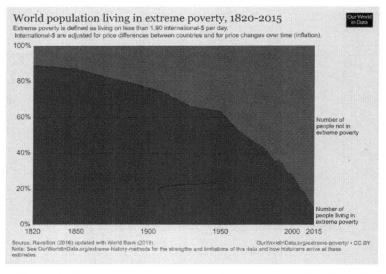

Figure 3: Extreme poverty over the last two centuries, Oxford Martin Programme on Global Development (University of Oxford)

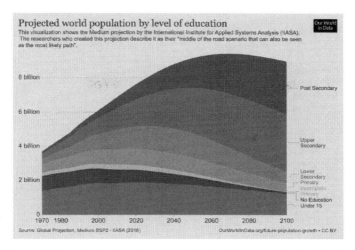

Figure 4: Level of education over the last two centuries, Oxford Martin Programme on Global Development (University of Oxford)

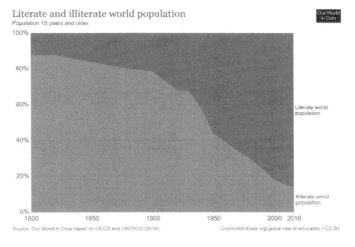

Figure 5: Literacy over the last two centuries, Oxford Martin Programme on Global Development (University of Oxford)

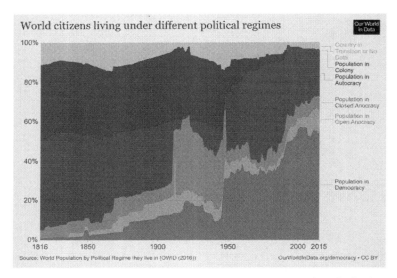

Figure 6: Political regimes over the last two centuries, Oxford Martin Programme on Global Development (University of Oxford)

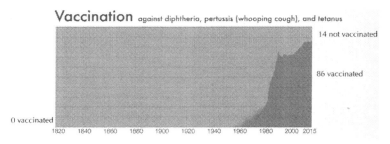

Figure 7: Vaccination over the last two centuries, Oxford Martin Programme on Global Development (University of Oxford)

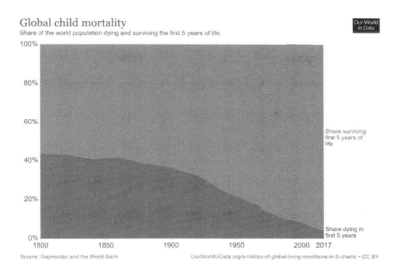

Figure 8: Child mortality over the last two centuries, Oxford Martin Programme on Global Development (University of Oxford)

Each area shows dramatic and continuous improvements. So, it's puzzling for the researchers also to find that more than nine out of ten people do not think that the world is getting better. They blame this on media coverage of events such as plane crashes, terrorism attacks, and natural disasters. But is this fair? We know from their own statistics that most people are now educated. Are nine out of ten people really so naïve as to overlook massive social improvements during their own lifetime because they read about bad things that happen in the world?

Statistics are inherently tricky. Personally, I've held a grudge against them ever since a school career assessment concluded I should become a statistician. At the time, this didn't seem like a thrilling ambition — could any job possibly be more boring? And how could you change the world with numbers? Now, having come across people who do exactly that, I am coming around to the idea (although it's too late in the day for me to make career choices). Statistics can be exciting, leading you to real human stories, and powerful, helping you make a difference. They can also be misleading and dangerous.

The process of observing the world and turning those observations first into data, then into information, then into knowledge, and finally into wisdom, is fraught with difficulty and open to challenge at every stage. Statistical methods are not easily understood by the layman and can be used in arcane ways to create multiple versions of any truth, including versions that seem opposite to one another — they are like a lens, that sharpens your view of one point in a picture while blurring the rest of it. A good example is poverty.

A press release from the World Bank in 2018 picked up on the statistics above, declaring with pride that the percentage of people living in extreme poverty globally fell to a new low of 10 percent in 2015.[1] Compared to 1820 when poverty is estimated to have been around 95 percent,[2] this is impressive. However, the World Bank also finds that poverty reduction has slowed or even reversed for many nations, and the disclaimer at the end of their statement acknowledges that "Access to good schools, health care, electricity, safe water, and other critical services remains elusive for many people, often determined by socioeconomic status, gender, ethnicity, and geography. The multidimensional view — wherein other aspects such as education, access to basic utilities, health care, and security are included — reveals a world in which poverty is a much broader, more entrenched problem. The share of poor according to a multidimensional definition that includes consumption, education, and access to basic utilities is approximately 50 percent higher than when relying solely on monetary poverty. Moreover, for those who have been able to move out of poverty, progress is often temporary: Economic shocks, food insecurity and climate change threaten to rob them of their hard-won gains and force them back into poverty. It will be critical to find ways to tackle these issues as we make progress toward 2030."

Other research supports this more pessimistic view. A different research group at Oxford University, the Oxford Poverty and Human Development Initiative, reports that 17 percent of the world's population live in multidimensional poverty[3] and the Organisation for Economic Co-operation and Development shows 23 percent of us living in "fragile contexts", a number predicted to rise to 28 percent by 2030 and 34 percent by 2050.[4] The concept of fragility as promoted by the Organisation for Economic Co-operation and Development is largely about environments perceived as risky due to violent conflict, forced displacement, natural disaster, or other external causes. The majority of fragile contexts are situated in sub-Saharan Africa (35), followed by the Middle East and North Africa (9), Asia and Oceania (10), and Latin America and the Caribbean (4). However, many people living outside fragile contexts, in developed economies such as the US and Europe, also feel themselves to be living on a knife edge.

A useful tracker of such trends is the recent rise in importance of benevolent funds in the UK. Some of these were created by Victorian philanthropists to provide assistance to struggling gentlefolk, such as families in which the breadwinner had died, or to alleviate the condition of the starving and destitute of the parish. Others predated trade unions in offering crisis support to members of occupational groups, such as sailors, vicars, accountants, actors, musicians, and engineers. Many have now rebranded to adopt names more acceptable to modern ears — for example, the Society for the Assistance of Ladies in Reduced Circumstances is now the Smallwood Trust, and the Distressed Gentlefolks' Aid Association renamed itself Turn2Us.

Benevolent funds report a surge in demand, with half a million people coming to them for help and hardship grants in 2018-19[5] — and the type of demand is changing. They once catered mainly for people nearing end of life, but now their beneficiaries are younger, often fully employed but having never been able to amass savings to cover them for unexpected events. With the decline of the welfare state (about which more below), many people of working age are just about managing. A sudden illness, job loss, or family emergency can trigger a spiraling crisis, just as it did in the nineteenth century and earlier. Charles Dickens became one of the wealthiest men of his age, with a net worth in today's money of about 85 million dollars, but was a lifelong workaholic and social reformer after the formative experience of being sent to stick labels on bottles in a blacking factory at age 12 when his father, mother, and younger siblings were incarcerated for a debt of 40 pounds.

Large-scale research released in 2017 showed that 30 percent of the UK population are "living below an adequate standard of living and are just about managing at best".[6] At the time of the report, the number of such people was increasing dramatically. Between now and 2050, it may go up or down, and the story may be different from one developed country to another. However, as a densely-populated and highly-developed country, the UK of today seems a reasonable yardstick for future expectations. To get an idea of how many people will be economically fragile in 2050, how many people should we apply this 30 percent figure to?

We'll avoid double counting of people in fragile contexts by looking only at a few economies: North America, Europe, China, and India. All these will be developed by 2050, and none include fragile contexts. By 2050 the total world population is projected to be 9.7 billion and the population of our chosen areas to be around 3.2 billion[7] — applying the 30 percent rule and doing the sums, 10 percent of people on the planet in 2050 will be economically fragile even though they do not live in a fragile context. Adding this to the 34 percent who will be living in a fragile context, three decades from now, we can reasonably assume that 44 percent of people on the planet will be living on some form of knife edge.

If this number-crunching gave you a headache, apologies, but we've come out the other side with a lot to think about. There's a big difference between 10 percent, the one tenth of the world that will be in financial poverty by 2050, and 44 percent, the almost half of the world that will be living at high risk in 2050. Which number should we use as a guideline to judge where society is going? And just as importantly — does the rise in fragile living mean that in some way we have changed direction, back in certain respects towards 1820?

It is hard to answer such questions definitively using statistics, since multidimensional fragility is a new concept, and at this time only a few years of data have been gathered and analyzed. However, while the formulation of the problem may be new, the issue itself is as old as human society, in which there is an eternal tension at play. We expect certain things from the decision-makers in society, and in order to provide them, they need us to provide certain things in return — money in the form of taxes or its equivalent in the form of labour. History could be interpreted as the story of how societies compete for these things with their richest members. If you have more wealth than you need to cover living expenses, you can put it to productive use by investing in trade for profit or property for rent. Success will make you less inclined to pay tax and more able to avoid doing so, as well as in more need of a workforce and more able to pay for it. Your way forward will be made easier by the travails of those who only have just what they need to cover living expenses, since circumstance will at some point derail their lives, offering you a chance to obtain their property and labour at bargain prices. How different decision-makers have tried to maintain society in the face of competition with private interests for tax revenues and workforce is the story underpinning all of human history.

It's interesting to look back at how the earliest Bronze Age societies recognized the way in which external events turned people who are just about managing into people who are not managing at all, others used this as an opportunity to accumulate wealth, and the resulting oligarchic power destabilized society leading eventually to its breakdown. I'll explore this later on. However, modern people who are at risk from external events, whether in a developing or developed economy, don't need a history lesson to know the risks of their personal situation. They are like

Victorians in having no safety net. After what economists call the Second Great Contraction in 2008 (the first being the Great Depression of the 1930s) followed a decade later by the global coronavirus pandemic, fragility is up close and personal for many people everywhere. They may appreciate intellectually that economic growth over the last two centuries has massively improved living conditions worldwide, but at the same time see for themselves how some of the forces that generated such changes are now acting in a counter-productive way.

So, there is no reason to be complacent. Rather, we must examine current mega-trends closely to understand their impact and the direction of travel. This does mean we have occasionally to set our brains to work on the numbers. Often the devil is in the detail, and statistics by their nature obscure details. It also means bringing numbers together from different sources, and asking what lies behind them, so as to get a bigger and richer picture that tells a human story.

It's worth noting, for example, that even the contexts identified by researchers as fragile are mostly in middle-income countries, so understanding the direction of travel isn't about looking at changes in standard of living as measured by things like being educated or owning a washing machine. Fragility is more closely connected to a holistic concept, wellness. This book discusses the nature of wellness (which is not the same as healthiness or happiness), its costs, and the social, political, and economic changes that are affecting it globally. The book also proposes a path to making life better for people — a path that you, reader, can help your own community take at local level, wherever you live in the world.

Apart from occasionally hurting your head with statistics, and hopefully making up for it by entertaining you, this book aims to do several things.

First, if you're interested in progressive thinking, either as a supporter or as an opponent, it will save you time. In the last couple of decades, important new ideas have emerged in biology, psychology, sociology, healthcare, economics, politics, and other social sciences. These ideas are inter-related, have wide-ranging impact, and stem from solid research. If you would like to get up to speed without working your way through a reading list, and to have a simple explanation of how different ideas fit together, this book will provide the overview you need. If you then want to learn more, the **Further reading** section suggests some books to get hold of.

Second, this book isn't just a summary but also a practical plan of action. Any community — and I'll discuss this word in depth along the way — can follow the guidance in this book to make life more fulfilling for its members, by becoming what I call a supercommunity. The book helps you do this by providing short descriptions of what to do, with examples showing why it works. You can share this information with people and organisations in your own community, and it will help you all get started.

Third, this plan of action and the theory of collaborative work that underpins it are innovations, supported by a new way of financing good things that opens up a huge global investment market. Some of the original ideas covered here are explained in books, papers, and articles I've published along the way, but this book brings it all together for the first time, omitting the parts that most people aren't particularly interested in, such as underpinning mathematics and accompanying technologies.

Fourth, and finally, both the plan and the theory are based on my personal experience of working with hundreds of organisations of many types, worldwide, as what might loosely be called an enabler of project success. This could be considered action research, but I'm not an academic. Although I was encouraged to follow that path on completing university studies, I felt strongly at the time that this would be the wrong thing for me personally. Back then I didn't really understand why, but thirty years later, having worked with academics from various disciplines, I think it was because the need to become sufficiently expert in one discipline to succeed professionally makes it very hard to do true cross-disciplinary research.

It makes life much easier for teachers to divide knowledge into distinct subjects for the purposes of education, but this makes it hard to find well-rounded answers to the big problems, such as how to deal with global inequality of wealth and the low wellness this causes across society. It also makes it hard to get research grants for a topic that doesn't fit neatly into any particular subject, such as how people from different organisations can work together productively. Having said this, my first training was as a mathematician (the school careers advice wasn't too far off the mark, was it), and the approach to problem solving that you learn from studying maths has always been incredibly helpful.

Mathematicians are trained to deal with difficult problems by looking for patterns of structure and behaviour, then drawing on wide-ranging assortments of tools to draw conclusions from these patterns. The basic method is to welcome complexity. Having lots of detailed examples that are apparently different from one another is not bewildering but essential to a mathematician, since it makes it possible to see what, at heart, all the examples have in common. This book deals with a particularly wicked problem — how to reshape social life so as to benefit more people, without upsetting any apple carts along the way, and without relying on the magical injection of large amounts of money or support from governments or corporations. We will see that the trick is to start small, to put trust in those around us, and to believe in the power of collaborative action.

Trust and belief in others really matter. The book proposes that in order to increase the number of people who believe life is actually getting better, we need to create more cohesive and caring communities. An important aspect of multidimensional poverty is lack of community connection, which this book claims is not only vital in itself but automatically leads to other benefits such as better living conditions and a healthier ecosystem. The long journey of civilization from the first cities in the ancient Near East to the Internet, gene editing, and artificial intelligence has left many people without a strong sense of what it is to live in a community, but this sense is not by any means lost — and restoring it is a project we can all take part in.

Introduction

What this book is about

To become antifragile, communities need to develop local modifications of the market economy based on social enterprise, in which participants aim not only to make profit but also to benefit people and the planet.

Industrialization of society over the last few hundred years has brought people together from across the planet. But has economic growth brought people together locally? And although living standards have gone up enormously, for many of us it could all be taken away, without warning, at any moment.

For business to deliver its real potential value to humanity, we have to find a way to trade that is profitable to shareholders but delivers more than profits to shareholders. Business has to organize itself so that its effects also include building wellness for those with life challenges, helping grass roots organisations work together effectively, and diverting towards good things more of the vast funds invested into global capital markets. Business can and must restore to the centre of daily life the magic that makes humans human: our social relationships with one another.

Many people know from experience that feeling part of a community is a vital part of a fulfilled life, and this is borne out by research showing that in fact community connection is the most important factor of all.[8] What may be a new idea to modern people is that those without high wealth — which is most of us — will have to start looking at local, rather than national or international, resources for the support they need in order to thrive, and that where such resources do not yet exist, they must work together with others in their community to help create them. Political and economic forces have combined to leave states without the means to provide fully for citizens who face life challenges, and most corporations without the need to help, so the best thing we can do is face up to this, change our expectations, and work out how to turn the situation around. In particular, communities need to adapt for their own purposes the market economy that is moving national resources into private hands, and help develop local modifications of this economy based on social enterprise, in which participants aim not only to make profit but also to benefit people and the planet.

Models are emerging for this way of making things work, including diverse new forms of ownership, but large parts of the picture are still in flux, including fundamental aspects such as how the money flows and how the impact of social changes should be measured. Some cities are experimenting with new ways of creating and maintaining their infrastructure by developing what is known as a circular economy — after years of sustained effort in cities such as Cleveland, US and Preston, UK, evidence suggests that this has multiple benefits, including for the most disadvantaged citizens, but there is a long way to go, with many questions still remaining about how best to integrate local and global markets. Benefits themselves are hard to measure, with a wide range of techniques on offer that range from monitoring community capitals — natural, human, and industrial enablers of value delivery — to assessment of local progress against targets such as the UN Sustainable

Development Goals. And what is a community anyway? If we look at geographic communities, what size are we talking about, and is it measured in people or area? What about communities of common interest such as faith, or of common challenges such as disability or migration?

More generally, reliance on community rather than government is a huge shift for most people in the developed world, as well as for many in the developing world, since most of us have grown up with certain fundamental expectations. We tend to assume that part of a government's duty is to provide its citizens with things that we call human rights, and that tax revenues give it the resources with which to pay for this. This notion is almost as old as civilization itself, but has changed a lot over five thousand years, continues to do so, and some recent changes have been counter-intuitive, with impacts that may be enduring. To see this, let's take the long view and get some proper context. We'll start with a deal that is as old as history — tax for rights.

The long story of human rights

In order to prevent inequality that led to social breakdown, early societies protected individuals from unmanageable debt. Human rights go further in some ways now but no longer include debt protection.

Much of what we know about the first civilizations relates to records of how complex and diverse taxes were collected, since this was the subject of many early written records. A good example is the first known civilization of all, the cities that began developing around 3300 BC along the banks of the Tigris and Euphrates rivers in the area of

modern-day Iraq. Clay tablets surviving from ancient Mesopotamia describe taxes on livestock, the boat trade, fishing, even funerals, and a particularly onerous tax called
"burden", under which each head of a household owed the
government several months of labour service per year. If he
were lucky, he might spend this time harvesting the government's barley fields or digging silt out of canals. If he
were unlucky, he had to join the army and fight wars
abroad, perhaps never to return home at all.

Mesopotamia was what we would nowadays call a high
tax economy, but it wasn't a one-way deal. In return for
their contributions, people were provided with certain protections by the king. We have a good description of the deal
between state and citizen in the laws set down by the Baby-
lonian king Hammurabi, who reigned from 1792 to 1750
BC. His Code, inscribed on a seven-foot-tall black pillar
that you can see on display in the Louvre Museum, Paris,
goes into some detail about taxes and the penalties for non-
payment. For example, the penalty for abandoning your
field, orchard or home because of the labour obligation and
running away was forfeiture of your family's land and livelihood. This is among the least gruesome of Hammurabi's
favored punishments, which often demanded removal of
the guilty party's tongue, hands, breasts, eye or ear. Death
was another popular choice by Hammurabi. However, his
Code also establishes rights relating to property, divorce,
and even minimum wage — for example, in the extensive
regulations relating to health care.[9]

In ancient Babylon, there were several types of physician, what we would nowadays call specialists, who had to
make their services available to all — they were only allowed to refuse service to a patient deemed likely to die.

Fees were standardized, with a sliding scale based on ability to pay and seriousness of the procedure. For example, the fee for eye surgery ranged from 10 shekels for a gentleman (equivalent to a year's income for a craftsman) to 5 shekels for a freeman (a year's rent for a middle-class dwelling) to 2 shekels for a slave (about what it cost to make a wooden door).

There was no extra charge for medications, so prescriptions were free. Slaves were as entitled to health care as anyone else, and their masters had to pay. What is more, fees were payable only if the outcome was successful, and if a physician erred either by doing something wrong or omitting to do something right, his fingers or hands were cut off — a fairly strong encouragement for high quality of care. Similar injunctions applied to veterinarians, so even animals (or at least animal owners) figured in this early vision of rights.

Figure 9: The Code of Hammurabi

A particular focus of Hammurabi's Code was protection of individuals from unmanageable debt. In ancient times, there was a clear distinction between loans that made productive use of capital by financing trading ventures (denominated in silver) and debts that people fell into in times of hardship in order to meet living expenses and tax payments (denominated in grain). The first economies recognized that every now and then the latter got out of control due to what we would now call Acts of God – harvests would fail due to drought, storms, or pests, farmers would be called away to war, disease would lay people low, raiders would decimate the countryside, and so on. Following such events, there was a tendency for people to take out loans to cover taxes and subsistence. Since such loans did not generate profit for the debtor, often they could not keep up with interest payments and had to default, resulting in private means of subsistence falling into the hands of moneylenders and people selling themselves and their families into debt bondage. This not only caused misery but also a growth in private wealth at the expense of state tax revenues, as well as a decline in the free population able to serve in armies. The effect was social turmoil as opportunistic tribes attacked border territories. What we would now call multidimensional fragility resulted in instability, so the Code of Hammurabi and other laws of the time laid out various protections against those who sought to profit from economic distress.[10]

Only the owner of a field could harvest it, not a creditor – meaning the debtor paid their rents or taxes before paying down debts. Creditors could not foreclose on land on which taxes were payable. Creditors could not collect grain debts on the threshing floor or from the granary without the owner's permission. Laws such as these aimed to prevent debt obligations removing people's livelihood, except in cases of negligence or where punishment was warranted. In ancient economies, rulers would also proclaim general debt cancellations when it was necessary to restore society to a stable state. By these means the Near East preserved widespread economic prosperity for over two thousand years, until wealthy private interests started to gain the upper hand in the middle second millennium BC. I'll return to debt later.

The Code of Hammurabi is the best-known Sumerian code now but was itself descended from earlier ones,[11] so the tax-for-rights story goes back pretty much to the dawn of civilization. Hammurabi's Code is the ancestor of religious stipulations such as those found in the Old Testament (600-400 BC), which come closer to what we understand now as human rights.[12] For example, only the first four of the Ten Commandments mention God and the fifth is about respecting your parents. The last five are instructions not to murder, cheat on your spouse, steal, perjure yourself, or seek to acquire other people's property — the memorable reminder in the King James Bible not to covet thy neighbor's ass, much loved by schoolchildren but sadly removed from modern translations. All these are responsibilities people have towards each other under modern legal systems. These and other rules of justice in the Old Testament apply to friend and stranger, free and slave, man and woman, young and old, rich and poor, healthy and disabled, employers and employees, widows and children. They even apply to foreigners.

Figure 10: The oldest extant copy of the Decalogue, dated between 30 and 1 BC

Similar codes are found in varying form among other ancient religions. Thousands of years ago, civilizations took it as the duty of those in authority to provide an economic and social justice system that maintained the sanctity of life and showed compassion for those who suffer, but this was only the start of a long journey. The bar for human rights ratcheted up several notches in the revolutionary seventeenth and eighteenth centuries, with the English Bill of Rights (1689), United States Bill of Rights (1789), and French Declaration of the Rights of Man and of the Citizen (1789).

Of the many associated books, the most famous is "Rights of Man" by Thomas Paine (1791), which gained the author a death sentence in his home country, England, to which he never returned. Paine had a gift for making himself unwelcome — American intervention got him out of French revolution imprisonment and into the fledgling United States, where he then alienated even more people by publishing a diatribe against organized religion. Only six people attended his funeral, but his readership was wide and his key ideas endured. The new conception of rights set out by Paine and others went further than justice and terms of employment, to stipulate that government responsibilities included financial support for the poor, universal education, provision for the elderly, and assurance of employment.

Over the next hundred years, these Enlightenment ideas gradually normalized, and gave rise to government welfare programs. In the late nineteenth century, Germany under Bismarck introduced pensions and various forms of insurance for workers, partly to stop them emigrating to the to the United States where wages were higher. Similar reforms aimed at quelling popular unrest were introduced in the United Kingdom by the Liberal government of the early twentieth century, along with free school meals and labour exchanges that helped people find work. In both countries, a strong motivation for reform was the emerging electoral threat of socialism. Then as now, political leaders were terrified of the idea that the state might take the means of production out of private hands and plan centrally how the resulting outputs were distributed, which went against liberal economic principles of using markets to allocate resources, and was unlikely to benefit the vested business interests on whose support they relied.

The ideas most closely associated with state largesse in the twentieth century are those of John Maynard Keynes, generally considered the founder of modern economic theory. The debate continues over whether or not Keynes was a liberal who wanted to save capitalism or a (non-Marxist) socialist.[13] However, the politicians who initially accepted his ideas were quite clear about their own position. US President Roosevelt came to accept Keynes' views, introducing a far-reaching welfare program during the Great Depression, but always defended himself staunchly against accusations of being a socialist, claiming his actions were in defense of private enterprise: "It is following tradition as well as necessity, if Government strives to put idle money and idle men to work, to increase our public wealth and to build up the health and strength of the people — and to help our system of private enterprise to function."[14]

Figure 11: John Maynard Keynes, generally considered the founder of modern economics

Despite all attempts to stave off socialist power, the United Kingdom elected a Labour government after World War Two, which immediately introduced structural reforms to implement William Beveridge's vision of a society entirely without poverty. This first socialist government in the UK didn't last long, but its ambitions persisted, and in the 1960s the United States followed suit. President Johnson's State of the Union address on 8 January 1964 introduced "Great Society" legislation with the stirring words, "I have called for a national war on poverty. Our objective: total victory."[15]

Other countries joined Johnson's war, at least in principle, collaborating to create documents such as the Universal Declaration of Human Rights (1948), European Convention on Human Rights (1950), and International Bill of Human Rights (1976). The economic, social and cultural rights recognized in articles 22 to 27 of the latter go well beyond finances and health to include the right to social security, the right to work, the right to equal pay for equal work, the right to a standard of living adequate for health and well-being, the right to education, the right to rest and leisure, and the right to participate in the cultural life of the community.[16] Even downtime activities were now considered a human right. Unfortunately, however, this utopian project didn't last long.

A new conception of human rights

The economic shock of the 1970s led to commercial interests determining government policies. The rules of society are now shaped by businesses, whose access to a global workforce means they can disregard social concerns.

Helped by the economic boom of post-war reconstruction, by the 1970s it seemed that an epic historical journey was finally coming to fruition. States were intervening as necessary throughout the lives of their citizens, financially and otherwise, so as to ensure their holistic welfare from cradle to grave. However, a counter-current had been brewing for decades, and as it came to the forefront, perceptions shifted of the rights that states were expected to protect. We can follow this evolution by looking at the changing reception given to the ideas of one of the twentieth century's most influential thinkers.

The economist and political writer Friedrich August Hayek was born in 1899 and lived until 1992, so he grew up in the democratic, if militaristic, environment of the long European nineteenth century's tail end, but began his adult life in a world ravaged by totalitarian regimes, a step change that set the direction of his life. Like many intellectuals of his generation, he was drawn to socialist ideas in his youth. However, on starting postgraduate studies in the 1920s, Hayek was exposed to new economic thinking emerging in his native Austria, and had a damascene conversion to free market ideals. He became a radical figure, and remained out of sync with his times for much of his life.

Figure 12: Friedrich August Hayek, author of "The Road to Serfdom" (1944)

Hayek didn't see political views as a line running from communism and its milder version socialism on the left, through laissez-faire economics in the centre, to conservatism and its more extreme version fascism on the right. He saw only two distinct viewpoints. On the one side Hayek saw liberalism, in which producers worked together informally to keep the world's economy on an even keel, simply through participating in dispassionate market transactions. They set their prices based on detailed knowledge of what local consumers would pay, and the market itself (given the necessary autonomy by governments) ironed out fluctuations in supply and demand quickly and effectively. For the world to become a self-regulating system, it was vital for everyone to play the market in what liberal economists considered to be a rational manner, by which they meant acting out of pure self-interest.

In Hayek's liberal world everyone retains complete freedom of thought and action, in contrast to the other possible world he saw — any political arrangement in which governments intervene in markets. Hayek described socialist economic planning aimed at even-handed distribution of national outputs and fascist war machines aimed at creating powerful nation states as cut from the same cloth, both leading inevitably to thought controls by totalitarian government: "The most effective way of making everybody serve the single system of ends towards which the social plan is directed is to make everybody believe in those ends."[17]

Hayek's short and powerfully argued book "The Road to Serfdom" sold in the millions and was widely praised, but it took a long time for policy makers to be convinced of the argument. In a world decimated by world wars, with a depression in between, the victorious governments felt they had a strong role to play in rebuilding a fair and prosperous global society. And no-one wanted more populist uprisings. So, governments of the winning states not only intervened socially to create the welfare and healthcare schemes described above, but also economically to invest in new infrastructure and maintain price controls that kept businesses in the black. Three decades of economic growth ensued, and in developed countries such as the UK and US, people had, as British Prime Minister Harold Macmillan enthused in

1957, "never had it so good".

From the 1930s to the 1970s, governments saw them-selves as the key players in the economic health of their countries. This was a dramatic shift from mainstream eco-nomic ideas until then, which held government to be un-productive, and despite strong arguments then and again now for government being a key value creator,[18] it was to be short-lived. The pendulum swung back in the economic chaos of the 1970s, when inflation and unemployment raged across the developed world. The root cause, as it is today in the Eurozone, was trade imbalances — what hap-pens when some countries export much more than they import. This wasn't a new problem.

At the Bretton Woods Conference held by the Allied powers in 1944 to set out a new international order for money and finance after the second world war, Keynes had proposed the creation of a common unit of account for international trade, the Bancor, with rules governing its use that would protect the global economy from trade imbal-ances through collaboration among nations worldwide. Keynes' system was clever and farsighted but out of tune with the political climate of the day. The dominant player was the US, which saw itself as responsible for winning a world war and was in no mood to hand over the reins to an international coalition.

An indication of US thinking about foreign policy in the 1940s can be gained from a report by US Policy Plan-ning Staff in 1948, top-secret at the time, which observes: "we have about 50% of the world's wealth but only 6.3% of its population. This disparity is particularly great as between ourselves and the peoples of Asia. In this situation, we can-not fail to be the object of envy and resentment. Our real task in the coming period is to devise a pattern of relationships which will permit us to maintain this position of disparity without positive detriment to our national security. To do so, we will have to dispense with all sentimentality and day-dreaming; and our attention will have to be concentrated everywhere on our immediate national objectives. We need not deceive ourselves that we can afford today the luxury of altruism and world-benefaction."[19]

Keynes' plan was rejected, and the conference decided instead to make the US dollar the basis of international stability, establishing a system that tied the exchange rates of major currencies to the dollar and fixed the value of the dollar itself. From 1944 onwards, the US Federal Reserve guaranteed to exchange thirty-five dollars for one ounce of gold — the gold standard. The associated set of rules became known as the Bretton Woods system.

The Bretton Woods system worked for as long as the US economy boomed, and countries that received dollars for their goods were willing to use them to make investments in dollars, returning dollars to the US for use by Americans. However, in the 1960s, the costs of the Vietnam war together with purchases of foreign goods by Americans from growing economies like Germany and Japan were breaking this virtuous loop, leaving an increasing number of dollars in circulation. Since the amount of gold held by the US government was not increasing at anything like the same rate, the ratio of dollars to gold began escalating out of control. The real price of the dollar sank further and further below the official rate, so countries like France started sending dollars to the US Federal Reserve, asking in return for gold at the standard price. In a sudden declaration in 1971, the "Nixon Shock", the US abandoned the gold standard and let the dollar settle to its natural, lower level against other currencies.

The impact was huge – particularly on the price of oil, on which the entire world economy depended. Not only did a cheaper dollar mean that American companies had to pay more for oil, but Arab oil producers had always spent the "petrodollars" in which they were paid on dollar investments. Suddenly, an American political decision coming out of the blue had made their investments worth much less. To make up their losses, Arab nations put up oil prices, further exacerbating the pressure on industry. For a brief period, they also refused to sell oil to nations supporting Israel, which raised oil prices even more dramatically — from the start of the oil embargo in October 1973 to its end in March 1974, the price of oil rose from three to twelve dollars per barrel globally and even more in the US.[20] Industrial growth was already tailing off as post-war reconstruction slowed down, and such oil price rises were the nail in the coffin. It was unclear how to get the world's developed economies back on track, but one thing was certain — the war on poverty was starting to seem like an expensive luxury.

As politicians struggled to find a way forward, Hayek's ideas came back into focus. A new generation of economists argued that the best way for governments to solve the problem was to stop trying, and let business sort it out. If states were to ensure that less money was available to spend – "reduce the money supply", an approach known as monetarism, implemented by increasing interest rates so as to make bank loans more expensive – while at the same time increasing the freedom and security to operate of businesses, then free market mechanisms would swing fully into gear and get the economy back in shape. Milton Friedman, who won a Nobel prize for economics in 1976, two years after Hayek won the same prize in 1974, claimed to see only three functions for government: military defense of the nation, enforcement of contracts, and protection from crime, especially crime involving property. "When government-- in pursuit of good intentions tries to rearrange the economy, legislate morality, or help special interests, the cost come in inefficiency, lack of motivation, and loss of freedom. Government should be a referee, not an active player."[21]

Figure 13: Milton Friedman, author of "Capitalism and freedom" (1962)

The argument set out in Friedman's influential polemic "Capitalism and freedom" is not as unvarnished as the quote above suggests — for example, in the interests of creating a more effective workforce, he argues for government investment in education through a voucher system.

However, the effect was to move the focus of human rights from civil and political protection towards economic freedom. For the new thought leaders, generally known as neoliberals, the essential rights that a government should focus on protecting were economic, relating to property, trade, contracts, and wealth rather than to human welfare and dignity. For example, the aim of the World Trade Organization (of which more below) is "raising standards of living, ensuring full employment and a large and steadily growing volume of real income and effective demand, and expanding the production of and trade in goods and services, while allowing for the optimal use of the world's resources in accordance with the objective of sustainable development, seeking both to protect and preserve the environment and to enhance the means for doing so in a manner consistent with their respective needs and concerns at different levels of economic development."[22]

Neoliberals believe that a rising tide lifts all boats — that maximum market freedom opens the door to economic growth which in turn brings corresponding improvements to the human condition generally. They went much further than their antecedents in their vision of a minimal government. The original liberals of the eighteenth-century enlightenment had recognized that not everyone owns a boat, and presented a far more nuanced view of the role of the state that could hardly be called laissez-faire. Although fiercely critical of established religious and charitable foundations, they focused on inventing new institutions and new policies for social reform, and felt government had an important role to play in protecting the weakest in society.[23] Adam Smith, for example, considered the founder of economic liberalism, was strongly in favour of policies to main-

tain high wages, writing in "Wealth of Nations": "No society can surely be flourishing and happy, of which the far
greater part of the members are poor and miserable. It is
but equity, besides, that they who feed, clothe and lodge the
whole body of the people, should have such a share of the
produce of their own labour as to be themselves tolerably
well fed, clothed and lodged."

Figure 14: Adam Smith, author of Wealth of Nations (1776)

Smith also gave a long laundry list of government responsibilities. Public services for Smith started with basic

duties as preserving the cleanliness of roads, preventing the spread of fire, operating patrols to watch for hazardous accidents, preventing the spread of "leprosy or any other loathsome and offensive disease", and conducting public works to build and maintain roads, bridges, canals and harbors. This was only the beginning. In Smith's eyes, government should ensure the "cheapness or plenty of provisions", educate not only the youth but people of all ages, and even encourage "the frequency and gaiety of publick diversions". It might surprise some devotees of privatization, for whom Smith is a hero, that he felt government should run the post office.[24] For all that he extolled the virtues of economic growth, Smith believed government should be extremely careful not to pass power into the hands of merchants, describing them as "an order of men whose interest is never exactly the same with that of the public, who have generally an interest to deceive and even to oppress the public, and who accordingly have, upon many occasions, both deceived and oppressed it."[25]

The founders of liberal economic thought took care to highlight some principles that are absent from neoliberal theory. Government innovation and intervention lies at the heart of any successful market economy. For one thing, the infrastructure on which all industry depends is created and maintained by government – not just roads, rail, and ports but an educated and healthy workforce, a safe society, and the legal and justice mechanisms that provide businesses with freedom to operate. For another, there is no such thing as a truly free market. All markets are bounded by the laws and regulations that define their scope, which are culturally specific and change over time. As Cambridge University professor Ha-Joon Chang points out, "there is a huge range of restrictions on what can be traded; and not just bans on 'obvious' things such as narcotic drugs or human organs. Electoral votes, government jobs and legal decisions are not for sale, at least openly, in modern economies, although they were in most countries in the past. University places may not usually be sold, although in some nations money can buy them – either through (illegally) paying the selectors or (legally) donating money to the university. Many countries ban trading in firearms or alcohol. Usually, medicines have to be explicitly licensed by the government, upon the proof of their safety, before they can be marketed. All these regulations are potentially controversial – just as the ban on selling human beings (the slave trade) was one and a half centuries ago."[26]

Markets are social mechanisms. They exist in a society, so must play by the same rules. The question is whether society or the market shapes those rules. In the last forty years, market forces started rewriting the rules of society for their own ends. To an extent, this was not a new thing. The great trading economy of Venice, which employed modern production methods such as specialized workers and a moving assembly line long before the industrial revolution, shaped its societal structures to suit a wealthy merchant class. The difference between medieval Venice and the Western world in the 1970s is that the former was a smaller world, in which merchants lived close to the general populace and knew well that social unrest would damage their business interests. Workers in the Venetian Arsenal belonged to highly structured guilds, whose members all lived together in neighbourhoods and were bound by strong social ties. Long before unionization, the workers of medieval Venice were able to exert social leverage, and since everyone knew this, they rarely needed to. "Each guildsman pledged his loyalty to the state but there was a reciprocal arrangement, a species of social contract, in matters of justice."[27] By contrast, the globalized trading environment of the 1970s was based on a highly mobile labour, a potential workforce numbering in the billions, so theorists were able to persuade regulators that trade was the only thing that mattered. Don't worry, they claimed, we just need businesses to make plenty of money and social infrastructure will then take care of itself. In practice, it didn't really matter whether social infrastructure flourished or not, at least to businesses, since there were always more workers available.

Twentieth-century advances in communication and transportation created an environment in which a genuinely new approach to society could be tried out. Before the late 1970s, the only attempts to put neoliberal ideas of the 1960s and 1970s into practice were under the Latin American dictatorships of Chile in 1973 and Argentina in 1976. However, Margaret Thatcher (UK Prime Minister 1979-90) and Ronald Reagan (US President 1981-89) were convinced of the possibilities, and a new era began — the era we live in now.

The monetarist aspect of neoliberalism has been debated fiercely by economists in highly technical arguments.[28,29] Restricting the money supply may decrease inflation (when people have less money to spend, prices go down as vendors compete for sales) but businesses having less money to invest also tends to increase unemployment, and not only exacerbates recessions but causes new ones. Monetarists argue that restriction of the money supply inevitably coincides with such downturns from time to time but is not their cause.

More generally, monetarist ideas are challenged by research into the ancient origins of money.[30] Money seems to have originated not as a unit of exchange for traders, for whom it was cheaper and easier to price deals using standard commodities, but rather as a unit of account for taxation, which is why nearly all countries throughout history have issued their own currency (and may explain some of the challenges faced by countries that share a currency, such as in the European Union). In the ancient Near East, merchants set prices for thousands of years in terms of commodities, such as grain by volume and silver by weight. Switching to money actually increased the overall cost and difficulty of trade for society, especially across borders. However, issuing money made it easier for rulers to maintain armies. Rather than procure food, clothing, and other necessities for soldiers, all they had to do was pay them in money, and demand that citizens pay their taxes in money. Farmers and traders didn't have any particular use for money themselves, but needed it once a year when taxes came due, so were willing to exchange valuable goods like food and clothing for money at markets.

An emerging school of thought that aligns with this understanding of money is Modern Monetary Theory. Its proponents claim that neither lending by banks nor Keynesian-style spending by government generates inflation, since governments can use taxation to increase the demand for their currency.[31] This simple idea reflects not only the origins of money in antiquity but also the writings of foundational economists – Adam Smith is clear that "A prince, who should enact that a certain proportion of his taxes should be paid in a paper money of a certain kind, might thereby give a certain value to this paper money"[32] and similar views are expressed by Keynes.[33] It also has the virtue of matching the data, including recent events that puzzled monetarists, such as why injections of funding in response to the financial crash of 2008 did not generate inflation. Modern Monetary Theory offers a way forward for policy makers concerned about social justice and climate change to spend the money required, as well as to redistribute wealth in society.

However, despite the venerable history of these ideas, the options for government spending offered by Modern Monetary Theory are not yet a reality for most of the world's governments, at least in its current formulation. Mainstream economists still reject the approach, and its application has not yet been worked out for developing countries that cannot borrow or issue debt in their own currency on international markets. Until a seismic shift in attitudes takes place, and possibly even then, neoliberalism has set a course from which countries will find it hard to deviate. After following its precepts for decades, modern states have sold off their assets.

Selling off the state

Increasing freedom from taxation and regulation combined with privatization of national resources mean that the largest economies in the world are now corporations, leaving states deeply in debt with no way out.

Governments have long helped businesses grow without expecting anything in return. Mariana Mazzucato shows how the basic research and development that stimulates industry is often undertaken by government.[34] These fundamental investments may or may not be prohibitively expensive for business to undertake by reinvesting profits – either way, there seems no logical reason for government to miss out on a fair share of the eventual proceeds. Yet this behaviour is only the start of the enthusiastic generosity that governments show towards businesses in today's world.

Figure 15: Mariana Mazzucato, author of " Entrepreneurial state"

Since the 1980s governments of more than 100 countries have moved thousands of state-owned enterprises into the private sector marketplace — airlines, railroads, postal services, electric utilities, and many other types of businesses, valued in total at more than 3.3 trillion dollars[35] — and the process continues to accelerate. In 2015, for example, governments raised a record 320 billion dollars through privatization sales worldwide, substantially more than the 219 billion dollars raised in 2014, and easily exceeding the previous record of 265 billion dollars set in 2009.[36]

At the same time, states have reduced their own spending power by lowering corporate taxation. According to the European Commission Directorate General for Economic and Financial Affairs, between 1982 and 2004 the statutory tax rate fell in most of the countries for which data is available, often very substantially.[37] The same pattern has continued since then, with Deutsche Bank reporting in 2019 that "State finances are precarious yet companies are in great shape. That is partly because corporate tax rates have almost halved over several decades."[38]

Following neoliberal principles, governments have given corporations profit opportunity from relaxing regulations and selling off state assets while simultaneously charging them less in tax. The result is that corporations are now among the largest economies in the world.[39] Only 9 states have more revenue than Walmart, and of the top 100 global revenue generators, 71 are corporations. It's an irony that the anti-socialist project that Hayek so eloquently evangelized has resulted in 70% of the largest economies in the world being centrally planned.

	Country/Corporation	Revenue (US$ bn)		Country/Corporation	Revenue (US$ bn)
1	United States	3363	51	General Electric (US)	140
2	China	2465	52	CSCEC (CN)	139
3	Japan	1696	53	AmerisourceBergen (US)	136
4	Germany	1507	54	Agricultural Bank of China (CN)	133
5	France	1288	55	Verizon (US)	132
6	United Kingdom	996	56	Chevron (US)	131
7	Italy	843	57	E.ON (DE)	130
8	Brazil	632	58	AXA (FR)	129
9	Canada	595	59	Indonesia	129
10	Walmart (US)	482	60	Finland	128
11	Spain	461	61	Allianz (DE)	123
12	Australia	421	62	Bank of China (CN)	122
13	State Grid (CN)	330	63	Honda Motor (JP)	121
14	Netherlands	323	64	Cargill (US)	120
15	South Korea	304	65	Japan Post Holdings (JP)	119
16	China Nat. Petroleum (CN)	299	66	Costco (US)	116
17	Sinopec Group (CN)	294	67	Argentina	116
18	Royal Dutch Shell (NL/GB)	272	68	BNP Paribas (FR)	112
19	Sweden	248	69	Fannie Mae (US)	111
20	Exxon Mobil (US)	246	70	Ping An Insurance (CN)	110
21	Volkswagen (DE)	237	71	Kroger (US)	109
22	Toyota Motor (JP)	237	72	Société Générale (FR)	108
23	Apple (US)	234	73	Amazon.com (US)	107
24	Belgium	232	74	China Mobile Comm. (CN)	106
25	BP (GB)	226	75	SAIC Motor (CN)	105
26	Mexico	224	76	Walgreens Boots Alliance (US)	104
27	Switzerland	216	77	HP (US)	103
28	Berkshire Hathaway (US)	211	78	Assicurazioni Generali (IT)	103
29	India	200	79	Cardinal Health (US)	103
30	Norway	200	80	BMW (DE)	102
31	McKesson (US)	192	81	Express Scripts Holding (US)	102
32	Russia	187	82	Nissan Motor (JP)	102
33	Austria	187	83	China Life Insurance (CN)	101
34	Turkey	184	84	J.P. Morgan Chase (US)	101
35	Samsung Electronics (KR)	177	85	Koch Industries (US)	100
36	Glencore (CH/JE)	170	86	Gazprom (RU)	99
37	ICBC (CN)	167	87	China Railway Eng. (CN)	99
38	Daimler (DE)	166	88	Petrobras (BR)	97
39	UnitedHealth Group (US)	157	89	Schwarz Group (DE)	97
40	Denmark	157	90	Trafigura Group (NL/SG)	97
41	EXOR Group (IT/NL)	154	91	Nippon Telegraph and Tel. (JP)	96
42	CVS Health (US)	153	92	Boeing (US)	96
43	General Motors (US)	152	93	Venezuela	96
44	Vitol (NL/CH)	152	94	China Railway Constr. (CN)	95
45	Ford Motor (US)	151	95	Microsoft (US)	94
46	China Constr. Bank (CN)	150	96	Bank of America Corp. (US)	93
47	Saudi Arabia	150	97	ENI (IT)	93
48	AT&T (US)	147	98	Greece	93
49	Total (FR)	143	99	Nestlé (CH)	92
50	Hon Hai Precision Ind. (TW)	141	100	Wells Fargo (US)	90

Figure 16: Revenue generation of states vs corporations, 2018

Deutsche Bank's claim that state finances are precarious is borne out by looking at number one on the list above, the US, still the largest economy in the world with Gross Domestic Product half again as big as that of China. In 2019, the US spent almost one trillion dollars more than it earned.[40] Numbers as big as this are hard to visualize, so imagine you had a very large sock — wide enough for a stack of one-dollar bills, laid flat, and long enough to take the US budget deficit in such stacks. The sock would be just under 68 thousand miles long.[41] You could wrap it around the Earth almost three times.

That's nothing compared to the total debt of the US. A sock of dollar stacks making up the 23 trillion dollars currently owed by the US[42] would be a million and a half miles long. You could loop it between the Earth and the Moon, three times over, and play cat's cradle. However, it's the deficit that is more worrying. The US, similarly to many of the largest national economies in the world, is like a household that doesn't have enough left over from living expenses each year to pay off part of its mortgage, so its total debt mounts up from one year to the next. In the arcane language of finance, the mortgage is sub-prime, and the household may end up in default. Between 1800 and 2009, this happened to countries at least 250 times due to foreign debt, and a further 68 times due to domestic debt.[43] Defaulters include most of the largest national economies in the world, and the US only avoided it in 1933 by legislating away its obligation to pay debts in gold. I'll discuss debt again in more detail below.

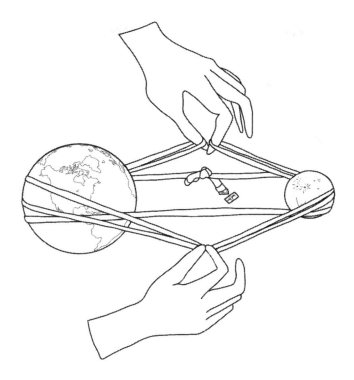

Figure 17: US debt in a sock of dollar stacks (image by Daisy Harrison-Broninski)

There is a backlash against corporate economic power, of course. The same Deutsche Bank report celebrating the great shape companies are in also warns that prominent US and European politicians are making higher corporate taxes a key part of their election platforms. Over 100 countries are working on proposals from the Organisation for Economic Co-operation and Development for a globally coordinated model of corporate taxation, under which corporations would have to pay tax in each country where they have activities and be subject to minimum tax rates.[44]

However, it will be very tough indeed to make any such collaborative action work as intended. Nations worldwide have been gradually hammering in the third and final nail in the coffin of state economic power since the end of the Second World War, when they signed The General Agreement on Tariffs and Trade (GATT) in 1948. Free trade has continued to evolve since then, up to and beyond the creation in 1994 of the World Trade Organisation. More agreements promoting globalized business have been brokered and more tariffs between countries removed, including on trade of information relating to banking, insurance, securities and finance. Recently, countries such as the US have started to move away from some aspects of free trade, but existing freedoms combined with a continual reduction of communications and transport costs in the post-war period mean that corporations can now operate from anywhere in the world, moving both operations and profits from one country to another when required.

Deutsche Bank accompanies its warning of a tax backlash by suggesting that corporations prepare for higher taxes by considering "their strategies around decentralization, capital expenditure, mergers and acquisitions, and changing performance metrics to prioritize return on assets."[45] The plain-speaking version of this is simple: move out of any country that dares to increase taxes on business. Even threats by companies to relocate can be enough to prevent such measures by government, and corporate pressure can also lead neoliberal administrations to weigh in on behalf of their country's business interests. A European Union attempt in 2018 to agree a Europe-wide 3 per cent tax on transactions brokered by online platforms, whose headquarters and offices often reside overseas, came to nothing after objections from Sweden, Denmark and Ireland, who feared US retaliation.[46]

Efforts to build international consensus on the issue have failed, and finance ministries in individual countries are now considering unilateral action, but it is possible that further corporate and US threats will scupper this too, in the end. There is good reason to believe that corporate power is here to stay, which would represent a watershed moment for the world - unless, that is, we've been here before and the situation somehow reversed itself, in which case we could learn from history. Is this a genuinely new phenomenon?

Public services by the private sector

Throughout history the rise of oligarchic wealth destroyed societies. Now, corporate power dominates political decisions, so privatization continues although the resulting public services are expensive and poor quality.

Looking back over the last 40 years, the rise of corporate power compared to government power brought about by neoliberalism seems like a dramatic shift. Looking further back throughout history, the balance of power between private oligarchic interests and the states in which they operated is a complex story, but the trend is always in the same direction. There were often swings as influence shifted between one side and the other, characterized by events familiar in modern times and arguments similar to those heard today, but societies throughout history generally started with an interlocking combination of public and private ownership of the means of production and commerce then moved inexorably towards accumulation in private hands. When this imbalance was allowed to escalate out of control, the result was often to destroy society.

As discussed above, states of the ancient Near East used temples to control vital means of production such as mills and metal working, while also sponsoring private commerce via at-risk loans to traders. For two thousand years, the growth of private wealth through usurious loans to households in years of distress was kept in check by debt cancellations and targeted laws, but eventually private wealth accumulated enough to weaken the power of rulers. Their ability to maintain borders weakened correspondingly, and social structure began to fall apart around 1600 BC, collapsing totally around 1200 BC.

During the early days of Imperial China, the Qin dynasty had a famous debate on monopolies vs laissez faire, the Discourses on Salt and Iron of 81 BC. The outcomes of the debate might be described as inconclusive, but in the end government relinquished control of monopoly industries to private business. People started to accumulate land, and two centuries later the Han dynasty ended after droughts, plagues, and famine led to a revolt against landowners who took advantage of rural distress to exploit workers. Three centuries of battle between warlords ensued.

Rivalry between oligarchic interests to whom the government of ancient Athens contracted out the exploitation of land, forests, and mines caused constant conflict during the early 6th century BC.[47] An attempt by the reformer Solon to reset debt and create a more equitable basis for trade failed, leading four years later to tyranny. Similarly, the Roman Republic let limited term contracts to an aristocracy of equestrian knights, the publicani, in what we would now call public-private partnerships.[48] Conflict between this class of oligarchs and the rural and urban workers that became indebted to them ended up destroying the Roman Republic.

The Byzantine empire had a heavily militaristic but financially successful centralized economy in which government collected high taxes, fixed interest rates, and exercised strict trade controls including prices and customs duties. Nevertheless, wealthy individuals, the dynatoi, gradually displaced peasant cultivators from their land, leading to emigration, reduced tax revenues, and widespread distress in cold winters. Eventually the empire felt threatened enough to introduce reforms during the 9th and 10th centuries that briefly restored balance, until a series of self-indulgent rulers came under the sway of aristocratic interests and a weakened empire fell to the Crusaders.

An interesting exception to the rule is the Republic of Venice, with which the Byzantines competed over territory. The longest lasting republic in history, existing from 697 AD until overthrow by Napoleon in 1797 AD, Venice introduced financial innovations not unlike those of the modern day, such as secondary markets for a wide variety of debt, equity and mortgage instruments, but made the merchant class and state almost inseparable via The Great Council. As discussed above, Venice had an unusually high level of social cohesion, which embedded those who accumulated great wealth into the operations of the state. Their power was restricted by law, and there was a common understanding that excessive exploitation of the workforce would lead to emigration or rebellion.

So, if the modern shift of state assets into private ownership without checks and balances is becoming truly entrenched worldwide, evidence from history is that this carries significant risk. It will have major impact on social outcomes because, unlike states, corporations are run solely for profit. Governments try to ensure that corporations act responsibly towards the communities in which they operate, as well as towards the ecosystem they inhabit, using instruments such as the Guidelines for Multinational Enterprises from the Organisation for Economic Co-operation and Development. However, ensuring adherence to such guidelines via legal means is difficult. As discussed above with regard to taxation, the nature and reach of the operations of transnational corporations renders them almost impervious to traditional jurisdiction.[49]

In today's world, the directors of corporations, including those that hold contracts to deliver public services, can make their own decisions about balancing human and environmental benefits with profits. Despite social pressures to act ethically, they have little choice but to favour the latter. Economists have been arguing since the 1970s that the duty of a corporation is to maximize shareholder value.[50][51] There are also strong incentives for corporate directors and managers to improve share price via practices such as share buy backs (using cash to re-purchase the company's own shares, rather than investing in development of products or services) that do not result in long term infrastructure improvement, economic growth, or benefit to society.[52] The double whammy of perceived duty and personal self-interest stretches far beyond profiteering business practices. Not only do corporations offer financial support to neoliberal politicians, but they commit huge amounts of money to influencing the political process, by lobbying for changes to the law that work in their favour.

The US Supreme Court established in 1976 that a corporation was entitled to make unlimited money contributions to political parties and political action committees, under the First Amendment right guaranteeing the right of an individual to freedom of speech. Looking behind the scene of American politics, the increase of lobbying since then is startling. In 1982 there were 89 corporate political action committees in the US. By 2009 there were 1598, with a further 1594 that were ideologically based. In 2014 there were around one hundred thousand professional lobbyists in the US alone, with spending on lobbying at over nine billion dollars per year, and much of this work has become unregistered "shadow" lobbying with no oversight.[53]

In the UK, there are different rules to the game but influence on public affairs from industry is no less pervasive. The Guardian journalist and outspoken commentator Owen Jones documented in "The Establishment" how in every area of UK public life, including officially non-partisan services such as the media, policing and justice, success is inextricable from actively supporting whatever range of views is currently in the political mainstream, and how this "Overton window" of political attitudes has moved dramatically from left to right over four decades.[54] Privatization of the National Health Service, now ramping up, would have been unacceptable even when privatization was all the rage under Margaret Thatcher. Jones describes the pervasive influence of think-tanks funded by corporate interests, and how a political career path typically includes close links with big business. Forty six percent of the most profitable companies in the UK have a member of parliament either as a shareholder or on the board of directors.

With lawmakers under such pressure to make and change laws in favour of private enterprise, the only constraints safeguarding provision of public services are those written into the contracts between the government agencies that pay for them and the private organisations that provide them. As anyone who has worked on such a contract knows, they are so complex that civil servants struggle to hold providers to account, especially over the long term when the original terms and conditions may be invalidated by changes in the external environment, due for example to climate or demographic change.[55] If you cannot assume that both parties to a public services contract share a common desire for public good, then the contract must nail down all the required outcomes exactly, but this is very difficult to do in a world that is not static — and since corporations compete on price for public services contracts, they are very careful to use contract wording to minimize their financial risk. The net result is that the contract winner conforms to the letter, rather than the spirit, of what is required by the public who rely on the services delivered.

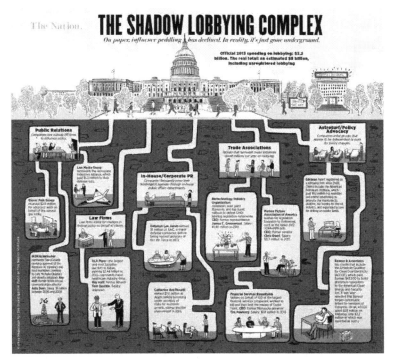

Figure 18: Shadow Lobbying Complex in the US (graphic due to Investigative Fund at The Nation Institute)

One wonders what a visitor from another planet would make of the current belief that public assets are best handed over to the private sector. "So, earthlings, although your governments and industries share the same labour market and the same access to cheap shared services, your plan is to improve public services by giving them to corporations whose aim is to extract profit? In order to encourage businesses to take them on, you are giving them monopoly power via inflexible contracts lasting decades? You know, of course, that it is more expensive for industry to borrow money than for government, a cost that will be passed on to taxpayers? That corporations must by law protect themselves against risk, which means inflating prices unnecessarily? That both industry and government will have to spend huge amounts of time drawing up contracts, the costs of which for both sides will be paid by government?" They would probably conclude that they should conquer Earth, just for our own good.

Detailed data on the cost efficiency of privatization is hard to come by, but Mariana Mazzucato illustrates what may be a general picture by comparing healthcare transaction costs in the US, which are around 30 percent of total healthcare expenditure, with the UK prior to marketization of the NHS, which were in the order of 6 percent.[56] While this is only indicative, it suggests that public service costs could be five times higher in a privatized system. It is easy, however, to find examples of poor public service delivery by the private sector. In the UK, examples include the G4S Olympic security failure that forced the army to step in,[57] the collapse of Britain's largest care home operator Southern Cross,[58] and the biggest IT failure in history, the National Health Service National Programme for IT.[59] A data-driven analysis of the performance of public services published by the Institute of Government in November 2019 finds a general decline in both quality (the standard of public service provided and how satisfied users are) and scope (the range of services provided and the number of people able to access them).[60]

Most of us depend to some extent on public services, which not only include resources we hope to need only rarely, such as policing, justice, and healthcare, but also support for everyday life that one would wish to take for granted, such as waste collection and road maintenance. How is the transition to private provision of public services affecting day to day life?

The impacts of corporate power

The rise of corporate power is creating human misery, exacerbated ever further as inequality grows unchecked. Debts are escalating out of control at both household and state level.

The increase in corporate freedoms from legislation and taxation, at the same time as sale of state assets to corporations whose managers are legally obliged to maximize shareholder profits, is having two main impacts.

The first impact is on the disadvantaged, who often depend not only on welfare but on a wide range of related public services. Again taking the UK as an example, the number of children who slipped into poverty from a working family rose more steeply from 2010-2017 than at any time for the preceding 20 years,[61] and more than half of children are growing up below the breadline in some neighbourhoods of the UK, where teachers find pupils sleeping rough behind bins.[62] Child criminal exploitation levels are back to Victorian times as gangs capitalize on a lack of youth facilities and school exclusions to groom children.[63] Patients with serious mental health problems are discharged in a way that was unthinkable five, let alone fifteen years ago, sometimes without warning.[64] Rough sleeping estimates show an increase of 165 percent since 2010.[65]

Globally, there are similar indicators of public services failure. Mental disorders continue to grow with major health, social, human rights and economic consequences in all countries.[66] One hundred million people worldwide are homeless, with one in four people on the planet living in conditions harmful to their health, safety and prosperity.[67] Controversially for some and terrifyingly for others, signs and impacts of climate change increased from 2015 to 2019, the warmest five-year period on record,[68] a change that affects the poorest people in the world disproportionally. One of the primary threats to human life as a result of climate change is food insecurity, which is greatest in the global south where people rely on small-scale agriculture and are more vulnerable to droughts, flooding and extreme weather.[69]

The second impact of corporate power on society is that the rich get richer. French academic Thomas Piketty became an international superstar of the economics world when he set out detailed proof in 2013 that, whether or not a rising tide lifts all boats, most people do not own a boat. Wealth is becoming increasingly concentrated in fewer hands. Piketty shows how society is returning to a pattern of wealth distribution last seen in the Belle Époque, when "as in most societies prior to the nineteenth century, wealth was highly concentrated in all European countries, with 80 to 90 percent of capital owned by the top decile and 50-60 percent by the top centile."[70]

In a long but surprisingly readable book that sold in astonishing numbers for an economics text, Piketty shows how although in the twenty-first century the middle class is wealthier than it was in the nineteenth, now owning between a quarter and a third of total wealth,[71] the years between World War Two and 1990 during which the level of inequality reduced significantly could be regarded as an historical blip: "global inequality of wealth in the early 2010s appears to be comparable in magnitude to that observed in Europe in 1900-1910."[72]

Figure 19: Thomas Piketty, author of "Capital in the Twenty-First Century" (2013)

The new level of inequality may be typical of society throughout history, but this doesn't mean we should ignore it. Inequality affects everyone in society from top to bottom – as Brother David Steindl-Rast reminds us eloquently[73], social gatherings don't really work if someone there is having a bad time. Economists of the right as well as left acknowledge it as a major problem that society must address, with Mervyn King, Governor of the Bank of England from 2003 to 2013, writing in 2016: "Inequality is one of the most important challenges to our economic system".[74] UK researchers Richard Wilkinson and Kate Pickett showed in 2009 detailed evidence that, "whether you classify people by education, social class, or income, people in each category are healthier if they are in a more equal society than people in the same category of income, education, or class in a less equal society."[75]

Some of this can be seen in statistics on life expectancy for the generation of Americans that started their working life under Reagan. The average wage of a full-time male worker is still significantly less than it was in the 1970s,[76] and as a generation of workers who lived through a forty-year slump in earnings reaches middle age, the impact on their health is starting to show. The post-war increase in life expectancy in the US reversed direction in 2014, with mid-life mortality reaching its highest rate since the second world war in 2017.[77] Major causes such as drug overdoses, suicides, and organ system diseases are common across all racial groups, and are best understood as long-term conditions whose effects accumulate over decades of poor life-style. In 2017, deaths of despair caused by alcohol, drug overdoses, and suicide stood at almost four times their level in 1999.

Wilkinson studied economic history, but both he and Pickett are epidemiologists by profession, and they track the growth and impacts of inequality with the patient, methodical attention to detail applied to monitoring the spread of an epidemic. They observe a particular effect, on the cohesion of society, which is the focus of this book. "There are few things more corrosive of a properly functioning democracy and of the market than corruption and unbridled greed. Although the international measures of corruption currently available were designed primarily to assess levels of corruption in poorer countries, they strongly suggest that one of the likely costs of greater inequality is increased corruption in government and society more widely ... trust and the strength of community life are weakened by inequality, and this is true not only of interpersonal trust, but also of trust in government — the difference between the attitude of Americans and Scandinavians to their governments is well known. In addition, international data and data for the American states suggest people trust government less in more unequal states. There is also evidence from societies where voting is not compulsory (as it is for instance in Australia) that voter turn-out may be lower in more unequal countries. Whether or not this reflects a greater separation of interests and an increasing sense of 'us and them' between people at opposite ends of the social ladder, it certainly suggests that too much inequality is a threat to democracy."[78]

This observation is borne out by separate research showing how the rise of neoliberalism has been paralleled by a dramatic decline in how much people trust their government.[79] In 1958, more than 75 percent of Americans said that they trusted the government most or all of the time. By 1985 the figure had dropped to about 45 percent. In 2015, it was close to 20 percent and in 2019 down to only 17 percent. More than 3 in 4 US citizens used to trust their government. Now, only about 1 in 6 does so.

Figure 20: Kate Pickett and Richard Wilkinson, authors of "The Spirit Level" (2009)

A particular impact of the rise in inequality is the corresponding rise of household debt. The International Monetary Fund reported in 2012 how household debt soared in the years leading up to the Great Recession of 2008. In advanced economies, during the five years preceding 2007, the ratio of household debt to income rose by an average of 39 percentage points, to 138 percent. In Denmark, Iceland, Ireland, the Netherlands, and Norway, debt peaked at more than 200 percent of household income. A surge in household debt to historic highs also occurred in emerging economies such as Estonia, Hungary, Latvia, and Lithuania.[80]

A similar pattern of increasing debt is repeated at state level. In the third quarter of 2019, the global ratio of debt to Gross Domestic Product hit a new all-time high of over 322%, with total debt reaching close to $253 trillion.[81] Well before the coronavirus crisis started, global debt was set to grow even faster in the following year, being estimated to exceed \$257 trillion by the end of March 2020. Jubilee Debt Campaign estimates that 27 countries are at risk of a public or private debt crisis, a further 20 at risk of a public debt crisis, and 35 a private debt crisis. In total this makes 82 countries, and the situation is worsening — in 2017 the figure was 79, and in 2015 a mere 71.[82] For many people, debt is a straightforward problem with strong moral overtones — the word generally used when a debt is abolished, forgiveness, implies that the borrower somehow committed a sin. However, anthropologist David Graeber shows in his monumental history of debt through the ages how this is a radical simplification.[83]

Throughout history, debt has been a cultural construct that is not by any means just about money, but rather a means of embedding participants into a complex social network, with patterns of behaviour and responsibilities that apply on both sides. In tribal societies, many debts are ritualized and symbolic, without either side envisaging any possibility of repayment. There have also been significant changes since ancient times in treatment of risk and interest. Loans to merchants by temples of antiquity to fund foreign trading ventures were void if the venture failed due to an event such as shipwreck or piracy, rather than being inherited as a liability by their families or resulting in confiscation of collateral such as a home. Also, interest was fixed – both sides agreed the total cost of the loan at the start. The unchecked escalation of compound interest, devastating to many families in the modern day, is a new phenomenon — for much of history it was regarded as deeply immoral and severely punished when attempted by lenders.

Figure 21: David Graeber, author of "Debt: The First 5,000 Years" (2011)

The modern view of debt as a simplistic transaction, and application of punitive terms to borrowers rather than to lenders, is at odds with a persistent pattern of debt forgiveness throughout the ages, going back as far as history itself. It was common for kings and emperors of antiquity to forgive the debts of all citizens at times when they needed public support, such as on accession to power or in times of war. In biblical times, all debt was cancelled every 49 years — this is the origin of the word Jubilee, which applied to the year in which it took place. When Jesus returned to Nazareth to "proclaim the year of the Lord's favour", he was reading from the scroll of the prophet Isaiah and calling for a Jubilee Year.[84]

In his summary of decades of research into how early civilizations in the Near East managed their economic affairs,[85] Michael Hudson (described by David Graeber as the most important economic historian of the last fifty years) shows how debt cancellation was a basic mechanism for maintaining social order in ancient times. "The idea of annulling debts nowadays seems so unthinkable that most economists and many theologians doubt whether the Jubilee Year could have been applied in practice, and indeed on a regular basis. A widespread impression is that the Mosaic debt jubilee was a utopian ideal. However, Assyriologists have traced it to a long tradition of Near Eastern proclamations. That tradition is documented as soon as written inscriptions have been found – in Sumer, starting in the mid-third millennium BC. Instead of causing economic crises, these debt jubilees preserved stability in nearly all Near Eastern societies. Economic polarization, bondage and collapse occurred when such clean slates stopped being proclaimed."

The clean slate tradition was a practical response to the reality of agrarian societies. Debt cancellation applied only to household debts, since these could easily escalate out of control when events interrupted the income flow of the debtor. Then as now, the fortunes of farmers varied from year to year – as discussed above, harvests would fail due to drought, storms, or pests, farmers would be called away to war, disease would lay people low, raiders would decimate the countryside, and so on. When this happened, farmers did not have enough crops surplus to their subsistence needs to pay taxes, rents, and other costs of living. They went into debt not by taking out excessive loans, but by not having the cashflow to finance their regular living expenses.

At such times, rulers dealt with the systemic issue by cancelling debts, starting with monies owed to themselves and their officials, and often decreeing that debts to private creditors such as landlords were also null and void. If government had not taken such action, farmers and their families would have been forced into debt bondage, giving family members and themselves over into slavery in lieu of payment. In the short term, this took away tax revenue from rulers as well as removing their ability to conscript soldiers and commandeer unpaid labour for basic infrastructure work such as maintaining city walls, building temples, and digging irrigation ditches. In the longer term, the net effect was to increase the power of wealthy merchants, creating an elite group in society whose oligarchic power would eventually exceed that of government.

This gave rise to tensions, of course, between the forces of government and the desires of merchant-entrepreneurs to obtain labour for their own ends by obliging people to work off debts – and then as now, the private elites won in the end. The balance of power between rulers and rentiers ebbed and flowed for two millennia until about 1600 BC, ending with a slow collapse in central authority that bears a strong resemblance to the present day, although events in the ancient world unfolded over millennia compared to only decades in modern times. The appropriation of land and public infrastructure, unmanageable escalation of household debt, and vast emigrations of antiquity are happening again now. Hudson describes as timeless these phenomena, the social tensions they cause, and the eventual domination of a merchant class. "The origins of Western civilization are to be found in the way Bronze Age Sumer and Babylonia, Egypt and the Aegean broke down and gave way to their successors. In Greece, local Mycenaean palace managers disappear from records in 1200 BC, reappearing

in the 8th century as basilae, concentrating land and hitherto palace wealth and authority in their own hands and that
of their clans."

Debt abolition for both nations and individuals still
takes place in modern times, but it is no longer a basic
structural mechanism. Now it is a last resort, applied as a
desperate measure when no other recourse is available and
treated as an exception rather than a rule. All Germany's
external debt was abolished in 1953 in order to enable the
country's economic growth. In 2005, following large scale
public campaigns, the total debt of 37 developing countries
was reduced by two-thirds. In 2015, the Croatian government made a deal with banks, telecoms and utilities opera-
tors to erase the debts of around 60,000 citizens to give
them a "fresh start". Such debt cancellations are not made
to ensure stability of autocratic rule, as they were in the
ancient Near East, but are intermittent interventions based
on social and mercantile instincts. Modern economists such
as Yanis Varoufakis who argue for debt forgiveness in the
Eurozone[86] make the case not only that overwhelming debt
arises from lenders taking advantage of borrowers but also
that it imperils the financial system as a whole. The latter
reasoning is based on Hudson's simple observation that a
debt that can't be paid, won't be paid. When a country has
unmanageable debt that is not forgiven, it is likely simply to
go into default.

In their 2011 study of financial crises over 8 centuries,
Carmen Reinhart and Kenneth Rogoff show that sovereign
defaults on external debt have been an almost universal rite
of passage for every country as it matures from an emerging
economy to a developed economy, a process that can take
centuries. France defaulted on external debt 8 times and

Spain 13 times in their early years. From 1800 until well after the second world war Greece was in almost continual default, as it now looks possible to end up being again, and Austria had an even more stunning record of defaults. Portugal, Egypt, Russia and Turkey have long histories of default, as did nations now defunct such as Prussia and the early Italian city-states. The long story of external debt default at national level gives the lie to any belief that market economies are getting any better at sustaining debt-driven growth, and in 2008 we saw as plainly as possible that developed economies are no more capable of avoiding crises than emerging ones. "Our immersion in the details of crises that have arisen over the past eight centuries and in data on them has led us to conclude that the most commonly repeated and most expensive investment advice ever given in the boom just before a financial crisis stems from the perception that 'this time is different'... Each time, society convinces itself that the current boom, unlike the many booms that preceded catastrophic collapses in the past, is built on sound fundamentals, structural reforms, technological innovations, and good policy."[87]

Tellingly, Reinhart and Rogoff make it clear that while some nations appear to have left sovereign debt default behind, every economy in the world is still vulnerable to the impact of bad debts in the form of banking crises, which also unsettle financial stability at global level. In the wake of 2008, even the mainstream financial establishment is starting to predict a new approach to debt. Mervyn King, former Governor of the Bank of England, wrote in 2016, "It is evident, as it has been for a very long while, that the only way forward for Greece is to default on (or be forgiven) a substantial proportion of its debt burden."[88] Despite this

recognition, global financial rules are too firmly embedded
to change rapidly – like steering a supertanker, any change
in direction will be slow to take effect. Both Greece and
Italy still have their debts, and most households worldwide
cannot look forward to the fresh start provided to Croa-
tians. Nations and individuals should not rely on external
financial solutions any more than they would be wise to
count on structural change that reverses the growth of
transnational corporate power. Rather, they need to find
their own way forward — and it is critical that they do so,
since the primary aim of the founders of neoliberalism, to
safeguard individual freedoms, is now generating societal
movements with very different ends in mind.

The emergence of neoconservatism as an evolution of
neoliberalism is introducing back into public life reactionary
forces that seek to put a check on diversity of race, sexuality, and faith. At the same time, populist movements seeking
to counter some of the effects of financial inequality are
making acceptable again forms of belief such as nationalism
and eugenics that led to war in the last century, alongside
protectionist economic tactics that run counter to almost all
mainstream thought. These trends may not lead to another
world war, but the consequences of bringing back attitudes
once thought outdated will run deep throughout society.

Having faced up to the situation, this book sets out a
way that communities can start to deal with it. The technological and economic changes that are making us all more
connected are not only forces for national asset stripping,
corporate tax evasion, and manipulation of political opinion
by powerful vested interests. Communities can take advantage of powerful, low-cost technologies and create new
forms of finance that galvanize people to work together in a

different way, and lay the groundwork for a hopeful future.

How communities can look after themselves

We can create a better society without extremism by building supercommunities, which adopt emergent behaviours to become antifragile whether or not new sources of value provide economic growth.

This book goes on to claim that we can at least partially remedy poor public services provision, financial inequality, and environmental degradation without extremism, by tackling the effects at local level and seeking to build what I call supercommunities. It sets out a simple strategy for doing this, including how to build consensus at local level and coordinate corresponding action.

The first discussion provides a fully holistic vision of wellness, which is fundamental to a thriving community. I'll discuss what wellness isn't, including how it relates to illness, and explore what it is, introducing the concept of positive psychological capital. I'll show some of the different kinds of intervention into wellness, and look at how to intervene on behalf of the neediest in society, arguing that they should be the main focus.

The topic of the section after that is the heart of this book — community. I will explain why community is different from constructs such as neighbourhood and family, and look at the many kinds of communities and many ways in which an individual can connect with them. In particular, I will discuss the relationship of community with wellness, describing how to use community to improve your own wellness along with that of others.

The next section sets out in plain language the theory

of collaboration I developed in my previous book. The theory is formal, meaning that it is underpinned by definitions of things and their relationships, but here I'll keep things down to earth. I'll look again at common words such as "conversation", and explore simple, practical ideas that are useful in any working life.

After that, there is a section about ownership. I'll look at who is involved in ownership, and survey old and new forms to see how each can be useful to communities seeking to improve the lives of their members. The section shows how transformative it can be for a community, and explores different ways to participate. I'll describe a simple visual technique for exploring interventions into the life of your community so as to improve its human, natural, and industrial assets. The section concludes with a discussion of new forms of finance that are transforming communities worldwide, including an innovative new mechanism with the potential to unlock the vast power of global capital markets for good things.

Measurement is the subject of the penultimate section, which discusses how to track the impact of change. You can't get where you want to go unless you know where your destination is, and have a way of working out when you've arrived. There are different techniques for measuring the wellness of people in a community and of the community overall. These can be used in combination as an integral part of a journey towards wellness, without generating extra overheads or costs.

The book concludes with a summary of how to start transforming your own community, or communities, into supercommunities. The section includes illustrative stories and advice, concluding with observations on personal transformation. Becoming more involved with your community may require you to learn new skills and is quite likely to change your own life significantly. However, all you need to get going is the willingness to become what in Yiddish would be called a macher — someone that makes things happen in their community. In this section, you'll find a summary of how to succeed in making a difference locally. And to make a difference globally, we just need enough people to step up at local level.

The Afterword offers some final thoughts. It is followed by a nutshell summary of the ideas in each section of the book that you may find useful as an aide memoire, as well as to set the many ideas presented into context.

The book aims to be useful. It is non-partisan, I hope — being about community doesn't make it communist, being concerned about social justice doesn't make it socialist, recognizing the need to maintain community capitals doesn't make it capitalist, and placing importance on traditional values doesn't make it conservative. The collaboration principles set out here have a mathematical underpinning,[89] so could be considered a form of social science, although the book does not belong to a particular discipline such as anthropology, sociology, psychology, politics, history, or economics (and like them is not in a position to apply the scientific method). It does draw from research in all these areas, choosing and simplifying key ideas in order to tell a story that may help us think about things in a useful way. As Mariana Mazzucato writes about economic value: "How we discuss value affects the way all of us, from giant corporations to the most modest shopper, behave as actors in the economy and in turn feeds back into the economy, and how we measure its performance. This is what philosophers call 'performativity': how we talk about things affects behaviour, and in turn how we theorize things."[90]

Stories can be more reliable than truths, since they are more flexible. I always recommend to people a marvelous little book called "Proofs and Refutations" collecting the last writings of the Hungarian philosopher Imre Lakatos. His short Socratic dialogues between a teacher and pupils, each named after a letter of the Greek alphabet, show in an entertaining way how any assertion about the world will always have a counter-example.[91] Simple answers can't be trusted, and however complex you make them, a new exceptional case will always pop up.

Figure 22: Imre Lakatos, author of "Proofs and Refutations" (1976)

If this book describes any form of general approach, it is autopoiesis — a word describing any organism that maintains itself by restructuring its own operations in response to environmental changes. An autopoietic system has behaviours that emerge as required, allowing it to survive in a chaotic world by continually re-imagining its internal order. We'll see below how the concept of autopoiesis emerged from the study of animal communication.

Autopoiesis is related to ideas about uncertainty promoted by Nassim Nicholas Taleb, showing the extreme impact of rare and unpredictable outlier events (Black Swans)[92] and the necessity to thrive and grow when exposed to volatility, randomness, disorder, and stressors (to be antifragile)[93]. Taleb emphasizes in particular the advantage of being able to benefit from Black Swans rather than be undone by them. However, the route to antifragility that Taleb suggests is financial in origin. His barbell strategy is to make sure that 90 percent of your capital is safe by investing it in risk free assets, which have just enough return to protect you from the effects of inflation, while placing the remaining 10 percent in very risky investments that represent bets at high odds — paying out handsomely on a Black Swan event, for example. In Taleb's own case, he was fortunate in that the financial crisis of the late 1980s occurred early in his career as a trader — his approach paid off, leaving him not only financially independent but with concrete proof of his ideas (and he did well again from the next worldwide financial crash, in 2008).

Taleb's approach is focused on personal profit from disaster rather than maintaining general welfare — how to be one of the winners, not the losers - and does it even apply to the more complex and holistic effects of financial inequality on communities, such as low wellness and environmental degradation? Barbell strategies have been developed in areas other than finance, such as transportation planning, but the concept is basically a linear one, of maximizing the value of a particular resource such as money. We will see that the notion of resources has been applied to communities in the form of community capitals, an idea we will discuss below. However, measuring such resources is much more complex and multifaceted than measuring an amount of money. Community capitals are also closely inter-related to one another, not least by human relationships that in themselves could be considered a form of resource, and again are very hard to measure numerically.

Unfortunately, there is no magic bullet such as a barbell strategy for financial inequality and its effects on wellness and the environment. The problem is a more human one than managing a financial portfolio, and thus both more challenging and, to me at least, more interesting and exciting. Communities in the modern world will not thrive by adhering to any fixed way of life, but rather by remaining aware of what is going on around them, and allowing their members to reform — literally, to re-form — their own interactions to meet new challenges as they arise. New challenges are not going to stop emerging, so sustainability through internal reconfiguration is critically important.

We need this new form of community evolution since the traditional means of providing new resources to society, economic growth, is not a reliable means of addressing social issues in the short or medium term. There are two main sources of economic growth.

Harvard University researchers write, "In economics, it is widely accepted that technology is the key driver of economic growth of countries, regions and cities. Technological progress allows for the more efficient production of more and better goods and services, which is what prosperity depends on."[94] However, the benefits of new technologies do not accrue evenly across society. As discussed above, governments have long helped develop new technologies then handed them over to businesses for exploitation without expecting anything in return. This may change, but basic research in the new technologies that will transform industry in the new few decades – space exploration, nanotechnology, gene editing, artificial intelligence, and so on – has already been done under the old arrangements. For the foreseeable future, the profits resulting from new technologies will flow into private corporate hands, rather than being state revenue that can be used to improve social outcomes.

The second source of economic growth is to some extent illusory, since it consists of moving resources from one place to another, and recording growth in the latter. Taking the long view, and looking at the world as a whole, much of what we might consider to be past economic growth was always based on extraction of resources in other countries, so could be interpreted as redistribution rather than an overall increase in personal productivity. Throughout history, empires have swelled their coffers by the exploitation of natural and social resources in newly conquered or colonized territories. The colonial powers of the West granted freedom to many of their colonies in the first half of the twentieth century, but were still able to generate economic growth from reconstruction in countries devastated by world war, which funded the Western social reforms of the 1940s, 1950s, and 1960s. Once this slowed down, the globalizing reforms introduced by neoliberalism provided new sources of revenue from investment into developing countries (about four fifths of US domestic profits during the period 1980 to 2010 were generated from investment abroad[95]). Despite President Trump's claims that "we're going to see economic growth of 4, 5, and maybe 6 percent", in 2019 the largest economy in the world, the US, grew by only 2.1%.[96] This is less than the 2.4% average during the second term of his predecessor President Obama, and may well reflect a long term downwards trend.

Wherever economic growth comes from in future, it may not be powerful enough to act as the transformative source of value needed to address social issues. Piketty acknowledges that historic data cannot be precise, but shows how global economic growth as an average per person has always been low. Even in the last hundred years, it reached only the unimpressive maximum of 1.6 percent. His table below shows that the world economy has grown through the ages mainly by increasing the population, which on a planet that has now become overcrowded is not an aim we should continue to seek. Piketty predicts that growth in the centuries to come is likely to return to the even lower level it had before the twentieth century.[97]

What would be the effect on Piketty's calculations if you were to factor in the massive depletion of natural resources extracted to fuel industrial growth over the centuries? It may be that economic growth is an illusion, or worse, that in fact financial growth and the corresponding growth in social infrastructure has always been balanced by an environmental debt passed on to future generations. Economics may be a zero-sum game, or even a shell game that can't be won.

Table 2.1: World growth since the industrial revolution			
Average annual growth rate	**World output**	World population	Per capita output
0-1700	**0.1%**	0.1%	0.0%
1700-2012	**1.6%**	0.8%	0.8%
incl.: 1700-1820	*0.5%*	*0.4%*	*0.1%*
1820-1913	*1.5%*	*0.6%*	*0.9%*
1913-2012	*3.0%*	*1.4%*	*1.6%*

Figure 23: Table 2.1 of "Capital in the Twenty-First Century" (2013), Piketty

This seems startling. Surely the massive technological developments of the last three hundred years, and the corresponding transformation of daily lives worldwide, must have generated more output than this? Piketty's data and statistical methods have been debated by economists, as one would expect, but there is little real pushback on his main findings. A possible explanation emerges when you think about horses as compared to tractors for powering agriculture. Horses are not only better for the environment than tractors, producing less greenhouse gases and pollutants, but also more energy efficient.[98] In other words, one tractor may produce more output than one horse, but subtract the costs of producing and maintaining tractors from the equation, and the world would have achieved more economic growth overall had we simply increased the number of horses. Industrial advancement can be very wasteful of resources.

Research in the US showed that if the country switched to horse power, it would need 23 million horses to cultivate its 147 million hectares of farmland. Taking into account that horses make fertilizer, reproduce themselves, and eat raw food, 11 percent of US cropland would have to be given over to growing their feed. If you do a similar calculation for tractors, they require 26 percent of US cropland to sustain themselves — in other words, tractors are more than twice as expensive to run as horses, for the same output. Similar research in Sweden concluded that tractor-based agriculture consumes 67 percent more energy than horse-based agriculture.[99] A recent investigation into the use of bullocks for agriculture in India recommended that their use be promoted, and research undertaken into new designs for the accompanying equipment.[100]

Could the world switch from tractors back to animal power for agriculture? We'd need more horses, for a start, and they'd need to be carthorses (or bullocks, or oxen). We'd also need more farmers, and they would need to be more highly skilled — it's a lot harder to plough with a team of horses than to steer a modern tractor. Other agricultural jobs that have been replaced by machines would need to be re-learned, such as hedging, ditching, and walling — all of which improve the landscape and create natural habitats that encourage a diverse ecology. There would also be a lot more grunt work involved. Horses drop fertilizer on the field, but not evenly, so it would need to be spread out. Horses need to be taken care of, seven days a week, and sometimes into the night. We'd need more veterinarians and blacksmiths too.

People might consider such jobs to be more or less fulfilling than staring at a computer screen in an office cubicle. They might be more or less rewarding financially, once you take into account the relative cost of living and differences in lifestyle between city and country. Some people might object to the re-introduction of animal labour on a large scale. Such a move would be radical, disruptive, and I'm not arguing for anything like it here. Rather, I'm trying to show that we can't grow our way out of the current situation, since growth is returning to its historical slow or even zero rate – and anyway, most of the benefits brought by growth don't accrue to governments. To whatever extent we start to reintroduce older ways of working and living, low economic growth in a world where most of the resulting profits flow to corporations presents a potent challenge.

New sources of value may emerge from space exploration, nanotechnology, gene editing, artificially intelligent machines replacing humans in the workplace,[101] or other technological developments, but if present-day levels of inequality continue, only a small percentage of the population will see their personal wealth increase from such innovations. Even we hope for a society that moves towards more equal distribution of wealth, future industrial advancement may do little more than maintain the twentieth century average rate of growth, which shared out equally across the population of the planet will do little to improve the lot of those in greatest need.

So, neither political nor economic forces seem set to solve the problems of the planet. Even supposing that future political movements dedicated to restoring the social reforms of the mid twentieth century come to power, and there is more general acceptance of progressive economic ideas that enable their mission, there is no reason to believe that they will have access to the resources they need. Such economic growth as there is in the next century will benefit mainly the few, and there are powerful forces aligned against moves by states to increase their fund base, such as bringing back high inheritance taxes on wealth or transferring privatized assets into some form of public ownership.

This may seem to be a gloomy vision, but facing facts is the first step toward change, and if you see it as a call to action, it is a hopeful thing to do. I've always wondered why some useful words vanish from language — whatever happened to "lest"? — and others never appear at all. In English, we could really use a word for turning crisis into opportunity. Taleb's neologism, antifragility, is about creating structure that generates a positive response to crisis, but there is also a personal side – a state of mind that sees difficult situations as potential sources of unexpected advantage, and responds by using them as a spur to move forwards differently. Strategists from Sun Tzu onwards stress the importance of choosing a battleground on which you can win, and in a war on fragility most of us may gain more from a fight at community level than from pressuring our elected representatives to act at state, nation, or global level. There is enough uncertainty about the future of the social contract between government and citizen that it makes sense for communities to assume they are effectively on their own for the long haul, and start taking action now to make themselves as antifragile as possible, not least against the effects of climate change.

As a prescription for thinking long-term in a short-term world, philosopher Roman Kzrnaric sets out "design principles for deep democracy".[102] Alongside political and legal safeguards for the well-being of our descendants ("guardians of the future" and "intergenerational rights"), he recommends civil society participation in deliberative assemblies to shape policy on long-term issues ("citizen assemblies") and radical devolution of power to cities from national level ("self-governing city-states"). This is a hand-book for implementing the latter two mechanisms, with the qualifier that its recommendations can be applied by communities of any type or size.

If enough communities take up the banner, adapting common ideas and approaches to their own specific needs and becoming supercommunities, they will be thinking local but acting global. Acting with what specific aim in mind, though? Fragility is such a broad concept. In order to make a real difference to real people, we need to hone in on the thing that fragility most affects. We need to understand wellness.

Wellness

What wellness isn't

Wellness is not the same as absence of illness, and is not a purely medical concept but more holistic. Definitions vary, and attempting to standardize wellness may lead to undesirable intervention into private life.

The UK National Health Service describes homeopathy as follows. "Homeopaths believe that homeopathy can help with any condition that the body has the potential to repair itself. The practice has two essential principles: 1) That a substance that can cause symptoms of illness will cure those same symptoms if given in extremely small doses. For example, a very small amount of caffeine might be used to treat insomnia. 2) The more you dilute a substance, the more you increase its power to treat symptoms that it would otherwise cause. The dilution of the substance must be performed in a very specific way, with an increasing number of dilutions resulting in the solution becoming more potent."[103]

The website goes on to quote a description of the process from Ben Goldacre, author of Bad Science. "The typical dilution is called '30C': this means that the original substance has been diluted by 1 drop in 100, 30 times. On the Society of Homeopaths site, in their 'What is homeopathy?' section, they say that '30C contains less than 1 part per million of the original substance.' This is an understatement: a 30C homeopathic preparation is a dilution of 1 in $100\hat{\ }30$, or rather 1 in $10\hat{\ }60$, which means a 1 followed by 60 zeroes, or — let's be absolutely clear — a dilution of 1 in 1,000,000,000,000,000,000,000,000,000,000,000,000, 000,000,000,000,000,000,000,000. To phrase that in the Society of Homeopaths' terms, we should say: '30C contains less than one part per million million million million million million million million million million of the original substance.' At a homeopathic dilution of 100C, which they sell routinely, and which homeopaths claim is even more powerful than 30C, the treating substance is diluted by more than the total number of atoms in the universe. Homeopathy was invented before we knew what atoms were, or how many there are, or how big they are. It has not changed its belief system in light of this information."

Ludicrous practices such as homeopathy get wellness a bad press. Wellness is often linked with alternative therapies, and while some of these are genuinely worthwhile, others take commercial advantage of impressionable people via products and services that are not only useless but may even be dangerous. Homeopathy has zero effect on health so at least its only impact is on your wallet.[104] Ear candles, however, do not in fact purify the blood, strengthen the brain, or cure cancer, but may well burn you, cause bleeding, or puncture your eardrum.[105] The Universal Medicine cult thrives on donations, legacies, and paid treatments such as burping out bad spirits, despite claiming that disabled children were evil in a former life, exploiting vulnerable women through male-performed therapies such as breast massage and manipulation of the pubic bone, and being led by a tennis coach who was found by a Supreme Court to make fraudulent medical claims, prey on cancer patients, and have an indecent interest in girls as young as ten.[106]

Wellness as a concept may have been partially co-opted by the lunatic fringe, but has a respectable pedigree. The medical community has understood for a long time that being healthy is different from not being ill. The World Health Organization proposed in 1948 that health should be linked to "physical, mental, and social well-being, and not merely the absence of disease and infirmity".[107] The Faculty of Public Health of the Royal Colleges of Physicians of the United Kingdom now defines three overlapping domains in which public health practice should operate, including health improvement and health protection alongside health services.[108] Health improvement includes reducing inequalities, dealing with employment and housing, reinforcing family and community, improving education, and intervening in lifestyles. Health protection not only works to counter the effects of infection, emergencies, radiation, chemicals, poisons, and environmental hazards but also aims to provide cleaner air, water, and food and help prevent war and social disorder.

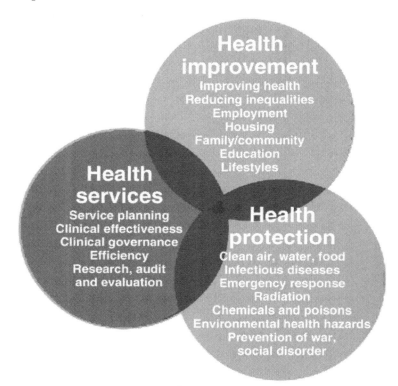

Figure 24: Domains of public health practice

Despite this understanding being widespread in the medical community for a long time, doctors in the UK still complain informally to one another that the National Health Service is effectively a National Illness Service, focused on responding to symptoms one by one rather than promoting a holistic approach to, and providing support for, a better lifestyle. They think it makes more sense to help people avoid becoming patients. For example, physicians are well aware of the cost of treating psychosomatic complaints, not just in appointment time but for the expensive and unnecessary tests they are obliged to run on a daily basis. The Royal College of Psychiatrists estimates the cost of Medically Unexplained Symptoms to be three billion pounds every year to the UK, which is 50 pounds per year for every man, woman and child in the country.[109] Another source of frustration for General Practitioners (GPs) in the UK is the need to prescribe antidepressants. Despite research in 2005 showing that 78 percent of GPs believed an alternative treatment for depression would be more appropriate,[110] usage in the UK doubled over the next decade.[111]

Public Health England knows all this, of course, and runs campaigns aiming to make people more proactive in their own wellness. However, these campaigns take a medical rather than a holistic approach, showing you how to check your health and offering guidance on how to improve it by moving, sleeping, and relaxing more, smoking and drinking less, and eating better.[112] Most of us know intuitively that this isn't the whole story. The social and psychological elements of wellness make it much more than being fit, well rested, and well fed. Most people would not thrive if they were marooned on a desert island, even if they had shelter and could find plenty to eat.

However, it isn't so easy to say what is missing from this kind of purely medical approach. It is not enough to list areas that affect wellness, as in the three public health domains. Yes, surely housing and education are good, and poisons and war are bad, but how can we assess the impact of such things on an individual person and come up with an overall statement about their wellness?

Different attempts at doing this tend to come up with quite different solutions. In order to assess the success of their rehabilitation programs, the US Substance Abuse and

Mental Health Services Administration took a holistic approach to wellness by considering it from eight different angles, or dimensions:[113]

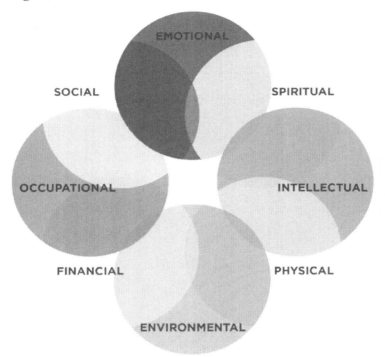

Figure 25: Eight Dimensions of Wellness, US Substance Abuse and Mental Health Services Administration

By contrast, rehabilitation practitioners in the UK created a quite different way of looking at aspects of wellness. The UK Association of Mental Health Providers no longer use the ten-point Mental Health Recovery Star they developed, but it makes an interesting comparison. The eight dimensions created in the US describe capacities that you have — intellectual, social, financial, and so on — whereas the recovery star created in the UK describes aspects of your life such as work, relationships, and responsibilities:

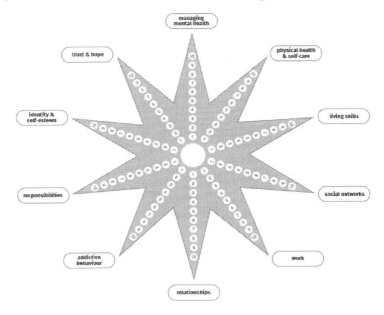

Figure 26: Mental Health Recovery Star, UK Association of Mental Health Providers

It is not obvious which of these two approaches is better, and there is no clear relationship between the two. The physical dimension corresponds partially to the "physical health & self-care" point of the star, except that it doesn't mention self-care. Similarly, the social dimension sounds a little like the "social networks" point of the star, but again the mapping is not exact. There are many other such approaches, all of which come with their own sophisticated measurement tools, and again none of them correspond closely to one another. The fact that research and evaluation by practitioners has given rise to such different ways of thinking about wellness suggests something important — that any attempt by a particular government agency to assess the wellness of their clients might not be the best way to define what wellness actually is.

The eight dimensions picture is labelled as a way of defining wellness, and the recovery star is often interpreted in the same way, but each was designed simply to measure the success of specific government programs — rehabilitation from substance abuse, certain types of mental health provision, and so on. Government agencies have to measure their outcomes, of course, but this book addresses a different challenge, a much more wide-ranging question of how communities can help people improve their own wellness, proactively and with local support. There is no reason to think that our answer will look the same as theirs.

In particular, we are not seeking a definition of wellness that can produce standardized results such as those from a physical checkup. A full set of clinical health tests will generate a set of numbers including your systolic and diastolic blood pressure, cholesterol reading, blood sugar levels, and more. A medical professional can then interpret these numbers for you, applying complex rules to prescribe drugs and other measures that may alleviate or prevent physical illness for you. Is this the same model we would wish to apply to improve your wellness?

We might try to do exactly that if, for example, we wanted to create the equivalent of a national health service for wellness — a ministry of life, which intervened in every area of your existence. Suppose your wellness checkup showed that your housing was unsatisfactory — a wellness professional might prescribe home improvements that you should put in place, perhaps suggesting paint colours that would suit your temperament. If the problem was your marriage, they might prescribe relationship counselling or even, depending on the numbers, a divorce. This seems dangerously close to a nightmare vision of thought control by a totalitarian government. Data is vital, of course, but before trying to collect it, we need to examine our intentions. If we are not careful, the means will determine the ends.

The classic example of data collection leading to unfortunate outcomes is eugenics. Originating in analysis of aristocratic family trees by the English scientist Francis Galton (1822 — 1911), eugenics is based on the idea that you can distinguish heritable traits of humans, classify them for desirability, then control human breeding so as to preserve only the good ones. Proponents often had a grand vision: the establishment of a perfected human race. In practice, eugenics was based on preventing certain people from reproducing.

This didn't apply only if you had a mental or physical disability. You were deemed unfit to have children if you were illiterate, or scored badly in intelligence tests. People who were alcoholic, aggressive (if male), promiscuous (if female), or judged by the standards of the day to show criminal or deviant tendencies were also excluded from contributing to the future of the race. Others who didn't make the cut were members of minority groups such as African-Americans, Hispanics, or indigenous people. Generally, it was thought best to remove the poor from the gene pool whenever possible.

In the twentieth century, this chain of thought led not only led to Nazi extermination programs that killed millions but to drastic state intervention in family life by other countries. In the US, for example, powerful interests commissioned research and influenced policy to promote eugenics. Charities funded by the Rockefeller family funded the National Committee on Mental Hygiene, which raised awareness of mental illness and lobbied for psychological supervision of child development.[114] The Carnegie-funded Eugenics Record Office and the Draper-funded Pioneer Fund helped bring eugenics ideas into prominence, making psychology courses into vehicles for eugenics propaganda. A graduate of the Record Office training program wrote: "I hope to serve the cause by infiltrating eugenics into the minds of teachers. It may interest you to know that each student who takes psychology here works up his family history and plots his family tree."[115]

This led in due course to laws empowering doctors to sterilize people believed were unsuitable to reproduce. From 1907 to 1963, the US forcibly sterilized 64,000 people.[116] Canada was slow by contrast, starting twenty years later and only ever managing to sterilize around 2,800 people by force between 1928 and 1972.[117] Sweden, however, sterilized 21,000 people by force from 1941 to 1976, an impressive total for a country whose total population is under two percent that of the US.[118] Japan carried on for another twenty years after even Sweden threw in the towel, sterilizing 16,500 people between the passing of a National Eugenic Law in 1940 and its eventual abolishment in 1996.[119]

Forced sterilisation is now illegal in all these countries, thankfully. Nevertheless, eugenics is an idea that refuses to go away, rearing its head again in modern times with the emergence of techniques for gene editing that can affect not only you but also your descendants, and even thought leaders such as Richard Dawkins wondering "whether, some 60 years after Hitler's death, we might at least venture to ask what the moral difference is between breeding for musical ability and forcing a child to take music lessons."[120]

Putting aside the obvious moral issues with tactics such as forced sterilization, eugenics is bad science. There is no objective way to partition and score human characteristics. Eugenicists are particularly keen to remove from the gene pool the individuals that they feel to be antisocial, but this is a meaningless classification, saying more about the people making the judgement and about social conditions such as housing, education, and nutrition than about the people being judged. Positive qualities such as sporting or musical ability are just as culturally specific, and their emergence in an individual is just as affected by a range of environmental and emotional factors. A strapping six-foot youth with perfect pitch might have a head start in playing hockey or the double bass but no interest in doing either, or lack the personal qualities necessary to succeed.

It is also quite likely that such an engineered person would have unexpected characteristics that no-one wanted. We now understand that genes are expressed in complex and variable ways, even when it comes to medical conditions such as physical disability or susceptibility to certain forms of cancer. Genes are not a blueprint but a recipe, and the way in which they affect the development of an organism is dependent on a wide number of environmental factors that are difficult to understand, let alone control.[121]

If any further evidence against eugenics is needed, we

will see in the discussion of collaboration theory below that the human brain evolved as it did because of the inherent advantages of teamwork, and effective teams need a mixture of personality types. A eugenic future in which different races of humans are bred to play specific roles within teams, like ants in a nest or bees in a hive, is a depressing enough thought to deter most of us from believing that genetically engineering could perfect the human race once and for all.

The pernicious idea that you could breed people for wellness obsessed many psychologists from the nineteenth century until late in the twentieth century. However, there was one who, even at the height of the mania for eugenics, saw a different way forward.

What wellness is

Positive psychology explores how becoming self-activated can help you flourish. PsyCap captures the importance of Hope, (Self-)Efficacy, Resilience, and Optimism in overcoming challenges and achieving goals.

Our children learned about Maslow's Hierarchy of Needs in the village primary school, which goes to show how deeply embedded in society the idea has become. In 1943, American psychologist Abraham Maslow proposed that you can understand how healthy human beings manage their needs by grouping them into levels, although his original paper didn't include the image of a pyramid that afterwards became associated with the idea.[122]

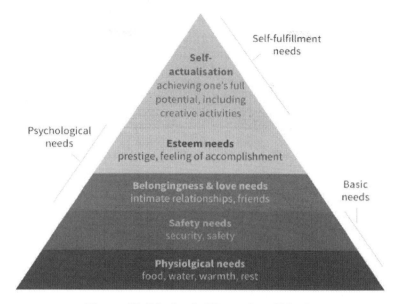

Figure 27: Maslow's Hierarchy of Needs

The Hierarchy of Needs aims to show how people are motivated. Maslow recognized that most of us feel a mixture of different needs at any one time, but argued that people tend to prioritize each level in turn. He felt that initially you are most motivated by physiological needs such as sustenance and warmth. Once these needs are met, your focus moves up level by level through safety and human interactions towards prestige and creativity.

Maslow's real interest was in the top of the pyramid, needs for self-actualization, which enable a person to reach their fullest potential. He believed that only about 2 percent of people would ever develop the qualities necessary for this, such as honesty, independence, awareness, objectivity, creativity, and originality.[123] Towards the end of his life, Maslow developed the notion of a sixth level. "Transcendence refers to the very highest and most inclusive or holistic levels of human consciousness, behaving and relating, as ends rather than means, to oneself, to significant others, to human beings in general, to other species, to nature, and to the cosmos."[124]

These ideas have been widely criticized. Academics attack Maslow's methodology — he studied only people he admired, such as the iconic genius Albert Einstein, social reformers Jane Addams, Eleanor Roosevelt, and Frederick Douglass, and the healthiest 1 percent of the college student population. They deplore the absence of any supporting evidence then or now for people being motivated in the way Maslow described. Critics also point out that Maslow's ranking is subjective and debatable. For example, he treated sex as a physiological need along with food and breathing.

People are certainly less predictable than Maslow's hierarchy suggests. Every love song tells the story of someone willing to place a relationship above their basic needs. The machinations of royalty throughout the ages prove how prestige has always motivated some people more than relationships. The sufferings welcomed for the sake of holiness by ascetics and the penury that artists put up with for art's sake show how some people will prioritize above everything the sixth level Maslow eventually added.

However, none of this has dented the massive influence of the Hierarchy of Needs. Business books and management consultants have made use of it since the 1960s, and the Hierarchy is still well-known enough in the Internet age for a meme to go viral that shows a new bottom level need, for Wi-Fi. To understand why the Hierarchy endures, we need to set it into the context of Maslow's life and his more general thinking.

Figure 28: Abraham Maslow, creator of the hierarchy of human needs

Abraham Maslow (1908 — 1970) was a poor Jewish kid from an unhappy family of first-generation immigrants in a rough area of New York.[125] Outside the home, anti-Semitic gangs chased him, throwing rocks. Inside it, he grew to hate his mother: "What I had reacted to was not only her physical appearance, but also her values and world view, her stinginess, her total selfishness, her lack of love for anyone else in the world — even her own husband and children — her narcissism, her Negro prejudice, her exploitation of everyone, her assumption that anyone was wrong who disagreed with her, her lack of friends, her sloppiness and dirtiness..."[126]

Maslow lifted weights, studied hard, became an academic, and raised a family with his childhood sweetheart.

He was six years old when the first world war started, and at thirty-three with two children, ineligible for the 1941 draft in the second, but became horrified by war. In 1951, he left New York for Massachusetts to become head of psychology at Brandeis University, which ten years later helped him establish the American Association for Humanistic Psychology. Maslow had overcome his own past to find fulfilment and peace, and believed his colleagues should be helping others to do the same.

Maslow thought most psychologists were looking in the wrong place for an understanding of human behaviour. Since the emergence of psychology as a scientific discipline in the nineteenth century, research, conferences, and therapies had focused on the analysis and treatment of abnormal behaviour and mental illness. Maslow wanted to know more about positive mental health. "It is as if Freud supplied us the sick half of psychology and we must now fill it out with the healthy half."[127]

Leading approaches of the time included psychoanalysis, which focuses on unconscious repression of traumatic events, and behavioural therapy, which tries to help people break learned thoughts, beliefs, attitudes, and behaviours that are damaging. Maslow's ideas led to new ideas and therapies based less on the detection of mental disorders and more on personal empowerment. He believed that people possess the necessary inner resources for personal growth and healing, so the purpose of therapy is simply to unblock their use. The continuing popularity of his ideas, despite criticism from academics, shows how deeply the approach speaks to people. It is almost as if the details don't matter. The intention is the important part. Focusing on self-improvement seems to help people think constructively about their lives.

Rather than continually re-examining the past, humanistic psychology focuses on the here and now. Therapists encourage people to take personal responsibility for their actions (both good and bad), to believe in their own personal value whatever they have experienced, and to strive to become happy through personal growth and self-understanding. As you might expect from an approach that emerged in the 1960s, this sounds like an idealistic New Age vision — and like some other ideas of the time, it had a brief academic heyday in the 1970s before moving into the world of self-help books, fads, gurus, and accessories. However, towards the end of the century another group of academics returned to the ideas, giving them new terminology, new credibility, and new therapy tools.

Psychologist Martin Seligman was born in 1942, so is from the generation after Maslow, and could be considered to have inherited his mantle in the promotion of wellness to psychologists. Seligman's first major research was into the psychological condition in which a person or animal learns through experience to behave helplessly in a bad situation, even when they actually have the power to do something about it. Seligman argued that mental illnesses such as depression can be caused, at least in part, by feeling out of control.[128]

Figure 29: Martin Seligman, founder of the positive psychology movement

This interest in self-activation, or lack of it, infuses Seligman's later work. Like Maslow before him, Seligman came to focus less on mental disorder and more on well-being and happiness. Seligman led this approach back into the mainstream in 1998, when he became president of the American Psychological Association, and chose as the theme for his term "positive psychology". Like Maslow's humanistic psychology, positive psychology sets out to re-dress an imbalance in which practitioners focus too much on relieving misery, and develop interventions targeted mainly at mental illness. Positive psychologists explore how therapists can intervene in a patient's life to help them "flourish".

Seligman distinguishes three forms of flourishing. In the pleasant life, you experience good emotions and understand how to amplify them. In the good life, you engage with your activities fully and enter a state of flow. In the meaningful life, you gain a sense of purpose by contributing to something bigger than yourself. It turns out that the benefits of the pleasant life only endure if you also have a good or meaningful life.[129] Research by positive psychologists also shows that people who flourish are not more religious, fitter, richer, or better looking. They don't have more good events and fewer bad events. They are more social, typically being in a romantic relationship and having a diverse friend set, but this not the cause of their happiness.

Seligman separates well-being into five different elements, which he gives the mnemonic PERMA:[130]

- **P**ositive Emotion. Feeling good, positive emotions, optimism, pleasure and enjoyment. Remember to adopt a positive perspective as often as you can.

- **E**ngagement. Fulfilling work, interesting hobbies, "flow". Find the things that make you happy and engaged.

- **R**elationships. Social connections, love, intimacy, emotional and physical interaction. Focus on your relationships with family and friends, and find ways to connect.

- **M**eaning. Having a purpose, finding a meaning in life. Search for meaning and lead a life of purpose.

- **A**ccomplishments. Ambition, realistic goals, important achievements, pride in yourself. Savour your accomplishments and strive for a life of further achievement.

Used in therapy, PERMA has been shown to produce minor improvements to quality of life, helping people count their blessings, act with more kindness, set personal goals, show gratitude, and focus on their personal strengths. A review of its impact concluded that "effect sizes are small, but still significant for subjective well-being and psychological well-being, indicating that effects are fairly sustainable."[131] This level of impact makes a real difference to some but might not be enough to help people with deep, complex wellness challenges.

For one thing, Seligman is a psychologist, not a social worker — he studies the mind, not money, safety, or other material concerns that have a massive impact on wellness. For another, he and his colleagues are setting out to redress a balance in psychology, which has traditionally focused on helping the miserable become less so rather than helping the happy become more so. His work is not targeted at people who are really suffering. As a result, PERMA doesn't include the basic needs of Maslow's hierarchy, which may be your main concern if you have radical wellness issues and need to turn your life around in a big way. Those among us who face life challenges beyond their control cannot make progress without wraparound support that is practical, detailed, and tailored to their personal situation. We'll return to this below.

PERMA may not provide everything that some people need, but another tool of positive psychology may have wider application. Before we come to PsyCap, though, it is worth noting that positive psychology has its critics. Some point out the importance of recognizing negative things about yourself and of real problems that may be affecting your mind. More generally, evidence is missing for the categorizations made by positive psychologists, just as it is for the Hierarchy of Needs. It seems to be very difficult to get people to agree what wellness is. Standing back from the modern-day discipline of psychology, this may be an impossible challenge.

Academics in psychology or any other field must define what they are talking about, or their writings will be meaningless. However, the chances of positive psychologists gaining the universal, lasting agreement of mankind on a definition of wellness are slim, since people have already been discussing it for thousands of years in books of religion and philosophy without coming anywhere close to a consensus. Wellness encompasses complex notions such as happiness and self-fulfillment. It relates to many things, each of which has multiple aspects — outlook on life, relationships, work, spirituality, health, and so on. The relative importance of each aspect to a person may be influenced by where and when they live, as well as by their family background and personality.

There is also a feedback loop between our good or bad experiences of life — in a personal relationship or at work, for example — and the attitudes we adopt, such as remembering to be positive and finding ways to connect. Winning in a sports match, attention from someone you respect, or a family member getting the all clear in a medical test will leave you in a positive state of mind, ready to engage, full of purpose, and at the end of the day you might decide to bring an unexpected gift home for your partner. A split note in a trumpet solo, forgetting your lines on stage, or arriving late for an important meeting might put you into an unhelpful one — nervous, lacking confidence, and not as mindful of other people's feelings as you would like to be. The situations we find ourselves in, or put ourselves in, give rise to complex, intermingled responses, and these responses then make a difference to our situations.

A formula such as PERMA is a thinking tool for psychologists, on which they can base the design of interventions. It allows a therapist to separate your responses into categories then help you adjust your attitudes going forward. This doesn't mean that your brain is using PERMA to create your responses. Inside your head, it is much more complicated — good emotions are entangled with a fulfilling job, love can give meaning to life, ambition leads to optimism or the other way around, and so on ad infinitum. Everything is mixed up with everything else, in ways that are highly personal and vary throughout our lives, as well across cultures and throughout history.

Luckily, we don't need a perfect definition of wellness or a complete understanding of how the human brain generates it in order to help people change their lives for the better. What this book will make use of from positive psychology is not its definitions but one of the tools it has produced. Just as Maslow's pyramid entered business thinking, so too is positive psychology being adopted by organisations concerned about the personal development of their staff. They are looking at the characteristics of organisations — for example, to help improve the way an organisation functions in a crisis — and of their staff, to try and understand what attitudes and behaviours lead to higher performance in the workplace. The latter has given rise to a notion so simple and general purpose that anyone can use it, whatever their circumstances, to improve their own wellness. It is called positive psychological capital, or PsyCap.

PsyCap aims to release the HERO within. HERO is used here not only as a metaphor but also as an acronym, for **H**ope, (Self-)**E**fficacy, **R**esilience, and **O**ptimism. Hope is feeling determined to achieve goals and planning to reach them. (Self-)Efficacy is your confidence in being able to accomplish this plan. Resilience is how well you recover from stress, conflict, failure, or the other challenges that inevitably arise along the way. Optimism is what motivates you — the underpinning expectation that your life really will improve, and that you will overcome obstacles along the way. Optimistic people often try to turn obstacles to their own advantage.[132]

PsyCap is (please excuse the technical language) really neat, in my opinion. For a start, it is not actually about organisations and employees at all, but plain common sense that anyone can use to turn around their personal journey through life. If you are going to get somewhere, you need to decide where you are going and find it on a map (Hope), feel able to make the trip (Self-Efficacy), deal with upsets along the way (Resilience), and believe you will reach the destination (Optimism). What's more, the approach works without needing all the academic psychologists in the world to agree on a definition of wellness, or neurologists to define exactly how the brain works. If you can work out what you want to achieve, PsyCap tells you, and the people who care about you, the state of mind you need to develop in order to get there. We'll talk later on about help from other people in acquiring a positive state of mind.

First, though, let's talk about what goals a person might want to achieve. What wellness goals should you put in your HERO plan? As you might expect, your route to wellness depends on who you are.

Intervening in wellness

Some people cannot increase their wellness without access to, and help in using, practical as well as psychological resources - the poor in particular, since early disadvantage lowers your ability to thrive unaided.

Wellness is a common human aspiration, but different humans face a different level of challenge in achieving it.

Martin Seligman explains some of the ways in which positive psychologists help people overcome wellness challenges. He calls these interventions. In his 2004 TED talk, "The new era of positive psychology", Seligman describes three examples: beautiful day, gratitude visit, and strengths date.

"Just to sample the kind of interventions that we find have an effect: when we teach people about the pleasant life, how to have more pleasure in your life, one of your assignments is to take the mindfulness skills, the savoring skills, and you're assigned to design a beautiful day. Next Saturday, set a day aside, design yourself a beautiful day, and use savoring and mindfulness to enhance those pleasures. And we can show in that way that the pleasant life is enhanced.

Gratitude visit. I want you all to do this with me now, if you would. Close your eyes. I'd like you to remember someone who did something enormously important that changed your life in a good direction, and who you never properly thanked. The person has to be alive. Now, OK, you can open your eyes. I hope all of you have such a person. Your assignment, when you're learning the gratitude visit, is to write a 300-word testimonial to that person, call them on the phone in Phoenix, ask if you can visit, don't tell them why. Show up at their door, you read the testimonial -- everyone weeps when this happens. And what happens is, when we test people one week later, a month later, three months later, they're both happier and less depressed.

Another example is a strengths date, in which we get couples to identify their highest strengths on the strengths test, and then to design an evening in which they both use their strengths. We find this is a strengthener of relationships."

How you feel about the value of these interventions will depend very much on your needs. Let's illustrate this by imagining some people with different wellness issues.

Suppose you are in your late twenties, with the family background, education, and contacts that you need in order to thrive, but are blocked from doing so by psychological issues, as well as physical symptoms that you suspect are really psychosomatic (migraines, backaches, digestive problems, and so on). You need to get your head together and start enjoying life.

One way to do this might be therapy sessions with a positive psychologist, who may recommend interventions such as those above. Counselling will take a few months, and during this time your work may continue to suffer. You might even lose your job, or need to take time out. However, this doesn't matter too much — you have a university degree and can tap a social network to get back on track when you've got your head together.

Another example. You and your partner had just retired and were both looking forward to the next stage of life when your partner suddenly died. You have minor mobility issues but can get about unaided. You volunteer in a charity shop, and your children visit occasionally, but apart from that you don't see many people and have no enthusiasm for your old shared interests. You don't feel that excited about anything these days.

Again, positive psychology could really help you. You have plenty to live for, even if you can't see that just now. Interventions designed to restore your love of life may well enable to you work through the stages of grief and come out the other side with a new way forward.

Other people with low wellness, however, find themselves in radically different situations. Here are three more examples.

Suppose you are a single mother living on a run-down housing estate, with low-paid care work that only just covers the bills even after working long hours, and an alcoholic ex-husband who can sometimes be abusive. You dream of qualifying as a dental nurse, but your first priorities are finding child care to cover your working hours, ensuring both your child's safety and your own, and getting your home into a livable state. However, you never get time to sort any of this out, and feel that you are running from pillar to post every day without making any real progress.

Or suppose you left the armed forces with a disability and anger management issues. You would like to form a steady relationship, which means adjusting in various ways, not least to your new physical capabilities. You also need to find both a new occupation and new pastimes. Your passion was always playing football, but that's not an option any more. If you are to get a job and hold it down, you'll have to come up with a new way to have a bit of stress-relieving fun at evenings and weekends — and avoid doing so via alcohol, which is not so easy when all your old mates drink heavily.

Final example — you left a children's home two years ago and after a period living rough, doing whatever it took to get by, have managed to get off drugs and are selling the Big Issue. You hope for a room in a hostel but don't know what the next step might be. You never got any qualifications, still struggle with low self-respect, and don't have the faintest idea what your aptitudes might be. Next year your sister gets out of the home and you're worried about her. It's hard to see where to start.

People like these last three examples have more to deal with than low psychological wellbeing. They also have serious practical problems and need access to resources in order to solve them, as well as help in making use of these resources. Otherwise, they will not thrive and there is a limit to how long they can even keep their heads above water. The feedback loop discussed above, between experiences of life and personal attitudes, typically sends people into a downwards spiral that is hard to break out of. When someone is struggling to keep their head together, their performance at work and their behaviour outside of it are both likely to suffer. This increases their stress level and decreases their self-esteem, causing them to behave even worse, and things to go still further out of kilter.

Creating a beautiful day or making a gratitude visit is unlikely to make a long-term difference to people struggling with real practical problems. They often accept that their mental attitudes could be better, and welcome offers of mental health counselling. However, they know very well that they won't be able to sustain good mental health until they have a way forward with their practical issues. In the meantime, they might even welcome informal help as much as (possibly more than) professional therapy, both for moral support day to day and to have some assistance with in dealing with the authorities over housing, work, finance, justice, and so on. We need to think about interventions in a much broader way than helping people change how they think about things, and recognize the importance to society as a whole of doing so.

Just as we now view debt as a moral failing of the borrower, rather than of the lender as people did in older societies, there is a modern tendency in some quarters to consider poor people in bad situations as having brought it upon themselves in some way, and therefore to be less than fully deserving of help. However, it's important to recognize what a different start in life some people get compared to others, and how much impact this has on their ability to cope unaided. The previous section described how political and economic forces are returning financial inequality to nineteenth century levels. This is generating a corresponding inequality of wellness. In fact, there disparity of wellness may be even greater, since financial privilege brings both psychological and physical advantages that are not obvious or easily measurable.

Let's start with a minor illustration of this: music education. Most of us value music for its own sake, just as listeners. What has been proven in recent years is how valuable it is for children to learn to play an instrument, and how it affects all areas of personal development. A comprehensive review of research in 2015 shows that music does more than any other extra-curricular activity to improve your life chances.[133] As you might expect, learning to make music makes you a better listener, but it also improves your memory for things you hear, and makes you more proficient with language (written as well as spoken). Playing an instrument improves your ability to think in three dimensions, which is a key enabler for mathematical skill. Musical ability leads to better scores in intelligence tests and in all school subjects, as well as enhancing your creativity. It helps you learn to concentrate, focus on goals, and think about several things at once.

Music brings other psychological advantages that give you a head start in life. Musical performance provides a sense of accomplishment, and practicing increases your determination and persistence. Musical achievement increases self-confidence and self-respect, as well as making you more aspirational. Working with others in a musical band or ensemble develops social skills, helping you feel that you belong and showing you how to work as part of a team. Similarly, this encourages emotional intelligence, improving skills such as empathy, sensitivity, tolerance and ethical understanding. Overall, playing music makes you less stressed and less anxious.

The readily observable advantages of music education are corroborated by evidence from neuroscience.[134] This reveals that the corpus callosum — the mass of fibers connecting the two cerebral hemispheres — is significantly larger in people who play music, particularly if they started early. This means that music helps coordinate the left and right halves of our brain. Musicians also have larger cerebellums, containing more and denser synapses. Musicians have better motor skills. Learning to play music also increases the concentration of what is called gray matter, which is responsible for information processing. Study music, and you'll become better at thinking generally.

Despite all this, growing inequality means that less and less children from disadvantaged backgrounds have access to music education. In the UK, for example, government funding cuts to state education mean that many British schools have been forced to drop music (along with other arts subjects) from the curriculum in order to prioritize the STEM subjects of science, technology, engineering and mathematics. A report commissioned by the Musicians' Union in 2019 reveals that despite undeniable evidence for the benefits to every aspect of a child's development and wellbeing of learning music, provision remains patchy and children from poorer backgrounds do not have adequate access to music education. Children from families with an income of under 28,000 pounds per year are half as likely to learn an instrument as those from families with an income of over 48,000 pounds per year.[135]

Access to high value extracurricular activities such as music is the very tip of the iceberg when it comes to the wellness advantages of coming from a financially secure background. The bulk of the iceberg is not even the further physical, intellectual, emotional, and spiritual benefits that come from private lessons, school trips, and family holidays to ride horses, ski, sail, surf, visit museums and galleries, and explore foreign cultures — what is sometimes called cultural capital. The third part of the iceberg, the huge part hidden beneath the sea, is not directly related to money at all, but rather to the psychological influences on a child's development that motivate them to succeed in life — that unlock the HERO within, as PsyCap puts it.

Large scale research published by the Joseph Rowntree Foundation in 2010 concluded that children growing up in poorer families emerge from school with substantially lower levels of educational attainment, which "is a major contributing factor to patterns of social mobility and poverty", and the authors attribute this mainly to parental influences.[136] In early years, it makes a major difference if parents are able to create a learning environment in the home and spend time reading to their children. At school, children thrive the more that parents encourage them to aim for higher education and help them to avoid antisocial behaviour. Learned behaviours repeat across the generations: "Children's test scores are lowest when poverty has persisted across the generations, and highest when material advantage has been long-lasting."

Exactly the same conclusion emerged from more recent research in Germany, which concluded that "disparities in the level of parental investments hold substantial importance for [Socio-Economic Status] gaps in economic preferences and, to a lesser extent, IQ. In light of the importance of IQ and preferences for behaviors and outcomes, our findings offer an explanation for social immobility."[137] A child from a poor background is less likely to get the extracurricular activities, cultural capital, and parental support that not only equip them to succeed in life but make them feel they have a good chance of doing so. The gulf between them and the more privileged is much more than financial. Poor kids are less likely to have a sound mind in a sound body, and so are competing in the game of life with one hand tied behind their back.

You may be wondering to what extent poor people are simply less innately gifted. This awkward question has been the subject of much research and debate, with no conclusion either way.[138] However, what has become clear is that parental attitudes are a much stronger influence on future socio-economic status than parental intelligence.[139] Researchers across the spectrum are agreed that until society does something about this, meritocracy is an illusion.

Doing something about this is a sensitive issue, since it could be viewed as interference in family life. This is for policy makers to grapple with. Here, I am arguing only that we should act to alleviate the effects of a disadvantaged family life that emerge when kids become adults (and often, parents). There are two reasons why. First, it is unfair. A child gets no choice over the background they are born into. If as an adult they wish to raise the bar for themselves and their own children, that is an admirable ambition that we should all do as much as we can to support. Second, it's cheaper for society to help people with complex life challenges than to do nothing. The costs to society of leaving them to suffer are enormous, as we can see by examining current social issues in the UK.

The costs of low wellness

People who consume many government services generate massive cost to society. They are stigmatized as criminal or lazy but typically have long-standing health conditions that generate further wellness issues.

As described in the Preface, 30 percent of the UK population are "living below an adequate standard of living and are just about managing at best", a percentage that is increasing dramatically with rising inequality.[140] Being economically fragile means that any unexpected event can tip you over the line into dependence on state resources. As more people become economically fragile, the demand on such resources is growing, and the government is finding it harder and harder to keep up.

Research released in 2019, before coronavirus, predicts

that, by 2023-2024, UK government resources for social care will fall short of what is required by at least 10.4 billion pounds (the gap would be a mere 8.7 billion pounds if staff are not given pay increases in line with those planned increases for healthcare workers, but this would make it almost impossible to recruit).[141] The report outlines a terrifying future in which the entire social care system of the UK falls apart.

When it comes to the residential care of older people, "the amounts local authorities are able to pay towards someone's care are below the full cost of delivering care. Local authorities are increasingly reporting that providers are handing back contracts deemed unviable. The challenges facing providers is well illustrated by the recent news that one of the country's largest care home groups, Four Seasons Health Care, has gone into administration." More generally, the researchers describe the entire social sector as unsustainable, citing for example that, "There are just over 40,000 nurses working in adult social care but almost a third are estimated to have left their role within the past 12 months."

Despite this black picture, people who work in the social services have always understood very well how the costs could be reduced. They know from daily experience that a high proportion of their budget goes on a small number of clients with particularly complex needs. They also know that these people consume similar proportions of budget in other services. This is because people with the lowest wellness often have many different interactions with government.

Our example people — the single mother, ex-soldier, and Big Issue seller — are probably each dealing with multiple services including healthcare, social care, housing, police, justice, education, welfare, and more. This brings two types of cost to government. First there is service delivery itself — medical treatments including for Medically Unexplained Symptoms, prescriptions including for antidepressants, home visits, rental subsidies, case management, and so on. On top of that, the clinicians, social workers, police officers, teachers, and others involved all know that their work won't be effective unless it is joined up with the help that others are trying to provide. So, on top of doing their own paperwork they all try to coordinate with each other, writing documents, sending emails, making telephone calls, arranging and holding meetings. This is time-consuming, and not even very effective (we'll see below how to improve the collaboration required for wellness).

In the UK, the disproportionate costs of dealing with the neediest in society gave rise to the Troubled Families programme. At the launch in 2011, Prime Minister David Cameron claimed that "a relatively small number of families are the source of a large proportion of the problems in society. Drug addiction. Alcohol abuse. Crime. A culture of disruption and irresponsibility that cascades through generations. We've always known that these families cost an extraordinary amount of money, but now we've come up the actual figures. Last year the state spent an estimated 9 billion pounds on just 120,000 families. That is around 75,000 pounds per family."[142]

In 2012, a report on troubled families illustrated this further with anecdotal case studies. "The most striking common theme that families described was the history of sexual and physical abuse, often going back generations; the involvement of the care system in the lives of both parents and their children, parents having children very young, those parents being involved in violent relationships, and the children going on to have behavioural problems, leading to exclusion from school, anti-social behaviour and crime."[143]

Over the next few years, the Troubled Families programme descended into a storm of controversy, with accusations of poor data usage and the final evaluation of work from 2012-2015 finding no evidence of any impact whatsoever.[144] The lead author said in 2016, "As far as we can tell from extensive and voluminous analysis of tens of thousands of individual records, using data from local authorities, the Department for Work and Pensions, HMRC, the Department for Education and the Police National Computer, the troubled families programme had no discernible impact on the key outcomes it was supposed to improve at all. It didn't make people any more (or less) likely to come off benefits, to get jobs, to commit fewer crimes and so on."[145]

Nevertheless, a second five-year phase of the programme started in 2015, this time with a more rigorous approach, and an evaluation update in 2019 told a different story about the members of troubled families.[146] It turns out only 4.6 percent of adults and 2.5 percent of children had ever been cautioned or convicted by the police. Less than one in seven families have any member dependent on either drugs or alcohol. Three quarters of troubled families are happy in their relationships. Over half believe they eat healthily although one in five say they cannot afford to.

However, around three-quarters of troubled families have at least one person with a long-standing health condition and in around half the main carer is disabled. Just under half have children with special needs, and two in five have a member with mental health problems. About two thirds of adults in troubled families are out of work, for which the most common reason is mental health, and over half the families are on benefits. Troubled families aren't bad, but they have low wellness, and this keeps them poor.

There is an unfair stigma attached to the worst off in society, who are often labelled with derogatory terms such as chav, pilloried in the press, and mocked in social media.[147] It might make more sense to look at the other end of society to find the truly irresponsible, abusive, and criminal elements. The UK establishment, for example, has been rocked by scandals over the last decade. Secret memos released in 2011 showed the depth of engagement between oil companies and politicians prior to the illegal and unjustified Iraq war in 2003 that left more than 3.3 million people displaced and 6.7 million in need of humanitarian assistance.[148][149][150][151] Ten years later, the emergence of evidence for widespread child abuse over decades by prominent media and political figures, and for inadequate safeguarding by organisations responsible for child welfare, led to the creation in 2014 of the Independent Inquiry into Child Sexual Abuse to investigate child abuse in schools and children's homes as well as in major public institutions such as the BBC, Catholic Church, and Anglican Church.[152]

Internationally, the viral spread in 2017 of the #MeToo movement against sexual harassment and assault exposed not only criminal actions by powerful individuals but the wide prevalence of sexual violence in the workplace by people in positions of authority, and how often the perpetrators get away with it due to fear of reprisal. In the US, sexual harassment in the workplace is experienced by 25 percent of women, but only one out of four victims ever report it.[153] In France, less than one fifth of workplaces take any measures to prevent harassment.[154]

We saw in the Introduction how attitudes to government, commerce, and debt have changed in modern times. If Dante was born today, he would probably put usurers in heaven, not the lowest circle of hell, for contributing to Gross Domestic Product via the interest on their loans to business. By contrast, when the desperate people struggling to meet the payments on payday loans with an Annual Percentage Yield of 500% shuffle off this mortal coil, ten years earlier than the better off in society,[155] it might be out of the frying pan into the fire.

Troubled families are not the ones taking advantage of others in society. If they consume more than their share of state resources, it is because they are unwell. Given that the first phase of the troubled families programme misunderstood so badly the people they were trying to help, it's not surprising that it failed. Even the more data-driven second phase is making very limited progress, achieving at best minor improvements and more often mixed, insignificant, or even negative changes against the indicators it measures. In order to do better at reducing the costs to the state of the neediest in society, we need to find a different way to understand the problems they experience — a better description of the issues faced by people with low wellness.

Wellness wheels

Using a wellness wheel to show how practical life issues are interconnected enables people to work through their personal challenges and set achievable goals for each one. This is the first step towards PsyCap.

We've seen how Maslow and Seligman break down the psychological aspects of wellbeing in quite different ways. Similarly, there are many different ways to analyze the practical life challenges faced by people with the lowest wellness. I'll give one such way in a moment. First, though, let's qualify it.

The practical aspects of wellness differ according to where you live, when you live, how old you are, your background, your interests, your beliefs, and more. I would imagine that my great-grand-parents, poor Jews that escaped from Polish pogroms to the London East End in the 1890s, had different life aims and obstacles to the families evacuated from the Somerset levels during the months of flooding in winter 2013-2014 that ruined their homes, cars, farms, and other businesses. The young unemployed of rural India and inner-city Bristol may share an aspiration to work in high technology, but face different challenges in achieving their dream. The number of older people in New York who are at risk from being isolated is brought into public awareness every time there is a heatwave[156] — these people probably have different concerns to the 53 percent of people over 65 in Finland who are isolated, a group in which only 2 percent claim to be lonely.[157]

Having said all this, it is helpful to have a starting point, so here is a framework that I call a wellness wheel. It shows ten wellness issues, with arrows indicating one way in which the issues affect each other. There are many more inter-connections, of course, but trying to show them all would fill the picture with so much cross-hatching as to make it unusable. One major advantage of a wellness wheel is its simplicity.

Figure 30: Wellness issues and some relationships between them — a wellness wheel

Another advantage is in showing issues as a closed loop. This visual image is powerfully reassuring, since it tells the viewer that their issues, which they may feel to be multiplying out of control, actually form a coherent, understandable picture. Without the wheel, a person may feel themselves to be alone, facing a multitude of personal demons, all terrifying in different ways. This powerlessness is reinforced by wellbeing Web sites that let the user choose different types of help from a list — the list is usually so long, with entries that overlap in such confusing ways, that it is tempting to give up before you've even started. Anything you do will just be scratching the surface.

By contrast, a wheel symbol is comforting, which is why it appears so often in religious art — think of a Hindu mandala, a Native American medicine wheel, or the Celtic cult symbol.[158] The wellness wheel shows a person that they have basically the same issues as everyone else. The problem is simply that their life has gone off balance, so they need to get the wheel turning smoothly again. They do this by setting goals for the issues that are affecting them most.

For each issue in the wheel, there are many possible goals that an individual might have. The idea is for each person to create their own wellness plan, as the basis of H in the HERO of PsyCap, **H**ope — feeling determined to achieve goals and planning to reach them. First, the person chooses an issue affecting them. Then, they look through a standard list of related goals, choosing some goals they want to focus on and writing down why (by making the wellness wheel community-specific, this list can be kept reassuringly short). They also find resources that help them with the E and R of PsyCap, but we'll discuss this later on. After working their way around the wellness wheel, they will have a full set of goals they can start working towards.

This is not a one-off activity, but something they are encouraged to do regularly. As each person makes progress with their plan, they should update its goals, replacing ones they have achieved with new goals they are now ready to make a start on. Let's look at how this works, starting with one of the example people described above: the single mother living on a run-down housing estate, with low-paid care work that only just covers the bills even after working long hours, and an alcoholic ex-husband who can sometimes be abusive. We'll call her Sarah, and work our way around the wellness wheel, starting at the top. For now, we won't discuss how to implement Sarah's wellness plan. We'll focus on what she wants to achieve.

First up is Safety, for which Sarah chooses a number of goals. She is worried about being safe in the home, where some of the sockets have exposed wiring and some shelves are coming away from the wall. She is also worried about safety on the way to and from school for her children, since there are gangs on the estate, and they have been bullied in the past, including on the school bus. A third safety concern is the children's father — she wants them to have a good relationship with him, but knows he cannot be trusted to look after them properly if he has been drinking.

Next, Transport. There is a connection with the second Safety issue when it comes to how her children get to and from school, especially for activities after hours. Sarah also has her own issue, which is the time it takes her to get to work — she has to catch two buses, and the journey takes so long that she has to leave home before the children and does not arrive home until long after they do.

Then there is Learning. If Sarah could train as a dental nurse, she could get a job that was closer to home as well as being better paid and with more flexible hours. She would also like her children to do extra-curricular activities such as sport or music, but these have a cost, and would mean them finding a way home without using the school bus.

The fourth issue is Work. Sarah knows that even before qualifying as a dental nurse, it is possible to find work as a trainee. Her oldest child has also been asking about doing a weekend job, and ideally Sarah would like to help him find one that is useful to him later in life. He is fascinated by cars, and she wonders if garages ever take on unskilled occasional staff, for example to help with tire fitting or even just administration — this might help him get an apprenticeship one day, or it might just be useful work experience if he wanted to become an engineer.

Drugs and Alcohol are not an issue for Sarah or her children, but she is worried about her ex-partner. He says he is attending clinics, and seems better than he was, but how can she be sure?

When it comes to Eating, Sarah doesn't really know whether to worry or not. She does her best, but has always struggled with weight and body image, and though she often watches television shows about healthy eating, isn't sure where to start.

Physical Activity is definitely something her family could do better at. Sarah used to enjoy sport at school but now has no time to exercise. Her children would like to do more, but the playground near them is dirty and Sarah worries it is dangerous. She thinks they could do more sport at school but isn't sure what is on offer.

Meeting people isn't top of Sarah's list right now. She has a small group of childhood friends who get together when they can. At some point, she'd like to form a partner relationship, but feels too tired to think about it most of the time. She'd like the children to have more friends, though, and thinks a good way to do this might be through team sports.

Sarah never had much Culture in her life, so doesn't know what might be on offer or how much she would enjoy it. The school sometimes offers theatre trips to the children, but you have to pay part of the cost. This doesn't seem to be a priority right now.

Similarly, Sarah can't think about Helping others until she has got her own life into better shape. However, she would like someone to talk to who can help her with interactions with the authorities — she hasn't got a computer, finds paperwork overwhelming, and would be less nervous if she had someone with her when meeting people from government agencies.

Taken together, here are the issues and goals in Sarah's first wellness plan:

- Safety
  - Safety in the home (sockets, shelves)
  - Prevent bullying (of children on the way to and from school)
  - Prevent abuse (from alcoholic father)
- Transport
  - School journey (supervision of children, including for after-hours activities)
  - Commute (time taken)
- Learning
  - Upskilling (dental nurse training)
  - Extra-curricular activities (cost)
- Work
  - On the job training (some kind of work in a dental surgery)
  - Child's part-time work (ideally in a garage)
- Drugs and Alcohol
  - Monitoring a family member (the children's father)
- Eating
  - Healthy eating (guidance)
- Physical Activity
  - Exercise (non-time consuming)

- o   Children's activity (supervised, ideally team
       sports)
- Helping
    - o   Advocacy (moral support and practical help
           with agency interactions)

These 14 goals represent the first of what will eventually be many versions of Sarah's wellness plan. As she overcomes one goal after another, about which we'll talk below, she will update her plan to remove goals that have been achieved and add new goals that she now has the head space to start thinking about, such as meeting new people and starting cultural activities (which may be related). Before making the plan, Sarah felt she was faced by an overwhelming mixture of difficulties. After working her way around the wellness wheel, she can see that it is possible to break a huge problem into manageable pieces.

The real advantage of a wellness wheel is not that it's a universal solution for everybody. It almost certainly isn't — other people, living at different times and in different places to Sarah, might find another wellness wheel more helpful. Having said this, it's possible that our other example people with low wellness could use the same wheel as Sarah — they'll just choose different issues and goals. Consider our example above of someone who left the armed forces with a disability and anger management issues. We'll call him John.

John may not be as concerned about Safety as Sarah but Transport could be top of his list — for him, this isn't just about getting around outside the home, but also about moving around inside it (for example, on the stairs). John has similar concerns to Sarah about Learning and Work, hoping like her for work where he can learn on the job and sharing Sarah's eventual aim of getting a qualification. He'd like to find a new way to do physical Activity, possibly even to start competing again. Meeting new people and Culture are important for John if he is to avoid spending too much time in a pub going forward. He knows from talking to his mates that he has PTSD, and that someone Helping with this would make him less likely to get into trouble.

Then there is our Big Issue seller, who we'll call Sam. Safety is a big deal for Sam, who is worried constantly about being found and targeted by people from his time on the streets. He is hoping to be offered more permanent accommodation, so thinks Learning how to budget and save is important, in order that he can manage when the time comes. He needs some kind of rewarding Work, and hopes to do something connected with Helping others who have been through some of the same things that he has. Sam also thinks he should have counselling, since he has trouble thinking about relationships and is not sure about his own sexuality any more.

All these wellness plans are different, but they could all be chosen from goals on the same wellness wheel. However, it might be sensible to create different wheels for people in different countries, or for people with special circumstances such as asylum seekers, persons displaced by natural disaster, and victims of epidemics. Apart from the difficulty of maintaining a universal wellness wheel, it would be huge. We could possibly use the ten issues above in a universal wellness wheel, although there would be a lot of debate about this, but would have to include so many different goals for each issue that it would become difficult for peo-

ple to use. It would also be as de-motivating as the Web
sites that just show a huge list of issues.

The important thing is to have some kind of wellness
wheel that covers all the issues you personally face, including for each issue an associated list of goals that are meaningful to you. Having a structured way to work through
your life challenges, so as to choose the goals most important in your life right now, gets you started on your
PsyCap journey by providing a basis for the H in HERO,
Hope. This first step — making your first wellness plan —
is hard, though, especially for the people who most need
one.

If life has led you to a place of low wellness, you probably feel out of control, unused to planning for personal
success and with low expectations of achieving it. To help
you overcome negative emotions, you need help in making
your wellness plan, and you will certainly need further help
in order to carry it out. This is where community comes in.

Community

Community, neighbourhood, and family

Social cohesion and engagement are at a historically low ebb. Restoring the trusting, reciprocal relationships that characterize community will release forms of value that help remedy major social challenges.

Do you remember, when you were young, hearing (or overhearing) adult jokes that you didn't understand at the time? And how they stick in your mind? My Dad told me one that I didn't work out for years, and it's not even unsuitable for children! It's an old Yiddish joke, about a tailor in a shtetl, which is a small town in nineteenth-century Poland. These cultural details are irrelevant to my purpose here, so I'm going to tell an updated version.

A man sees a sign in a bakery window: "Kate makes cakes for nothing." So, he orders one of Kate's cakes — the fanciest one, naturally. But when Kate hands it over, she also presents him with a bill. The man expresses his indignation, and Kate explains that he misread the sign. It doesn't say "Kate makes cakes for nothing" (cheery voice). It says "Kate makes cakes for nothing" (with rise and fall on the last two words).

Confused? It took me years to work out that the sign wasn't offering customers something for free. It was an existential complaint.

Let's imagine a real Kate doing this, in a small town or city neighbourhood — and because this is about something that we have to some extent lost, let's put this into the past and imagine her doing this around the end of the nineteenth century. The story would be different, wouldn't it. First, Kate's family, friends, and neighbours would come into the shop, asking her what she meant by putting up such a sign — and they would have told her that she didn't make cakes for nothing at all. Without her, who would buy the jam that Mary and her daughters made? Who would supply the school and hospital canteens? What about the apprentices she had given a start in life? And think of all the poor people who had benefited from the charity donations she had made over the years.

But suppose Kate kept her sign up. Then people might have started asking her whether everything was alright, financially. Was there anything they could do? For example, they could ask around, and see if the council or police canteens needed any sandwiches or cakes making. If Kate said no, money was not a problem, they might suggest that she do something else apart from work all the time. Did she know about the talks at the town hall? Why not come to the dance on Saturday night? Perhaps she would like to join the church choir.

If this too made no difference, Kate could expect a visit from the vicar (priest, rabbi, imam, …), asking if there was anything she wanted to talk about. The interventions would continue. Kate had always been there for her community, and if she was making a public cry for help, they were going to be there for her.

This isn't a fable about bakers, about the nineteenth century, or even about small towns. It's a story about communities, and how they have always sustained themselves with give and take relationships. Small-scale societies only work if everyone contributes. In return, people can expect some kind of support in times of trouble. There is also an associated expectation that community members will by and large behave honestly towards each other, for the simple reason that transactions of any kind within a community have little or no anonymity, so it's hard to get away with doing anything else.

This way of working together on a daily basis is actually the best definition of community that I know of. Robert Putnam, in his landmark analysis of the decline in community cohesion in America over the last third of the twentieth century, "Bowling Alone", shows how a cohesive community releases value to its members, acting as what economists would call a type of capital: "social capital refers to connections among individuals — social networks and the norms of reciprocity and trustworthiness that arise from them."[159] He highlights the general benefits to society of communities being cohesive. "Civic virtue is most powerful when embedded in a dense network of reciprocal social relations" and that "not all the costs and benefits of social connections accrue to the person making the contact.". Putnam distinguishes between two forms of social capital. Bonding reinforces exclusive identities and homogenous groups, for which he gives examples including ethnic fraternal organisations, church-based women's reading groups, and fashionable country clubs. Bridging encompasses people across diverse social cleavages — his examples here include the civil rights movement, many youth service groups, and ecumenical religious organizations. "Bonding social capital constitutes a kind of sociological superglue, whereas bridging social capital provides a sociological WD-40."

Figure 31: Robert Putnam, author of "Bowling Alone"

Putnam identifies diverse powerful effects of social capital on the ability of individuals to achieve their aspirations. "First, social capital allows citizens to resolve collective problems more easily." I will discuss this when we come to the prisoners' dilemma below. "Second, social capital greases the wheels that allow communities to advance smoothly." Making arrangements, including for business purposes, is much easier, quicker, and cheaper if the parties trust one another and can dispense with precautionary legal safeguards, surveillance equipment, monitoring checks, compliance structures, insurance, and so on. Social capital also improves the flow of information, which in itself is a powerful enabler for productive cooperation. Trust and social networks help individuals, firms, neighbourhoods, and even nations flourish economically.

"A third way in which social capital improves our lot is by widening our awareness of the many ways in which our fates are linked." People who engage actively with others in a trusting way are more tolerant, less cynical, and more empathetic. The positive impact of trust is related to the difference that positive parental influence makes to a child's development, discussed above. The positive interactions and reciprocal behaviours that a child sees within their wider social context (school, peer group, and neighbourhood) have far reaching effects on a young person's attitudes, behaviours, and choices. The way we see people interacting when we are growing up sets our expectations for life and forms the basis for our own learned behaviours. "Social capital is second only to poverty in the breadth and depth of its effects on children's lives ... social infrastructure is far more important than anyone would have predicted in ensuring the healthy development of youth."

A particular beneficial outcome for children is educational success: "there is something about communities where people connect with one another — over and above how rich or poor they are materially, how well educated the adults themselves are, what race or religion they are — that positively affects the education of children. Conversely, even communities with many material and cultural advantages do a poor job of educating their kids if the adults in those communities don't connect with one another."

John Stuart Mill described in 1861 how engagement in civic matters increases our awareness of, and concern for, the rights of others. "Still more salutary is the moral part of the instruction afforded by the participation of the private citizen, if even rarely, in public functions. He is called upon, while so engaged, to weigh interests not his own; to be guided, in case of conflicting claims, by another rule than his private partialities; to apply, at every turn, principles and maxims which have for their reason of existence the general good; and he usually finds associated with him in the same work minds more familiarized than his own with these ideas and operations, whose study it will be to supply reasons to his understanding, and stimulation to his feeling for the general interest. He is made to feel himself one of the public, and whatever is their interest to be his interest."[160]

Mill goes on to excoriate the state of affairs that results when citizens are disconnected from the processes of government. "Where this school of public spirit does not exist, scarcely any sense is entertained that private persons, in no eminent social situation, owe any duties to society except to obey the laws and submit to the government. There is no unselfish sentiment of identification with the public. Every thought or feeling, either of interest or of duty, is absorbed in the individual and in the family. The man never thinks of any collective interest, of any objects to be pursued jointly with others, but only in competition with them, and in some measure at their expense. A neighbor, not being an ally or an associate, since he is never engaged in any common undertaking for joint benefit, is therefore only a rival. Thus even private morality suffers, while public is actually extinct. Were this the universal and only possible state of things, the utmost aspirations of the lawgiver or the moralist could only stretch to make the bulk of the community a flock of sheep innocently nibbling the grass side by side."

Another benefit of community cohesion is environmental. Children who grow up in a well-connected community have a more pleasant physical environment, as do adults, since public spaces are cleaner, people are friendlier, and the streets are safer. Poverty is not as important a limiting factor, because people look after each other more. There is less crime, because people of all ages take part in community activities and events, which tend to include a mixture of ages, and older people keep an eye on the development of younger people.

A further benefit of community is its impact on health, economic prosperity, and wellness, the relationship between which is a theme of this book. Social capital leads to better local health, both physical and mental. Joining a club cuts in half your risk of dying over the next year — its positive effect is as powerful as the negative effect of smoking. Regularly attending a club, volunteering, entertaining, or attending a faith group is as good for you as getting a college degree or more than doubling your income. "The more integrated we are with our community, the less likely we are to experience colds, heart attacks, strokes, cancer, depression, and premature death of all sorts." Conversely, loneliness is as bad for one's health as smoking fifteen cigarettes a day and moderate alcohol abuse,[161] and has twice the impact of obesity in causing premature death.[162]

We'll discuss recent research into the impact of community connection on wellness below, and see how it not only helps you in an everyday practical way but with what Maslow would have called higher needs.

Yet "more than a third of America's civic infrastructure simply evaporated between the mid-1970s and the mid-

1990s", a dramatic social trend with complex causes. Inter-related changes to the way Americans live, work, and enter-tain themselves, as well as generational differences in life aspiration, led to a more disengaged society in the US. Put-nam proposes that we reinvent for modern times civic vol-untary structures such as emerged in America around the start of the twentieth century, and concludes his study by recommending large-scale societal changes that could help — improvements to civic education, workplaces that are family-friendly and community-congenial, better urban de-sign, faith movements that are pluralistic and socially re-sponsible, electronic tools that encourage face to face inter-action, a growth in participatory cultural activities, and more participation in the processes of government.

Some of these proposals have become reality over the years since Putnam wrote in 2000, and not just in America. In 2003, the European Union introduced the Working Time Directive, giving workers the right to at least 4 weeks in paid holidays each year, rest breaks, and rest of at least 11 hours in any 24 hours. The Directive also restricts excessive night work, ensures a day off after a week's work, and pro-vides for a right to work no more than 48 hours per week. The UK initiative Create Streets helps town planners "de-velop high density, beautiful, street-based economically and socially successful developments with strong local support and which residents will love for generations."[163] Social media tools such as meetup.com and nextdoor.co.uk can help communities of interest and geography bond together face to face as well as virtually. But are new regulations and new products enough? And how could we do more for ourselves to meet the challenge, without relying on gov-ernments and corporations to lead the way?

The trusting, reciprocal relationships that characterize community release forms of value that can help remedy the two great social challenges of our time — economic inequality and climate change, both of which have widespread, damaging ripple effects for people everywhere. This book sets out a way for communities to take a structured approach to restoring their own social cohesion from within. It is a recipe for restoring some of the community cohesion lost in America and elsewhere since the 1970s, as well as for restoring other enablers of community value production that I'll explore later on, such as financial and natural capitals. A close-knit social fabric improves the life of its participants in many ways, and we can all help rebuild it.

But for a community to take action, surely you need to define who is in, and who is out. Community seems very like a neighbourhood, but people who live in different places can behave in exactly the same reciprocal, trusting way — and people who live near to each other can be antagonistic or simply have no connection whatsoever. Putnam shows how "suburbs, automobiles, and the associated sprawl" disrupt community boundedness. If you live in one place, shop in another, shop in a third, take your kids to school in a fourth, see the doctor in a fifth, and belong to a social group in a sixth area, which if any is your neighbourhood? Community also seems related to family in some ways, but many families do not have positive relationships, or any working relationships at all.

As with families, it is also hard to know where to place the boundary around a geographical community. A neighbourhood can be defined in many different ways — by postcode, according to political district, or using landmarks such as streets or train tracks. Louis Golding's novel "Magnolia Street" is a fictionalized version of his early twentieth century childhood on Sycamore Street in the Hightown district of Manchester, where gentile and Jewish communities living on opposite sides of the street had little or no contact with each other (in the novel, until a pivotal event involving the life of a child).[164] In a family, you don't need to go far across the family tree to find yourself connected by blood to people you hardly know or may never have even met. The difficulty of placing a boundary around community brings another question — does reciprocity and trust for insiders mean that you are less likely to behave with tolerance and consideration towards outsiders?

We'll see that while the boundary is often unclear, this doesn't matter as much as the conditioning of behaviour that results from feeling that you belong to something. If you grow up and learn to operate within a web of reciprocal trust relationships, this sets the tone for your life, and determines your basic attitudes — how you feel about other people and how you interact in society generally. You might find it hard to say exactly what you are a part of, though. What is communal about a community?

Types of communities

Communities take varied forms and can be fluid. It is belonging that matters. The human brain evolved through social behaviour, since reciprocal altruism delivers powerful benefits that are otherwise unavailable.

A group of people may be united by all sorts of different things. The illustrative story above is about living in the same place — a man-made settlement such as a city, town or village. A sense of living in the same place might also be felt by people across a territory that is delimited by a natural boundary such as a valley or river. Others may feel themselves to be part of a community because they share a profession, faith, or political belief. They may come together through a common cause — a human rights issue, geopolitical agenda, or specific problem they feel strongly about. The members of intentional communities such as collective households, cohousing communities, ecovillages, monasteries, communes, survivalist retreats, kibbutzim, ashrams, and housing cooperatives typically hold a common social, political, religious, or spiritual vision and often follow an alternative lifestyle. People may join a professional body, grass roots organisation, or political party in order to become part of a community, or feel that they became part of this community as a result of joining. People can be united by their sexual orientation, what they perceive as their race, having a common cultural background such as place of origin, or through a language that they are able to speak.

Some communities are not about daily life at all. People with a common experience may feel it to be binding — this could be a traumatic one-off event such as violence or bereavement, or a positive repeated occasion, such as a woodland retreat that they attend every year. Committed fans of a band or television series, or owners of a specific campervan or motorbike, may declare themselves to be a community and meet regularly to assert this. Even people who use a niche device feel bonded by it — aging nerds still reminisce wistfully about the Apple Newton, for example. Humans from quite different walks of life can find ways of forming themselves into a group, and the fact that they keep doing so says something important about us.

There is a huge academic literature that explores the

different types of community, but to get to the heart of the matter we must step away from listing examples, and look at how humans are shaped by a need for connection with others. There are arguments of various kinds that human evolution stemmed directly from our social nature, in fields ranging from neuroscience to game theory. Let's start with the science. The benefits of community life may explain how our brains work.

In his 1997 book "The Symbolic Species",[165] neuroanthropologist Terrence Deacon explores how human brains may have evolved through a symbiotic relationship with the development of language, which he calls co-evolution. Deacon argues that humans are unique because of our ability to give meaning to symbols and then to reason about them. Our brains can use language to represent whole systems of meaning, in which entities have properties and are related to one another in a coherent way. Some of these entities and relationships are grounded in everyday experience — using the word "tree" to represent a particular physical object in the real world, for example — but others are imagined from that experience, such as when we work out what is likely to happen in future, or explore what-if type ideas that lead to inventions such as tools as well as new discoveries about how the world works.

The prefrontal cortex is significantly more developed in humans than in apes, and Deacon identifies it as the area of the brain where most symbol manipulation takes place. Since our brains have evolved to perform this astonishing feat, human children are born with the ability to pick up languages. He believes that the uniquely powerful brain of a human arose directly from human use of language — or rather, they arose together, each stimulating the other in a virtuous circle. There is a feedback loop between brain size and human communication, that created strong selective pressure both for evolution of the prefrontal cortex together with for a corresponding growth in human social complexity. Human brains may be an internal reflection of the close-knit social bonds that characterize human communities.

We'll talk more below about what actually happens when humans communicate, seeing that it is not as simple as one person using language to transfer information from their mind into the mind of other people. For now, it is enough to note that language only exists because we group together in a different way to other animals. Humans have a far richer social life. Animals often have powerful relationships that we would characterize as emotional, but they don't have the layers of complex ritual and associated belief systems found in even the most primitive human tribe. Animal behaviour is determined by instinct, whereas each human community has its own way of understanding and interacting with the world, which it preserves between generations via the use of language. Myths are not just shared stories, but mechanisms for driving behaviour — people use them to pass on specific understandings, and maintain certain ways of interacting with each other and the world. These social mechanisms are possible because of the evolution of the human brain, and vice-versa.

This seems a compelling argument but does not explain a number of things. For example, why does our species dominate the planet? Language and brain size might go together, but this doesn't mean that either gives us a competitive advantage over much more physically powerful animals, such as big cats or mammoths. Human use of language also does not explain why all human societies have so much in common. Other researchers argue that through natural selection we have evolved not only the ability to create social mechanisms, but also specific psychological traits, and that these have become hard wired into the human brain. "Human culture could be much more varied and surprising than it is. Our closest relatives, the chimpanzees, live in promiscuous societies in which females seek as many sexual partners as possible and in which a male will kill the infants of strange females he has not mated with. There is no human society which remotely resembles this particular pattern. Why not? Because human nature is different from chimp nature."[166]

A particular form of psychological trait that we may have evolved through natural selection — in other words, because it leads to having more children — is reciprocal altruism. There is research in a number of fields showing the competitive advantages of being nice to each other. By leading to cooperative behaviour, it brings overall benefits that selfishness would not. Individual humans stand little chance against a big cat or mammoth, but by banding together, they can drive one over a cliff to its death, then feast on the carcass. The close-knit social behaviour that characterizes human communities may have become embedded in the physical way the human brain works. Not only have we evolved the ability to create social mechanisms, but we are driven to create social mechanisms that enable each of us to take other people's feelings into account, rather than operating via brutal rules that reward only the strong, punish the weak remorselessly, and are just as red in tooth and claw as nature itself.

A similar evolutionary mechanism may explain why

humans enjoy music so much. We certainly spend plenty of money on it. In the UK, spending on music streaming was over a billion pounds in 2019.[167] In the US, it was over 20 billion dollars, and total music revenues including from also CD sales, radio play, live events, and advertising are about 43 billion dollars per year.[168] Neuroscientist Daniel Levitin hypotheses that we cannot help being drawn to music since particular regions and pathways evolved in our brains specifically for making and listening to it.[169] If so, this may be due to the huge positive impact music-making has on child development, as discussed above in relation to intervening in wellness. A large part of this impact is due to the social advantages you get from learning to make music — how it trains you to work productively with other people, and get pleasure from doing so. Our species has learned to like music since it makes us more sociable.

Any hypothesis about the way humans developed through evolution can never be tested, but there is circumstantial evidence available from psychological trials and computer models that demonstrate the competitive benefits of cooperative behaviour. The classic test is the prisoners' dilemma. There are many forms of this, but here is a typical version. Imagine that you and your friend rob a bank. There are no witnesses, but police know you were in the area, so take you into custody and interrogate you separately. If you both testify that the other one did it, you will share the blame and get 2 years in prison each. If only one of you testifies that the other one did it, they will go free and the other one will get 3 years as the sole culprit. But if neither of you confesses, the police can only get you for loitering with intent, for which you will get just 1 year each.

The interesting thing about the prisoners' dilemma is

that whatever your friend does, it seems to be sensible for you to accuse them. If they have accused you, you will end up with 2 years rather than 3. If they haven't accused you, you will go free rather than spend a year in person. However, when psychologists set up trials for people to play games based on the prisoner's dilemma, they consistently choose not to accuse the other person.

The prisoners' dilemma gave rise to a branch of mathematics known as game theory. In his 1996 synthesis of the evidence for cooperative instincts having evolved in humans, Matt Ridley describes psychological experiments created to test the prisoners' dilemma. Game theorists initially attributed people's behaviour in trials to them not being strategically sophisticated enough to realize that accusing their partner was the only rational choice. Then game theorists upped their own game. They developed more realistic versions of the prisoner's dilemma that took into account people's memory of how other individuals had behaved in the past. This helped to show the logic underpinning playing nice, and why evolutionary pressure may have hardwired it into the human brain.[170]

I like to think about it in terms of apple trees and sheep. Let's imagine a village with an apple orchard in the centre, on common land where people also let their sheep graze. By convention, each year the villagers agree when the apples are ripe, then pick them together and share them out — after all, it's much safer to pick apples if someone else holds the ladder, and it's quicker if passes you up an empty basket on a rope each time you fill one. As experienced smallholders, they also have a good idea how many sheep the land can support.

There is nothing to stop anyone coming to the orchard

one night, before the communal apple picking day, and picking some apples just for themselves. It would also be possible for someone to put more than their fair share of sheep onto the land. The apples might not be quite ripe if picked early, so a little sour, and having too many sheep on the common land would mean that they all go a little hungrier, so don't grow quite as fat. However, the thief (for in both cases this is a form of theft) would have so many more apples and sheep that they would benefit more from these tactics than from playing by the rules. How often do you think this would happen?

Well, a few children might scrump apples, risking swift punishment from any adults that spotted them, but it's unlikely that many adults who lived in the village would steal apples or add sheep. In such a small world, the risk of being found out is high so they would probably be found out, or at least suspected. It is likely they would be ostracized, prevented from sharing the common land in future years, and even forced to leave the village. Any benefit they obtained from theft in one year would be outweighed by the loss of apples and sheep in future years, and possibly also by the expense of moving to a new village.

Perhaps someone from another village might steal apples one night? It is unlikely that an individual who did this would be able to remain anonymous, even if they lived relatively far away. Humans are good at spreading the word, and eventually they would be unwelcomed as residents in any village and as traders in any market. Possibly bandits might have a go — this could be compared to the raids that tribal communities make on one another for trophies. When making a personal decision, though, it is simply a safer and more reliable choice to avoid rocking the boat and be an upstanding community member.

More importantly, few human beings would think about this situation in terms of how many apples and sheep they could potentially acquire through theft. Much of their personal wellness comes from participating in the communal activity of nurturing apples and sheep together. They look forward to the days of apple picking and a joint trip to market, where they can enjoy honest labour, have a laugh together, and take shared pleasure from the rewards afterwards. It is a highlight of the year, and makes life feel worthwhile. Not many people would give much thought to disrupting the apple and sheep traditions through theft, and if anyone suggested this, they would probably feel more outraged than tempted. The apples and sheep are not just products, but an important way of binding the community together and giving meaning to the lives of its members.

If this tale seems like common sense, you may be surprised to learn that the exact opposite is held to be true in mainstream economics. "The Tragedy of the Commons" is a principle holding that where people have access to a shared resource, self-interest will inevitably lead each of them to take as great a share as possible, leading to the resource being exhausted and of no use to anybody. The idea gained common currency, as well as a catchy name, from an article published by ecologist Garrett Hardin in 1968.[171] He referenced "a little-known pamphlet in 1833 by a mathematical amateur named William Forster Lloyd", which set out a hypothetical example in which shared use of common land by cattle herders leads to overgrazing.[172] Hardin argued that governments needed to "legislate temperance". They should not rely on people feeling a sense of responsibility towards society — which Hardin argued was unhealthy, since it led to anxiety — but rather on law. Hardin was particularly keen that laws should be introduced limiting how many children people were allowed to have. "The only way we can preserve and nurture other and more precious freedoms is by relinquishing the freedom to breed, and that very soon".

There are well-known examples of the Tragedy of the Commons such as deforestation of the Amazon rain forest from unchecked logging, depletion of fish stocks in the North Sea from over-fishing, and degradation of air quality in China from industrial pollution. In all these cases, legislation at national and international levels has been introduced to remedy the situation. This approach has limitations, since it is not only expensive for governments to police large areas of land but also intrusive. Patrols, drones, and CCTV cameras have a cost and are often resented as invasive of privacy by people in the areas they surveille. An alternative approach is to view large areas of territory as comprised of numerous parcels, each of which is the responsibility of a community, since on this smaller scale the Tragedy of the Commons turns out not to correspond to reality.

Political scientist Elinor Ostrom was awarded the Nobel Prize in Economics in 2009 for showing how communities devise complex social schemes to maintain their common resources at optimum efficiency.[173] Matt Ridley gives an example of how this worked in medieval times. "Medieval commons were not disastrous free-for-alls. They were carefully regulated communal property ... an English medieval common was a complex spider's web of jealously guarded property rights held under the supposedly benevolent umbrella of the lord of the manor, who owned the common but only on condition that he did not interfere with the rights of the commoners. There were rights of common of pasturage, estovers, turbary, pannage, piscary and common in the soil. Translated, these were rights to graze, cut wood, dig turf, turn out pigs to eat acorns, catch fish, or take gravel, sand or stone. And these rights were privately owned by individuals."[174]

Ridley goes on to outline how some of these practices have continued into modern times. "To this day, many of the Pennine moors of the north of England retain the traditional medieval rule known as 'stinting'. Each sheep being grazed on the moor is free to go where it wishes, but the shepherd is not free to add any extra sheep. He possesses a certain number of 'stints', each of which entitles him to graze one ewe, and that sheep must be one that is born on the moor and 'hefted' to a flock already there (a hefted ewe is one that knows its place and stays within a short distance of the same spot all year; an unhefted ewe will wander). The number of stints is, in theory, calculated to ensure that the moor is not overgrazed. In the Middle Ages, most village commons were stinted this way." The Tragedy of the Commons may apply on a large, impersonal scale, but at community level, people are not such fools as to tolerate selfish behaviour. In fact, the human brain seems to have hardwired mechanisms to detect when people act unfairly, and we instinctively judge such people very harshly.

Biologists like Ridley see altruism emerging from self-interest. Cooperation leads to more success in reproduction, so cooperative behaviours have become embedded into our genes, and some of these behaviours manifest as altruism. "More important than wealth, education, community size, age, family status, and employment, however, by far the most consistent predictor of giving time and money is involvement in community life. Social recluses are rarely major donors or active volunteers, but schmoozers and machers are typically both."[175] We've met the Yiddish term macher already — schmoozer is another one. Robert Putnam uses it to characterize someone who spends time in informal socializing, as opposed to a macher who makes things happen in the community.

Additional circumstantial evidence for cooperative behaviour and community life being innate to humans emerged in the 1990s when anthropologist Robin Dunbar found a correlation between primate brain size and average social group size. Comparing the average brain size of primates with that of humans, and extrapolating from the primate results, Dunbar proposed that humans have a preference for living in close-knit groups of about 150 people.[176] He explained the "Dunbar number" informally as "the number of people you would not feel embarrassed about joining uninvited for a drink if you happened to bump into them in a bar"[177] (he didn't mean that you would be happy to join any group of up to 150 people, but that most people are on informal terms with about 150 different people). Hunter-gatherer bands are usually about this size, as are military fighting units – a company typically consists of between 80 and 150 soldiers. Managers know that everything gets much more complicated, requiring a more formal organisational hierarchy, when a business grows beyond 150 staff.

Being part of a community doesn't mean you like, or even get on with, everyone in it. You may not have chosen to be a member, but belong simply through an accident of birth or circumstance. You may not particularly like being a member much of the time, and feel frustrated that you don't seem to have a choice in the matter — the experience of some young people growing up in a strict faith community, for example. However, the instinct to seek fellowship does seem to be an innate human drive. As we will see below, happy people tend to be more connected. And since connectivity conditions both our behaviours towards others and the opportunities open to us, we feel the impacts of belonging (or lack of it, isolation) every day and throughout our lives.

Scientific research into the human brain suggests that humans are driven to form communities. They didn't come into being for external historical reasons. Agricultural communities may have grown larger in order to provide sufficient food for armies or bureaucrats, but hunter gatherers were forming into tribes long before that, and no doubt the earliest farmers saw a benefit in sharing seeds, tools, tasks, beasts of burden, and produce. Humans create communities because it's better than being isolated, and if they need to come up with explanations of what they have in common, will use their creativity. What communities appear to be based on might be better thought of as a means to an end, whether their identity is proclaimed in a myth or as the name of a quartier. We have a collective impulse to find something in common, since we all understand at an instinctual level that this brings shared social capital, which in turn brings each of us benefits without which we do not flourish as individuals.

We'll use almost any means to feel a sense of belonging. The first car my wife and I owned was a Citroën Dyane, a kind of 2CV with extra boot space. When we passed another Dyane on the road, both we and they would beep each other cheerily. Later on, we owned one of the first

Chrysler PT Cruisers, a car with retro American styling, and until they became popular in the UK, had the same experience. We never went so far as to attend rallies for these models, but no doubt they existed (probably still do) and we would have been made welcome. Even if people do not have much in common as individuals, they can meet at events celebrating a minor common interest and have a jolly time together, coming away with a life-affirming sense of belonging.

In the Introduction, I discussed the idea of autopoiesis. An autopoietic system is one whose behaviours emerge as required, allowing it to survive in a chaotic world by continually re-imagining its internal order. It is driven to exist and continue existing, so meets new challenges by creating and re-creating itself as necessary. A community forms and adjusts itself in exactly this way. Many communities have no fixed boundary at all, not even a fixed definition. Both its members and its rules change over time. Not everyone who lives in a town is part of its community, or stays there forever, and the town itself may well change its physical extent over time. Members of professional organisations come and go, and the membership rules may change for cultural, legal, financial, or other reasons. We sold the Dyane and had to stop beeping cheerily until we bought the PT Cruiser. Now we don't beep anyone, and I do miss it, a little — although we now belong to new communities that are not so beep-based.

A side-effect of this chop and change inherent to community life is that most people belong to more than one community, and their combination of memberships changes throughout life. When you are fifteen, you may be a Christian Trekkie roller-skater. By the time you are fifty, you may be a Buddhist Green party member who rides a Harley. If you sell your Harley and buy a Triumph, you might start riding with new bikers, or you might stick with old mates — it's up to you. It's also up to the other Harley riders, but small-scale society is often less hard line about applying rules than larger and more impersonal institutions feel obliged to be. They might still let you join them on the road (although you'll probably end up buying the first round when you get to the pub).

Communities are often tolerant of other communities with whom they co-exist, and flexible about their own membership rules, since few people belong to just one community. Most of us hold a number of allegiances simultaneously. We can happily feel loyalty to the place we grew up as well as the place we live in now, to old school friends and new work colleagues, even to members of a faith we no longer adhere to or owners of a car we sold long ago. Just as the experience of growing up in a trusting and reciprocal social world helps children to develop confidence and personal ambition, it also teaches them to accept other people for what they are and feel comfortable interacting with others who live differently.

In a village, small town, or neighbourhood, one often sees people who may have come out with intolerant views in conversation demonstrate surprising acceptance of others when they meet in person. Immediate social presence seems naturally to over-ride the assumptions you make and prejudices you hold. Louis de Bernières' beautiful, tragic novel "Birds Without Wings"[178] illustrates how people of different cultures can live together harmoniously for centuries, understanding how they differ but not feeling constrained by it, until external powers force them into division. Given support from above by public institutions and laws, this tolerance can easily extend to a wider sphere. The Ottoman Empire whose twilight is depicted by de Bernières was celebrated in the middle ages for bringing together people and ideas from different faiths.

In modern times, the enshrining of tolerance in law has led to the notion of a hate crime. In the US, an Act was signed into law in 2009 that created new penalties for crimes motivated fully or in part by the victim's actual or perceived gender, sexual orientation, gender identity, or disability. This bill expands a 1969 law that covered only race, colour, religion, or national origin, and only applied if the victim was engaging in a federally protected activity such as voting or attending school. In England, Wales, and Scotland, the Crime and Disorder Act 1998 penalizes hateful behaviour towards a victim based on the victim's membership (or presumed membership) in a racial group or a religious group — and in 2013, Greater Manchester Police began recording attacks on goths, punks and other alternative culture groups as hate crimes.[179] Hate crimes continue in both the US and UK, but such laws have come into existence because legislators recognise that intolerance has a social cost.

Most people are members of more than one community, so intolerance is damaging to the social fabric, since it causes tensions that can erupt into incidents in any place and at any time. Public services such as policing, justice, education, and health then have to deal with the fallout of vandalism, aggression, and violence. It is necessary for police and others such as teachers and managers to intervene on the ground, sometimes endangering themselves in the process. There are costs to dealing with after effects on physical and mental health, as well as in taking action to restore justice. Unease between people also has an economic impact, since it affects the smooth operation of a market economy. Employers will not necessarily take on the best staff or treat them fairly, and people may refrain from buying or selling out of prejudice. Intolerance damages the social fabric, and it is social fabric that defines community, so intolerance and community are polar opposites, in a sense.

Having said this, some communities are insular and distrustful of strangers. This is often because they feel under threat. Minority religious communities fear judgement by the outside world and consequent intervention in their way of life, such as in the schooling of their children. Activist communities have a mission to change society, not necessarily by legal means, so they expect that authorities will try to plant undercover operatives in their midst. Criminal gangs and networks are intensely suspicious of newcomers, as well as of existing members, since no-one really believes in honor among thieves. Insular communities typically prevent their members from belonging to any other communities at the same time. Here is the Jehovah's Witness explanation of why most Witness youths do not participate in extracurricular activities:

"Witness families already are pursuing a program of activities that centers around their worship. And parents are encouraged to include recreation in this family-oriented program. With parents arranging and overseeing the recreation and entertainment of their children, often participating right along with them, needed supervision is provided. ... Jehovah's Witnesses take seriously the Bible's warning: 'Bad associations spoil useful habits.' And, as noted before, we try to comply with Christ's statement to his followers: 'You are no part of the world.' (1 Corinthians 15:33; John 15:19)"[180]

Insular communities need to isolate their members since otherwise the innate human drive to form social bonds would lead their members to also join other communities. As these people started to take on the beliefs and practices of their other communities, they would naturally start to question why one set of ideas is any better than any other. Tolerance is naturally engendered by community membership, but only if you are free to belong to more than one community. As a result, community leaders who wish to ensure that their members commit to one fixed set of ideas don't encourage or even allow their fellows to join other communities. Since intolerance has a social cost, government has some right to intervene here. However, it must be done sensitively. Not all communities united by ideology regard contact with the outside world as necessarily being a "bad association", like Jehovah's Witnesses, but intervention must be sensitive and collaborative.

Faith-based schools are an interesting example of how insular communities are responding to modern challenges of diversity and plurality. A study in 2019 found that faith-based schools develop a variety of responses.[181] Some strengthen both religious and intercultural education, promoting dialogue between communities or values, ultimately developing a kind of civic-religious education, such as a French-Muslim engagement.[182] Others withdraw in one direction or the other, enhancing either multicultural values or religious education but not both – they respond to the challenge of modernity by strongly rejecting or accepting secularization.[183] An examination of Jewish schools in Montreal and how they cater to the diverse Jewish population in the city showed that all schools aim at strengthening simultaneously a Montreal, Canadian, and Jewish sense of belonging – the Jewish schools see their main challenges as making the religious part of their education relevant in today's diverse world.[184] A comparison of teachers working in public secular and private faith-based schools in Quebec found that their professional stance towards impartiality in teaching about religious and ethical issues does not differ in any systematic way.[185] In other words, the picture is complex and nuanced. This opens the way for intervention, if done carefully and in close partnership with communities.

By contrast, new rules and regulations that appear to be aimed at forcing integration unilaterally can lead to an extreme response, and sometimes to tragic outcomes. The Indian mutiny of 1857 is generally attributed to the introduction of the new Enfield rifle. In order to load it, the Indian soldiers serving under British soldiers (sepoys) had to bite off the ends of lubricated cartridges, which were rumoured to contain a lubricant including pigs' and cows' lard. This meant that oral contact with it was abhorrent to both Muslims and Hindus for religious reasons. There is no conclusive evidence that the cartridges did in fact contain lard, but the perception that the cartridges were tainted added to a growing suspicion that the British were trying to undermine Indian traditional society via Westernization.

A Western humanitarian movement in India had already led to deep reforms. Over the previous decade, efforts toward emancipating women had included removal of all legal obstacles to the remarriage of Hindu widows. Converts to Christianity were to share with their Hindu relatives in the property of the family estate. There was a widespread belief that the British aimed at breaking down the caste system. The introduction of Western methods of education challenged the beliefs of both Hindus and Muslims. Rifle cartridges apparently greased with lard were the straw that broke the camel's back. There were atrocities against civilians by both sides in the Indian mutiny, although British outrage at the murder of British women, children and wounded soldiers (including sepoys who sided with the British) led to reprisals on a scale and with a level of brutality far beyond anything managed by the rebels.

The Indian mutiny led the British to stop imposing insensitive social measures. The humanitarian measures that missionaries and others sought to promote might have been implemented faster by granting greater autonomy to the country they had colonized. When India gained its independence in 1948, one of the first things that Indians did for their own society was to ban caste discrimination and enshrine this in the Indian constitution.

Researchers generally advise a comprehensive integration strategy, in which integration is not imposed from above, but encouraged and fostered in workplaces and grass roots community institutions such as childcare and school settings, leisure centres, and shopping centres.[186] This works best if the members of insular communities are able to adopt mainstream professions and corresponding lifestyles, with membership of clubs, gyms, and so on, rather than being confined to what is effectively an economic and cultural ghetto. Once this happens, people naturally become closer simply through daily interactions, some of which will lead to close working relationships and to the formation of diverse friendship groups.

In other words, insular communities can be encouraged to open up, without imposing intrusive policies or regulations, simply by addressing wellness disparities between different communities. Doing something about wellness disparities means doing something for those who have least of it, and it turns out that wellness has a secret sauce.

Connecting with community

The strength of your community connections outweighs everything else when it comes to wellness. This is because community connection enables, or the lack of it disables, everything on your wellness wheel.

The Royal Society for the encouragement of Arts, Manufactures and Commerce (commonly known as the RSA) was founded in 1754 by a group of merchants in a London coffee house, and was granted a Royal charter in 1847. The RSA has an archetypal Enlightenment mission, to enrich society through ideas and action, and its slogan now is "21st century enlightenment". For its first 100 years the RSA encouraged innovation and excellence through an Awards scheme covering Agriculture, Manufacture, Chemistry, Mechanics, Polite Arts, Colonies and Trade. It went on to help improve education, creating the first public examination system in 1856 and music examinations in 1859, helping to establish Girls' Public Day Schools from 1872, and in 1876 creating a National Training School for Music that later became the Royal College of Music. The RSA helped bring women into the workplace with its typing and secretarial examinations (an approach that now seems dated, but nevertheless had an impact at the time) and demonstrated early commitment to environmental issues, offering awards for the reduction of smoke emissions from 1770.

Today, the RSA continues to offer awards and to support schools (for example, through its Academy programme), and uses publications and events to encourage social action by a fellowship network that is now global and 30,000 strong. In 2006, Matthew Taylor was appointed Chief Executive of the RSA. Taylor had helped to write the UK Labour party manifesto and pledge-card in 1997 and went on to lead the Number 10 Policy Unit. Since Taylor's appointment, a main focus of activity by RSA staff has become research with the aim of influencing public policy. In 2015, the RSA published a report on large-scale research into the value of what they call connected communities.[187] Taylor's Foreword to the report is written for a UK audience at a time when UK government was implementing controversial austerity measures. However, the message addresses the topic of this book directly by talking about the relationship between community support and central government funding for wellness, so I am going to quote from it at some length.

Since David Cameron became prime minister in 2010, the government has repeatedly espoused what we might loosely call a 'communitarian' philosophy. Most directly associated with the 'Big Society' mission of the coalition government, and present more recently in public service strategies such as the NHS Five Year Forward View and a raft of legislation from various government departments, such a philosophy puts forth the assumption — or at least the hope — that stronger, more civic-minded communities can contribute to making life better for local people whether the focus is on policing, libraries, health, the ageing population or people's happiness and quality of life.

For the past five years the RSA and our partners have

been working to test this philosophy by understanding and strengthening communities in locations around the country, from County Durham to the West Sussex coast. This effective total of 35 years' practical experience enables us to speak with some authority on the trend toward communitarian principles in public policy. As detailed in this report, we have found that the assumptions of the communitarian public policy are broadly correct. It is possible to stimulate more flourishing communities, and 'community capital' can be drawn upon to generate great social value. In the course of our action and research we worked with communities in a way that contributed to significant increases in people's wellbeing, created economic dividends and opportunities for employment, promoted active citizenship and — even over short pilot projects — generated financial savings for the health service.

And yet we must also recognise that the other defining trend affecting local communities and their relationship to government over these last five years has been that of austerity. Local authorities have experienced cuts in funding of 40 percent since 2010. This has had a direct impact on the reach and size of public services and their ability work with and support communities with, to take one example, 350 youth centres closing between 2012 and 2014 and widespread reductions in staff, facilities, activities and funding across many other areas. Ahead of the government's autumn spending review, local authorities are preparing for another round of budget cuts of up to a further 40 percent — a scenario in which the Local Government Association has warned that "almost all of councils' money would have to be spent on explicit statutory responsibilities like social services, waste collection and concessionary travel, meaning that the money available for all other services, such as libraries, road maintenance and leisure facilities would have been cut by 90 percent."[188] The particular budgets that are most able to deliver the communitarian goals of the government have been most directly exposed to cuts, and the risk is that the gap between stated government policy and realistic outcomes on the ground will widen.

We need to be honest about where the acceptable floor is below which public services do not have adequate funding to carry out government policy. The non-statutory duties of public services must not be seen simply as 'soft' extras that represent easy savings, but potentially crucial points of collaboration and engagement between the state and communities as well as strategic opportunities to prevent greater problems arising from social isolation. Our experience from the Connected Communities programme has led us to conclude that it takes engaged, deliberative, sometimes difficult work to release value from community capital. Effective communitarian public policy requires planning, careful engagement with people, the weaving and brokering of social networks, and ongoing support for communities. It cannot be assumed that we can simply cut back the state and expect perfectly-formed communities to spontaneously bloom and deliver the aims of the Big Society or to make up for funding shortfalls in the NHS.

Taylor references the "Big Society" initiative that David Cameron launched two months after his election as UK Prime Minister in 2010. This initiative aimed to develop new powers in support of localism, volunteering, and social enterprises. In 2011 the coalition government created a new bank to fund community-led initiatives ("Big Society Capital") and new legal powers for councils to support them (the Localism Act 2011). However, after 2013 the term "Big Society" was not used in public by Cameron or in any government statements. What happened?

Well, for a start, the final Big Society Audit published in January 2015 showed how central government had in fact undermined the initiative through cuts in charity grants, policies which favour the private sector in public services contracts, and restrictions on the right to challenge government policy through the courts.[189] On top of that, few people on either end of the political spectrum liked Big Society. The left perceived it as a stratagem for reducing the size of the state — Ed Miliband, future Labour leader and at the time a leadership contender, accused the government of "cynically attempting to dignify its cuts agenda by dressing up the withdrawal of support with the language of reinvigorating civic society".[190] The right, by contrast, saw it as giving responsibility to people unfit to wield it, with a commentator in the Financial Times expressing a typical view by remarking that "the state has so far invested very little in teaching the skills that could help people make a contribution".[191] So, undermined by its proponents and criticized from all sides, it is not surprising that Big Society sank.

It may have been destined to fail. I argued in the Introduction that long-term, global economic trends mean we cannot wait for central governments, whether in the UK or elsewhere, to build wellness through direct injection of funds into public services, but need to do something about it ourselves, at local level. The same economic trends may mean that we end up waiting a long time even for the supportive policy initiatives Taylor argues for. The outcome of Big Society in the UK may have been another inevitable casualty of neoliberalism.

There are also few good reasons to feel confident about the effectiveness of any public policy in a time when a US President impeached by the House of Representatives feels able to run for re-election, the view of the UK public that their political system is fundamentally broken is supported by careful analysis of its systemic flaws,[192] and repressive governments are being elected in countries from Brazil to Sri Lanka. Even the European Union, a constellation of democratic countries representing a quarter of the world's economy and aiming to promote economic and social progress, is in disarray. As one commentator described vividly at the end of 2018, "Parts of Paris are literally burning. The United Kingdom is consumed and divided by Brexit. Italy is led by an unwieldy left-right coalition that is resisting EU budget rules. Germany is contending with a political realignment and in the early phases of a transition to a new leader. Hungary and Poland have embraced the illiberalism seen across much of the world. Spain is confronting Catalan nationalism. And Russia is committing new acts of aggression against Ukraine."[193] The coronavirus pandemic has shone a spotlight on the inability of world leaders to protect their citizens, however developed their economy may be.

However, we will see below how new means are emerging to bolster localism, volunteering, and social enterprises through local action, without requiring intervention by central government. The planning, careful engagement with people, weaving and brokering of social networks, and ongoing support for communities that Taylor calls for may emerge from grass roots action rather than be delivered from above via policy.

Before we get to that, though, let's look at some of the evidence from RSA research into why we need it — the connection between community and wellness, which the report calls a wellbeing dividend. "Social relationships are essential to subjective wellbeing and life satisfaction — indeed, our research suggests that social connectedness correlates more strongly with wellbeing than social or economic characteristics such as long-term illness, unemployment or being a single parent ... People who said that they feel part of a community were the most likely to report high subjective wellbeing. People who said there was something stopping them from taking part in their community were the least likely to report high subjective wellbeing."

This is a significant finding. The strength of your community connections outweighs everything else when it comes to wellness. This is because community connection enables, or the lack of it disables, everything on your wellness wheel. "There is evidence that investing in interventions which build social relationships can improve employability, improve health (which has positive economic impacts) and create savings in health and welfare expenditure." The researchers also observe that this impact should be understood as a network effect that improves the life of different people in different ways. "Concentrating resources on networks and relationships, rather than on the 'troubled' individual as an end-user can have beneficial effects which ripple out through social networks, having positive effects on people's children, partners, friends and others. This 'positive contagion' has been evidenced in those activities which increase the capacity of social interventions to create greater benefits."

Robert Putnam shows the correlation between the decrease in civic engagement in the generations born after 1945 and their decrease in their mental health. Baby boomers (born between 1946 and 1964) and generation X (born between 1965 and 1980) experience far more suicide, depression, and malaise than their forebears. Martin Seligman points out that Amish communities, which remain close-knit, do not show this trend, although in other respects their mental health is similar to that of the wider population. Seligman links the growth of depression among young Americans to "rampant individualism" and "events that have weakened out commitment to the larger, traditional institutions of our society."

Below is an infographic from the RSA report, showing the interventions they evaluated in 7 different areas.

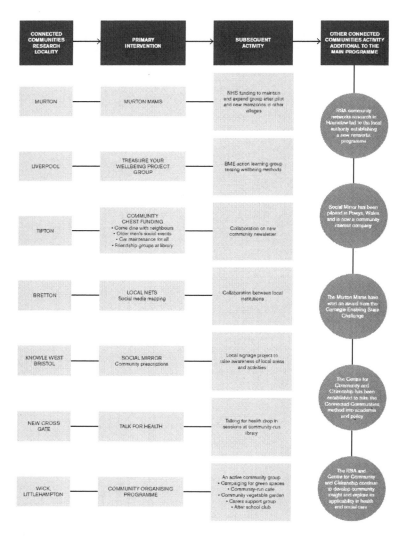

Figure 32: The Connected Communities programme at a glance

Broadly speaking, the interventions focused mostly on building social connectivity, rather than on addressing wellness wheel issues and goals directly. Murton Mams is a village social group set up to provide enjoyable and supportive activities for single mothers vulnerable to isolation and low wellbeing. Social Mirror is a digital tool used in an area of Bristol to identify socially isolated people and offer them the opportunity to take part in social activities. In the village of Wick, subject to high deprivation, a team of community organizers set up clubs, groups, and projects, and made plans to create a social space and community shop. In a deprived area of Liverpool with a high proportion of ethnic minority residents, workshops were arranged to survey local people about their life experiences. In a densely populated area of South East London, volunteers were trained in mental health counselling. Local community organisations in a Midlands town were encouraged to organize new groups, activities, and events. Residents who had voiced concern about local issues in a deprived town in the East of England were brought together with local organisations to engage in person.

Some of these interventions had mixed or inconclusive results. However, by and large they resulted in an improvement to local social relationships, which the RSA researchers describe as "community capital". They use this term to mean something slightly wider than the notion of social capital we used above to define community, taken from Putnam: "connections among individuals — social networks and the norms of reciprocity and trustworthiness that arise from them." Community capital also includes the benefits that individuals obtain from having particular social connections. This might come from belonging to an old boys' network that includes influential people. Alternatively, it might come from knowing people from your church, football club, or previous workplaces who trust you personally and are in a position to offer you work.

The RSA researchers make the point that community capital was lacking in the areas where they worked. Over half the people they surveyed didn't know anybody who could help them contact someone with local influence. They also note how a lack of diversity in networks can be damaging, limiting your access to different sources of influence or opportunity. This lends force to the claim made above that insular communities will often open up naturally over time, if they do not feel pressured to do so.

We've now met a few enablers of value that are referred to as capitals, and if it is getting confusing, please bear with me! In the Introduction, I suggested that social, financial and natural capitals together make up community capital, which makes my definition of community capital much wider than the relationship-based definition used by the RSA researchers. I will return to this below. In the discussion of wellness, we looked at cultural capital — the physical, intellectual, emotional, and spiritual benefits that come from a privileged family background. Another personal enabler of value that we met in relation to wellness is positive psychological capital, or PsyCap, which aims to release the HERO within — a state of mind in which you have the **H**ope, (Self-)**E**fficacy, **R**esilience, and **O**ptimism to improve your life. Thinking about all these things as capitals is making a parallel with the way that businesses operate.

The capitals of a business are the different kinds of thing it can draw on in order to operate. A shop needs a till to take payments and an alarm system to keep it secure (or at least a lock on the door). A factory needs machinery of various kinds. These businesses also need other kinds of capital. Some are obtained privately, such as financial cashflow and a skilled workforce. Some are provided by government for all to use, such as transport and telecommunications networks, and government may also contribute to workforce skills through public education. Some are natural resources, such as fresh air and rainwater. All of these capitals can be exhausted, damaged, or depleted by the operations of business, so they need to be maintained or replaced continually. Sustaining capitals has a cost, which can be higher than a business can afford alone, so it is not always paid by the businesses that use them. Government may step in to fund infrastructure, or the capitals may gradually be worn out. An example of how this is happening in to natural capitals is groundwater depletion, which is rarely assessed and poorly documented, but is becoming recognized as an increasingly serious global problem that threatens sustainability of water supplies and leads to land subsidence.[194]

In the same way, one needs to think about how to sustain community capital (however you define it), cultural capital, and PsyCap. The cost can be high, but if these capitals are not sustained, things stop working properly, just like they do for a business that doesn't service its equipment regularly or runs up unmanageable debt. The populist government of Hugo Chavez in Venezuela would have been able to fulfil its social welfare mission for longer had it maintained the infrastructure of the oil industry that generated over half of national income.[195] Investigation into the extensive pollution of the Thames and other rivers with untreated sewage between 2012 and 2014 laid the blame on "inadequate investment, diabolical maintenance and poor management" by the Australian bank Macquarie, which created a £2 billion debt for Thames Water after buying it in 2006 but used it only to benefit of the bank and its investors before selling the company in 2017.[196]

The RSA researchers are making the point that weak social relationships lead to low general wellness, which leads to people consuming public services. Therefore, government should invest in sustaining social relationships. Despite the failure of the Big Society programme, this message has not been lost on UK government, where the Office for National Statistics now has a group dedicated to monitoring aspects of what the RSA call community capital. Shown below are their latest statistics, for July to September 2019.

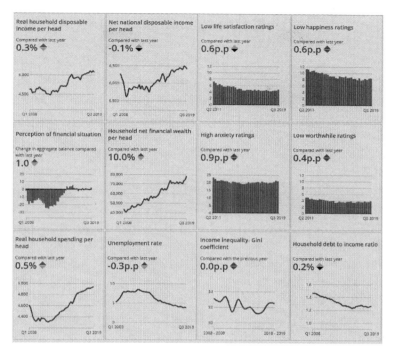

**Figure 33: Dashboard of well-being indicators, July to September
2019, UK Office for National Statistics**

The data are accompanied by conclusions such as that
life satisfaction fell due to growing concerns about future
employment prospects, the feeling that things done in life
are worthwhile also fell significantly, and anxiety remains
high, affecting about 1 in 6 people in the UK. General statistics and conclusions such as these show how hard it is for
central government to engage properly with community
issues. It may be possible to measure life satisfaction, meaning, and anxiety at national level, but as the RSA report
says, "the effects of social networks and the results of intervening to strengthen them are locally specific, unpredictable

and non-linear. Overly idealistic or one-size-fits-all approaches will achieve little; but deliberative, intelligent and participatory engagement with communities can generate significant advantages for all involved. Context is key, and bespoke local engagement is required to successfully facilitate the growth of community capital."

How can central government, detached by its nature from locally specific context, invest in bespoke local engagement? We saw in the discussion of wellness that people with the lowest wellness often have major health issues, which lead in turn to other issues including education and finances. This evidence from the Troubled Families review is supported by the RSA research, which found that low satisfaction with health was the most significant wellbeing variable. So, it might make sense to focus on health as a key driver, which is how these ideas are playing out into UK government policy. Let's stick with the UK for now to see how this is being implemented, and what might be missing from the current approach.

Community and wellness

A community can help marginalized people increase their wellness at low total cost by providing social rather than medical resources to help them thrive. However, some people need more than a social prescription.

From 2010 to 2014, I led a project for the UK National Health Service called NHS GATHER, whose purpose was to increase the adoption of useful innovations. It had long been recognized that innovation in healthcare was slow — a phrase often quoted at the time was 17 years from (laboratory) bench to (hospital) bed.[197] However, people were starting to understand that the issue was not turning an idea into a proven innovation. Junior doctors across the country were coming into the profession with fresh energy, and (along with some senior practitioners) were developing new clinical approaches, trying them out, proving their value methodically, writing them up in journals, and speaking about them at conferences. The problem was that although people could understand an innovation and see its value, they were put off from replicating it by the difficulty of introducing change. When more than a few people are involved in a change, as was usually the case, getting them all to work differently requires persistent effort over a long time, as well as a high level of social skill. Typically, no-one else was able to start using an innovation without extensive hand-holding from the originator, and while originators were keen to help, they didn't have enough time due to the pressure of their own daily work.

The RSA has noted that an improvement in social relationships within a community often stems from the efforts of key people, which they call ChangeMakers — people "who are particularly adept at influencing change through networks" and proposes that "Interventions that identify and target these individuals and seek to work strategically with networks around them can generate greater efficiency and carry positive effects through a population more quickly than would less strategic approaches."[198] There is an equivalent in a workplace context with regard to introducing new working practices — people that management theorists call Heroes, because they go so far beyond what is expected of them. Heroes work late and at weekends, pulling out all the stops in order to achieve a particular outcome. The healthcare innovators we worked with were all

Heroes — many had gone to extraordinary lengths to introduce a new approach about which they felt passionately.

What we did in NHS GATHER was select the highest value innovations (whittling it down first to 135 then finally to 34) and work with the originator of each one (usually it was a single person) to document not only the nature of the change and why it was worth making, but also how they made it. We asked about the stages they went through as they pushed the change into clinical practice. For each stage, we wanted to know what sort of people or organisations were involved, and the part each played in achieving the goals of that stage. For each activity carried out in a stage, we found out what the inputs and outputs were, who supplied the inputs, and who used the outputs for what. We put all this together into an Innovation Guide — a step by step plan for introducing the innovation into working practice.

We put these Innovation Guides online as templates. A hospital, surgery, ambulance service, or other clinical organisation could choose an innovation that they felt would be useful locally and download a copy. They then replaced the original people and organisations with local versions, and started using it as an online project plan. As they completed an activity, they uploaded the outputs (such as a set of documents), which were automatically made available to people whose activities had them as inputs.

NHS GATHER was based on the ideas in my first book,[199] which I'll discuss below when we come to look at collaboration. The system won an NHS innovation award but was swept away in 2015 as part of a wave of transformational change, being replaced by a scheme called New Models of Care. Rather than focusing on individual innovations as we did, the new scheme focused on sites that introduced entire new care models, joining up health and social care as far as possible, and working closely with voluntary and community organisations. 25 sites were selected as vanguards, to take a lead on the development of holistic approaches to healthcare that would act as the blueprints for the NHS moving forward as well as an inspiration to the rest of the health and care system.

It is too early to judge the success of this programme. There have been no blog posts for two years now,[200] and an independent evaluation in 2019 was able to conclude only that "there are some indicators where it is too early to say, and some evidence is mixed, but the overall direction of evidence is clearly in favour of the programme improving, or being likely to improve, services' effectiveness and efficiency."[201] It will be interesting to see what happens when other sites try to reproduce the approach taken by successful vanguards, now that there is no longer a system to facilitate the replication of change. However, it is clear that the NHS has come to understand the importance of community engagement in creating good health outcomes.

We learned the same lesson from evaluating hundreds of innovations in NHS GATHER. The ones that demonstrated the greatest step change in patient outcomes, and that we chose for Innovation Guides, almost invariably stemmed from treating health as part of a much wider wellness picture. Part of this was to recognise that critical factors other than medical intervention, such as being able to recover at home rather than in hospital. Delivering hospital care at home is a significant challenge, requiring a combination of sophisticated technology and complex collaborative effort. However, the financial savings are huge (in-patient costs range from £413 per night in a ward to £1932 per night in intensive care),[202] the benefits to patient quality of life are worthwhile in themselves, and innumerable studies show that home care leads to better, faster recovery. In a familiar environment, surrounded by family and friends, people are more active, sleep better, are less exposed to infection, and have more effective immune systems.

Another part of the wide wellness picture is the need to build a supportive network of people around a patient, including not only healthcare professionals but also professionals from other areas such as social care and education, as well as friends, family, neighbours, and volunteers from the community. This relates to the other benefits of community connectedness found by RSA research, in addition to a direct effect on wellness. They observed a citizenship dividend, whereby connectedness empowered people to act in the world, making them more confident, providing them with new skills, improving their employment prospects and increasing their interest in education and volunteering. The actions people took were often directed towards helping others through peer support networks.

The researchers also observed a capacity dividend. In the same way that a telephone network becomes more useful as more people get a phone, so too does a community become more effective overall as its members become more connected and empowered personally. This effectiveness shows itself through activities such as running a community library or helping people deal with authorities, and these activities have a further indirect effect on local wellness, since people feel better simply from having productive relationships with people around them. The final dividend is economic. Connected people are more likely to develop useful skills, do productive work as a volunteer, and acquire paid work. Connected communities are also better at joining up public services with community and voluntary organisations, reducing the overall cost to government.

These other dividends are essential to another mechanism that, along with hospital care at home, underpins new models of care in the UK NHS. This is known as social prescribing. The wellness wheel shows how health is only one part of wellness, and we discussed above how clinicians have long understood that a National Health Service should be more than a National Illness Service. Social prescribing aims to deal with those parts of wellness that are not purely medical, via what the UK NHS calls community-centred ways of working. There are different models for social prescribing, but most involve a link worker or navigator who works with people to help them access local sources of support that range across the entire wellness wheel, and may come from community or voluntary organisations as well as from services run or funded by government.

This type of help is particularly valuable to people who are marginalized. Despite often having the worst lowest wellness, those who find themselves excluded from society, discriminated against, or lacking power and control because of living in extreme poverty, can be the least likely to access and benefit from local services. Community-centred ways of working can help people engage with the resources available to them, and become what clinicians call self-activated — more in control over their lives. To see how this relates to PsyCap, let's look at how social prescribing works in practice.

Social prescribing is aimed at people with wellness challenges such as long-term health conditions, mental health issues, and complex social needs such as loneliness or isolation. Social prescribing is also known as community referral, because it generally starts with a doctor passing on (the term used in health and social care is referring) a patient to a link worker. Someone can also be referred to a link worker by a pharmacist, council worker, police officer, housing association, social worker, teacher, charity or anyone else who believes some of their needs could be met from community resources. Referral may happen on discharge from hospital, as a result of a job centre interview, or following a visit from the fire service. You can even refer yourself.

After referral, a link worker meets the person to discuss their needs, and helps them identify local resources that they could draw on to improve their wellness. This could range from social clubs and activities to financial advice, vocational training, community transport, befriending services, and much more, all depending on the person and what is available locally. The link worker may meet the person only once, a light touch approach known as signposting. This works best for people who are confident and skilled enough to find their own way to services. Alternatively, the link worker may follow up with the person several times over a period of a few months to review their progress and adjust their plan of action. Whether or not this sustained approach is available depends on the person and on the local budget for link workers.

If sufficient funding is available, link workers may also be expected to work with local organisations to help community groups get off the ground, make themselves known to local people, and sustain their operations. Some social prescribing organisations run their own community activities. For example, the service Health Connections Mendip in Frome, Somerset runs talking cafes, workshops on living with long term health conditions, and a healthy lifestyles programmes, as well as facilitating peer led groups where people set their own health and wellbeing goals.[203]

There is great enthusiasm for social prescribing, lots of anecdotal evidence for its value, and isolated hard evidence. A poster child is the social prescribing scheme Health Connections Mendip, based in the rural town of Frome in Somerset. A study into its impact over three years showed that while emergency hospital admissions rose by 29% across the whole of Somerset, in Frome they fell by 17% with a 21% reduction in costs.[204] Julian Abel, a consultant physician in palliative care and lead author of the study, makes the significance of this clear: "In terms of magnitude this represents 5% of the total health budget. No other factors were attributable to the fall in hospital admission rates." Dr Helen Kingston, who set up the service, was recognized by the UK Prime Minister with a Points of Light award.

However, while Frome has a small pocket of deprivation, it is not among the worst-off areas of Somerset.[205] Frome and its surrounding region Mendip actually score quite highly on most indices of deprivation.[206] Social prescribing in Frome has helped a lot of people, but most people in Frome are not facing a chaotic storm of serious life challenges — and for those that are, there is somewhere else to turn. Frome council works with local residents to counter poverty via the charity Fair Frome, which runs food and furniture banks, offers community lunches, and helps people who are homeless, facing eviction, or struggling with council tax payments.

The online Resource Centre of Health Connections

Mendip is a good indicator of the wellness problems that they focus on, showing programmes for social connectivity, physical activity, self-management of health, care for the elderly, and end of life planning.[207] Hard evidence is not so readily available for the benefits of social prescribing across a social spectrum where deeper issues such as poverty, trauma, and safety are prominent. The latest comprehensive analysis of social prescribing, from 2017, summarizes the evidence as "broadly supportive of its potential to reduce demand" for General Practitioner and hospital services but "the quality of that evidence is weak" and "the evidence that social prescribing delivers cost savings to the health service over and above operating costs is encouraging but by no means proven or fully quantified."[208] Let's take a closer look, since the picture is more complex than it might seem, and so needs careful interpretation.

The statistics that jump out are average reductions following referrals to social prescribing schemes of 28 percent in General Practitioner services, 24 percent in attendance at Accident & Emergency, and statistically significant drops in referrals to hospital. These numbers are often used to promote social prescribing.[209] Evidence for the resulting cost savings, however, is mixed. Social prescribing creates a higher cost of care per patient, but this should be considered against the broader benefit from improved mental wellbeing outcomes and higher rates of employment. Taking these into account, one study shows a return of £2.30 for each £1 invested into social prescribing.

Having said this, another study shows that social prescribing doubled the number of people who were subsequently referred to professional mental health care. This extra cost, of providing mental health services, was not included in the broader benefit calculation above. There is a question here — to what degree is social prescribing just shifting the burden of professional care from one part of the health service to another, rather than managing wellness issues in a more holistic community-centred way? Link workers may be duty-bound to offer therapy to all clients as an option, which may lead to social prescribing accidentally increasing take-up of medical rather than community services. Mental health services are already stretched beyond capacity, so this is potentially a serious issue. Social prescribing could be delaying the provision of mental health services to people with serious mental health problems, who need urgent help.

Another subtle point is that the headline statistics may be a self-fulfilling prophecy. The discussion section in the review of evidence says, "Any reported reduction in demand for health services applies only to the cohort of patients referred to social prescribing, and in one study, only for subgroups who completed the interventions. In some cases, patients who failed to engage fully with social prescribing had much higher rates of health service use both before and after referral … This point is pertinent to value assessments." This is an important insight, couched in complex language.

In plainer words, the authors are saying that social prescribing only meets the needs of some people, and for others, it may be making matters worse. This is the same point made when comparing Frome to an area of high deprivation. It is also the same point made in the discussion of positive psychology, to illustrate how creating a beautiful day or making a gratitude visit are unlikely to make much difference to our three examples of people with real practical problems — a single mother struggling with deprivation and safety, a disabled veteran struggling with employability and substance abuse, and a homeless person struggling with personal demons and family safety.

There are many people for whom the health service is a first port of call when they have problems of any kind. Around 20% of patients visit their family doctor for problems that are primarily social,[210] and 15% of family doctor visits are actually for social welfare advice.[211] Many of these people are lonely, isolated, bereaved, unfit, overweight, or have minor psychological issues. Social prescribing can make a huge difference by helping them connect to the people around them, and take part in groups and activities designed to overcome their issues. In Frome, this is making a significant improvement to local wellness, and reducing the costs of healthcare provision.

However, it is possible that the situation would be different in a more deprived area. Our three people with real practical problems might not even think of their family doctor as a source of help. If they did make an appointment and were referred to a social prescribing link worker, they might consider the social groups and activities on offer to be of limited use compared to the seriousness of their life challenges. Social prescribing isn't aimed at the most deprived people, who have the lowest quality of life, and place the greatest cost burden on public services. For both ethical and economic reasons, society must help them turn their lives around, but this means providing a different type of help.

Personal support networks

The holistic support needed for wellness can be provided at low cost via a personal support network – a group
of people who help you make your wellness plan, then provide help and encouragement as you implement it.

The clue is in the name, isn't it — social prescribing is
still prescribing. Unlike a family doctor, a link worker
doesn't prescribe drugs, but rather groups and activities.
There may be follow up sessions, but the model is the same
medical one, of treating life challenges like an illness, for
which you provide a cure to make it go away, or at least
find a way of keeping it under control. If the illness is long
term, the medical practitioner may help the patient become
self-activated, so that they learn to manage their own health
better — for example, diabetes or irritable bowel syndrome
are dealt with in this way. Either way, in between appointments the patient is on their own with their condition.

Practitioners in health and social care, like staff in other
public services from housing to policing who deal with the
public daily, are well aware that some people need support
that is more integrated and wraparound. What is called person-centred, coordinated care has become an international
mission for health services, with the World Health Organisation declaring in 2015 that "The provision of health services must go beyond an emphasis on the hospital sector
and specialist services towards a more coordinated approach that embraces primary and community care-led
strategies and has the potential to be a more cost-effective
way of delivering care." They propose "reforms to reorient
health services, shifting away from fragmented provider-
centred models, towards health services that put people and

their families at their centre, and surrounds them with responsive services that are coordinated both within and beyond the health sector."[212]

In practice, people find it hard to know what this means. A review of how person-centred, coordinated care is being delivered in countries from Sweden to Australia illustrated "a diverse and evolving community of practice" and concluded that "there is some common ground in global definitions of person-centred care, but much richness and diversity as well."[213] The review acknowledges that the movement is grounded in "a long tradition of efforts to improve the humanity, comprehensiveness and effectiveness of healthcare practices that extends back over many centuries." However, while person-centred care "has succeeded in rallying countless people across the world to a more humanist, holistic and sustainable agenda for change in healthcare" it is also the focus of continuing debate. "The phrase has not passed without challenge by those who find its meaning unclear, or who see greater value and clarity in other conceptual models and phrases." The debate can get political — for example, some feel that it has led to treating patients as clients, with connotations of market liberalism that may be contrary to true ethics of care.

The UK has implemented person-centred, coordinated care by providing patients who have complex, long-term care needs with a multi-disciplinary team that helps them to plan their own wellness: "I can plan my care with people who work together to understand me and my carer(s), allow me control, and bring together services to achieve the outcomes important to me."[214] This sounds quite like the wellness plan someone might make after working their way around a wellness wheel. However, the scope is limited to health and care services. Even though this includes services from the voluntary and community sector, it covers only a small part of the wellness wheel. As we saw above, from the person's point of view, issues such as safety, employment, and money are just as much a part of their wellness as health.

If you feel threatened in your home or at work, or are on a financial knife edge, this is going to weaken your immune system.[215] Stress makes your medical conditions worse. It might even be causing them. Medical professionals are well aware of this, of course, but are not trained or funded to intervene beyond the sphere of health or social care. Tackling a person's wider issues is beyond their remit, so they are not empowered to spend time on it. They also know that, without working within a professional guidance framework, any intervention they were to make might help rather than harm the patient.

Figure 34: Person-centred, coordinated care from NHS England

A more holistic example of how public services try to recognize individual needs for wraparound care is the support provided in the UK to some victims of domestic abuse. Cases where the victim is deemed to be at high risk are discussed at a meeting called a MARAC, or multi-agency risk assessment conference. First, relevant information is shared between representatives of local police, probation, health, child protection, housing practitioners, Independent Domestic Violence Advisors and other specialists from the statutory and voluntary sectors. Then, representatives discuss options for increasing safety for the victim and turn these options into a co-ordinated action plan aimed at safeguarding the victim.[216]

The MARAC approach takes into account a broader based set of issues than NHS multidisciplinary teams are able to, and delivers ongoing support for the person at risk.

However, it is time-consuming for the people involved, which includes many public servants. A typical MARAC deals with 15-20 cases but takes half a day and involves professionals from 10-15 agencies.[217] Despite reducing further violence against victims, saving about £6 for each £1 invested, and agencies involved considering the extra work to be worthwhile, the cost to government means a MARAC approach is used only to deal with domestic abuse, and even then, only with the highest risk cases. It could be likened to an expensive cancer drug, available to people with a specific life-threatening condition. None of our example people with major life challenges would be eligible for a MARAC.

People need holistic support, but support is complex and costs money. There is a growing understanding in the care services that people with the lowest wellness must become self-activated in creating and managing their own life journey — what I call their wellness plan. This leads to PsyCap — a state of mind in which you understand your life issues, have worked out a set of goals you are aiming for, and feel that they are achievable. However, professionals in health, social care, housing, policing, justice, education and other public services see from daily experience, as do people working in voluntary and community organisations, that people with the lowest wellness cannot achieve these goals without taking a fully holistic approach. There are two challenges that make this difficult to provide.

The first is economic — where to find the diverse resources you need to achieve your goals. These come from all around the wellness wheel so range from transport to safety to education to work and more. We've seen that being embedded into a close-knit fabric of social relationships

— a community — helps with wellness, a lot, but it is not everything in itself. Knowing people can help you find the local services you need, including community groups and activities, but only if they exist in the first place and are able to sustain their own operations. What is available to you depends on where you live, and as you might expect, there is less on offer in deprived areas.

After NHS GATHER, I went on to lead a project called Town Digital Hub, which provided digital hubs for communities — interactive Web sites where each community organisation could maintain information about the services it provided and people could add these services to their personal wellness plan. People could track their wellness in various ways, record how each service helped them reach their goals, and share feedback to help services improve. When we started creating digital hubs, it was startling to see that one small town had about the same level of local resources as a deprived city area with total population ten times the size. Anecdotally, some community groups in the small town were offering more support than local people needed, and they were looking out for new people to help. By contrast, link workers in the city were so overwhelmed with case work that they had little or no time to help create and develop the local services they needed to prescribe for people with wellness issues.

When we come to look at social trading, I'll show how even the most deprived communities can build the local resources that people need. It turns out that you can look at local resources from a perspective that not only helps people build and sustain them, but also enables them to do so without central government funding. This is because some forms of resource contribute not only to wellness but also to economic growth. Communities can create such resources by taking ownership of their economy, which means adopting holistic measures of economic growth and realigning local financial flows accordingly.

Before we come to that, I'll look at the second challenge to personal wellness — how to get the personal support you need to carry out a wellness plan. People who feel low wellness have not yet turned their lives around, which leads to them feeling the opposite of PsyCap. Even if someone with serious life issues has made a wellness plan, they probably do not feel empowered to succeed at first, and expect upsets to occur that will derail their progress. To overcome this, they need more than the plan itself. They also need sustained, wraparound support. In Town Digital Hub, we implemented this by helping people to set up their own personal support network.

A personal support network is a group of people who work together with you to make your wellness plan, then provide help and encouragement as you set out to implement it. As goals are reached, members of the personal support network congratulate you and help you update your wellness plan. When challenges are encountered, they help you overcome them by providing advice and enabling access to new resources. A personal support network typically includes professionals from a range of agencies, like a cut-down MARAC, but most day-to-day support is provided by members of the community — family, friends, neighbours, and local volunteers — which reduces the cost for government. All members of a personal support network know each other, and communicate regularly and openly.

Let's see how a personal support network might be important to our deprived single mother, Sarah. One of the first goals in her wellness plan is to prevent bullying of her children on the way to and from school. This can happen on the school bus, so Sarah has talked to teachers, who promise that they will talk to the bus company about installing CCTV on the bus and training drivers to nip incidents in the bud. Despite this, nothing happens, and her children feel increasingly anxious. Sarah doesn't want to nag teachers, fearing that she will lose their support. So, instead, she talks to a volunteer in her personal support network, an ex-teacher who has social connections with the school governors. A word in the right ear, and the promised actions take place, without any feathers being ruffled.

Another goal in her wellness plan is to find part-time work for her oldest child, ideally in a garage. Sarah has asked around locally, but none of the garages she has been into seem to have anything on offer. All the members of her personal network also start asking around, and taken together, this spreads the word to a lot of local people. Eventually, someone mentions it to the owner of a small van maintenance company, and after a couple of weeks, Sarah's son is offered a trial day.

Sarah is also finding it really hard to keep up her diet and exercise plan, since she is still very stressed, and never seems to have any time. But losing control of her weight just makes her feel worse about herself, and she knows she would have more energy if she was fitter. Sarah talks to a neighbor who has offered to support her. They go through her diet and make a couple of changes that allow her to have a weak moment every now and then. They also discuss fitness, and look together at the results Sarah was getting when was exercising regularly. Sitting with someone else who takes a more objective view, Sarah can see that actually she was making real improvement. She feels reassured that progress is possible, and determines that she will definitely find the time for exercise, even at the end of a busy day. The practical and moral support has made all the difference.

Finally, Sarah has been assuming her ex-partner is continuing to attend his alcohol dependency clinic. So, she is dismayed to be contacted by her social worker, who heard from a colleague that he hasn't been for two weeks now. Knowing his past anger management issues, the service thought it best to warn her. Sarah agrees that there is a risk, and they arrange to suspend his visits with the children until he starts attending again. Sarah doesn't have to get involved in this, so is insulated from any fallout. A month later, Sarah is advised that he has been attending again, seems to be back on track, and they agree to put visits in place, supervised for now.

A personal support network makes an almost immeasurable difference to Sarah. Without it, she would probably not get very far with her wellness plan at all. With it, she can turn her life around, steadily and safely. However, such wraparound support doesn't emerge from out of the blue. Communities need to encourage its development, giving people a good reason to take part. It turns out that taking part in a personal support network provides even more benefit to the members than it does to the person at the centre. Communities also need to ensure that personal support networks do their job properly, providing effective help to the person at the centre.

This would be a lot simpler if there was a set of rules defining the elements of collaborative work. Then communities could hand it out to personal support networks via an app or on a laminated card. We can get close to this, but it might be better to think in terms of guidance. As Imre Lakatos reminds us in the little book on proofs and refutations that I gave to my kids, it's impossible to define anything exactly.

Wittgenstein upset two millennia of philosophy by asking the simple question, "What is a game?"[218] Games have typical properties, but it's easy to find exceptions. We think of games as done for fun, often in leisure time, but this doesn't apply to the Olympics or professional sports. Many games are played by children, but not poker. Games usually have rules, but throwing a ball against a wall doesn't. Ring-around-the-roses is a game, but it's not competitive. Card games mostly involve more than one person, but not patience.

So, I talk about principles for collaborative work, rather than rules — best practices, typical of effective collaboration, that help you work together to achieve good outcomes. Let's see what these principles are.

Collaboration

Goals and roles

Taking on a role is not about tasks but about accepting responsibilities for achieving goals. You need to know about other roles in the team, and ensure that it includes a mixture of thinkers, doers, socializers, and leaders.

Other than the usual temporary jobs as a teenager, and a brief internship before university, my first real job, where I was given a staff number and paid a salary, was for an academically-oriented software house in the city of Bath, UK. It turned to be my last job as well. After a couple of years, I went independent — and it's now been three decades without a boss, so I am almost certainly unemployable! However, despite choosing to curtail my time as an employee so swiftly, I really enjoyed it. This was partly due to there being only about 120 employees at the time — in other words, I got there before the company grew beyond the Dunbar number in size, so most people knew most people, and there was a strong sense of community. The other reason was my first assignment. I was thrown in at the deep end on a UK government sponsored research project called IPSE 2.5.

The acronym stands for Integrated Project Support Environment. The aim was to build a system that people could use to manage software projects.[219] At the time, the late 1980s, the failure rate of software projects was high — only 16 percent delivered their expected outputs on time and within the allotted budget.[220] You may be surprised to learn that, despite the massive growth of the tech industry since then, we've not got much better at this. Three decades later, only 29 percent of software projects succeed, which is still less than one in three.[221]

The 2.5 in our project name referred to the expectation that it would be a transitional system, soon to made obsolete by advances in underpinning technology. The Japanese government had recently invested in an ambitious programme to leapfrog the West in computing. They were going to create artificially intelligent operating systems that would work out what the user wanted and then do it without programmers having to intervene.[222] We thought that although their "fifth generation" technology would take a while to deliver, it would probably change the requirements for a system such as ours. We'd fix this in IPSE 3 by introducing techniques from what were then known as expert systems.

In the end, both we and the Japanese failed to deliver anything of much value. We were all too far ahead of the game. Modern computing technology is built in layers. Few programmers today have much contact with the layers underpinning their own code — they probably don't know how most of these layers work, and may not even know what all the layers are. Few such layers existed then. The Japanese were trying to build artificially intelligent systems from scratch, coding from nuts and bolts in a language called Prolog without any of the frameworks that have emerged over the last thirty years. Similarly, we were using an iconic programming system called Smalltalk, which was legendary among and much-loved by programmers but far too low level to run projects with.

I loved IPSE 2.5, though. The project leads weren't

just trying to solve a real-world problem, they were trying to do it in a formal way. This means that they planned to start by creating a mathematical theory of how people manage software projects, and then use this to build a product that genuinely met needs. They would also ensure that the theory was fit for purpose before using it by proving its validity — although proving in this context meant mathematical proof, rather than demonstrating that it matched the real world. That would be for later, once we had a working system with which to run trials. But what should be the basis of the theory — the conceptual model of software project management at the heart of IPSE 2.5?

At this point, I turned up, fresh out of Oxford University with a double-starred first-class degree in Mathematics and a Masters in Computation. Great, they thought, and assigned me the task of developing the conceptual model. I was delighted to be offered such an interesting piece of work, but had absolutely no idea where to start. Not only had I never managed a project, I'd never worked on one. I hadn't done business studies, and didn't know the first thing about management.

Luckily, more experienced people on the project saw me floundering around helplessly and, rather than moving me onto something simpler and less exciting to do, they suggested ideas that might get me started. One of these ideas was a visual technique that other project members were developing, which showed people working together in a structured way to produce outputs (carrying out a business process) by taking on roles and having interactions.[223] To take part in a business process, you would be assigned a role. You could then pass things to someone playing another role using an interaction — think of this like sending an email, but only to one person. People playing roles in a process would often need to repeat their tasks and interactions several times in order to deliver the required products and services.

Other visual notations were emerging around then to illustrate business processes, and over the last three decades they have become embedded in standard business practice across the world. Most companies over a certain size maintain a set of diagrams representing all their business processes, from manufacture to sales to shipping, and everything else besides, including back office operations like payroll and hiring. Now it is even possible to feed a diagram into a software system that then automates some of the tasks and delivers messages for you — a result that the Japanese would probably have been happy with in the 1980s, although their real aim was to generate the diagram as well, something that even now we are still working towards.

So, pictures of business processes weren't unique back then, and certainly aren't anything special now. However, some aspects of our notation were different from the norm, and still are. For one thing, the notion of interaction in the diagrams we used was related to philosophical ideas emerging from biological research into the nature of thought and communication, which I'll explore below. For another, our notion of a role was more than a job title such as warehouse manager or salesperson. For us, taking on a role meant you gained access to a store of information that came with the duty you had been assigned — documents, databases, messages, and other information that you could draw on to perform the work. This was a first step towards capturing how, in the real world, a role is less about tasks and more about responsibilities.

When you are assigned a role on some kind of project, venture, or initiative, you may agree with other people specific work duties that could be described using tasks and interactions. If your role is project manager, for example, then you might have tasks to create a plan, monitor its progress, and write status reports. However, you also need to do things that are less tangible — your role is more than the sum of these parts. You have to stay in regular touch with project sponsors and staff, and ensure that everyone is working well together. You need to be aware of risks and issues as they emerge, then do something about them. If possible, you should create a harmonious working environment in which people are as productive as possible.

These are the goals of the role, and accepting it means agreeing to work towards those goals. Exactly how you are supposed to do this might not be written down, or even possible to define. For example, what does it means to create a harmonious working environment? Every project manager has their own way of approaching this, and it might change week to week depending on who is currently on the team, and what is going on at the moment. The important thing is that you commit to doing it. The approach you adopt in practice is up to you.

This notion of role is very different from other approaches to process description in industry, and a few of us explored the ideas for many years after leaving IPSE 2.5, both in our separate careers and on occasional joint projects. For me, the notion of responsibility was the most important thing we had uncovered. Then as now, people who were writing down process descriptions thought of a role as being defined by its tasks, whereas I had come to see that the tasks were just the visible tip of an iceberg. Underneath the water was hidden a whole set of other duties. Since these were not drawn in the picture of a process, people taking on a role generally didn't realize everything that they were supposed to be doing. As a result, things would go badly wrong for the projects they were working in — which might help explain why more than two out of three software projects still fail.

This isn't just about software projects, of course, but about any collaborative activity. Statistics are harder to obtain for more general types of project, but estimates suggest that somewhere between one half and two thirds of all projects fail to some degree or another, which is not much different from the outcomes for software projects.[224] Things go particularly badly when people who are working together are not employed by the same organisation, which is very much the situation when dealing with personal wellness. Environments like healthcare, social care, justice, and education are networks, in which people from many different companies or agencies often need to work closely together on a person's case. However, usually there is no way for anyone to see the whole picture, so it's hard for anyone to know when things are going wrong. Often those involved with a failed project cannot even work out the reason for failure afterwards. This relates to the original notion in IPSE 2.5 that roles had access to their own private store of information, parts of which they could share in a controlled way using interactions.

After trying out ideas about role-based processes for a decade through consultancy work, I started writing about them in the early 2000s. The American business guru Peter Fingar encouraged me to write a book, which led to the publication of "Human Interactions" in 2005. In that book, which I now think was rather impenetrable, I set out a formal theory of collaborative human work. In this book, you may be pleased to hear that I'm going to leave out the mathematics. We'll just look at what I call the five principles of Human Interaction Management. To make these easier to remember, I now refer to them as the 5 Cs — Commit, Communicate, Contribute, Calculate, and Change.

The first principle, Commit, is about taking on a role. If you are going to take part in collaborative work, you need to take one or more roles in that work, each of which is more than a set of tasks — it is a set of responsibilities. This means that you commit not so much to carrying out the tasks as to achieving certain goals, which may overlap with but differ from the goals of other roles you are working with. When it comes to the personal support network around a person, each person involved needs to commit to supporting specific goals of their wellness plan. You may not even bother agreeing tasks in advance, assuming that people will work out what they need to do as they go along.

Let's look again at the interventions that members of Sarah's personal support network made to help her with her wellness plan. The ex-teacher helped her prevent bullying of her children on the way to and from school, via a word in the right ear. All of the members helped with her son's part-time work, by asking around to see if there might be a job in a local garage. Sarah's neighbor gave her critical moral support with her diet and exercise plan. Her social worker proactively intervened to manage any risk to Sarah and her family from an alcoholic ex-partner who might have relapsed.

Each member of her personal support network committed to helping with certain goals as best they could, depending on her needs as time went on and on their own capabilities. This didn't mean defining tasks they would carry out, but rather agreeing that they would work as a team to help Sarah achieve those goals. The ex-teacher's goals included bullying prevention, the neighbor's goals included diet and exercise, and the social worker's goals included monitoring the ex-partner. Everyone committed to the shared goal of helping Sarah's children to find part-time work.

It's particularly important for people who are working together to know who each other are, and to understand which goals each person is working towards. We'll see below how this allows the right people to follow up issues and take action, for example when sending messages. Knowing who everyone is and what you are all responsible for is an essential basis of acting as a team, which is what the members of a personal support network are, even if they work for different organisations or are acting in an independent capacity.

Every team creates its own dynamic, but some teams are more successful than others. A characteristic of a productive team is having a good balance of personality types. I think about this using a model adapted from that of Meredith Belbin.[225] Belbin considers that a successful team needs a diverse mix of behaviours, which he divides into three groups of three. Each of the three groups contains three behaviours that share a certain propensity.

In the first group, we have behaviours related to thinking. These include highly creative people who are good at solving problems in unconventional ways, logical people who make impartial judgements and weigh up options dispassionately, and specialists with in-depth knowledge in certain areas.

Then we have a group who favour action. In this group are people with the necessary drive to ensure that the team keeps moving with focus and momentum, methodical people who like to make plans that they see through efficiently, and people whose nature leads them to scrutinize completed work to ensure it is complete, correct, and consistent.

The final group in Belbin's model is social by nature. Here we find those who seek out ideas for the team, versatile team workers who will behave however necessary to help the team operate smoothly as a unit, and coordinators who help ensure that the right people are focusing on the right things to meet overall objectives.

Belbin's groups are not meant as science, but as a practical tool in the workplace. So, I add a fourth group that I have found to be useful, oriented towards leadership. People in this group may be strategists who use their awareness of the operational context to shape strategic targets and set policies, executors who keep the team's work in line with strategic targets as well as policies and regulations, and team leaders that streamline daily work and remove any snags.

Thinking about yourself in this way, you probably feel that you personally have a blend of these behaviours, with some more prominent than others. Grouping tendencies as above is a handy tool for putting together balanced teams. Teams that are too focused in one direction may not be very effective. A team full of Thinkers or Leaders may never actually deliver anything, while a team full of Action or Social people may do things right but not do the right things. When you're forming as a team, it is a good idea for each member to score themselves informally against each of the twelve behaviour types above, then for everyone to compare notes to see whether overall you are too strong in one area or too weak in another. If so, you can then adjust the team membership to create a more balanced set of behaviours before anything starts going pear-shaped.

Thinking about the people in Sarah's personal support network as team begs a question. Teams are people who work together — they interact. Why, when, and how do they communicate with Sarah and each other? Is there something that tells them to get in touch with each other, and what happens when they do? To answer this, we need to look at the second principle of Human Interaction Management, Communicate.

Communication, conversations, and purpose

Communication coordinates behaviour as well as transferring information. To work well with others, have conversations for Context, Possibility, Disclosure, then Action and communicate about one thing at a time.

In the decade prior to IPSE 2.5, Chilean biologists Humberto Maturana and his student Francisco Varela were developing an idea that we've met a couple of times now — autopoiesis.[226] The idea became widely known due to Lynn Margulis and James Lovelock linking it to Lovelock's famous Gaia theory of the Earth as a living system.[227] An aspect of autopoietic theory was the idea that living systems, including humans, do not interact with each other by encoding information and sharing it (the basis of the cybernetic theory that gave rise to modern information technology). Rather, living systems trigger behaviours in one another. Something in the environment of an organism causes it to react, such as detecting a movement or sound by another organism, and it responds through a physical process that is part of its internal structure. "The frog with optic fibers responding to small moving dark spots does not have a representation of flies."[228]

Maturana and Varela refer to the frog's behaviour as structural coupling, and extend this idea to how humans communicate. We discussed above how human brains may have co-evolved with the use of language to describe the world around us. However, Maturana and Varela saw this symbolic aspect of language as arising from a more basic use in communication. For them, social communication isn't about transferring information from one person's brain to the brain of another person using symbols. Rather, we use language to coordinate our behaviour with that of other people, by sending signals that trigger the responses we want. We cannot control the responses of another person, but social groups as a whole develop behaviours by which members learn how to send signals that generate certain actions. Our structural coupling is more flexible than that of a frog, but it's the same basic mechanism.

According to this idea, the shriek of a prairie dog doesn't mean "Eagle" or "Snake", it means "get into the burrow, everyone", and its jump-yip is a reminder to others in the pack to stay alert. Similarly, when your boss stops by your cubicle to ask how the report is getting on, she may not be asking you to transfer your knowledge about work in progress into her head, but ensuring that you submit it by the end of the week. When a friend or colleague asks if you're hungry, they don't want to know how full your stomach feels right now, but hoping you will want to go to a café together. When an oboist plays an A before a concert, they are getting the rest of the orchestra to tune their instruments to the same pitch. Yelling "Dinner!" at the foot of the stairs makes whoever is upstairs come down.

This idea about communication was taken up by American computer scientist Terry Winograd and Chilean philosopher Fernando Flores, who applied it to software design. They argued that artificial intelligence research should focus less on putting models of the real world into a computer, and more on learning how to help computers conduct productive conversations.[229] They presented an example of a common process in the real world, the Conversation for Action.

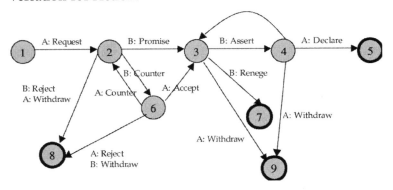

Figure 35: The basic Conversation for Action

This process shows how person A commissions work from person B. They do this by moving between states in a structured conversation. The conversation starts when A requests something from B, specifying the details of what they want. This moves the conversation from state 1 to state 2. B now has three alternatives. They can decline the request (moving to state 7), promise to provide it (moving to state 3), or make a counter-offer (moving to state 8) that

A is free to accept, reject or negotiate. After reaching state 3, both A and B are free to withdraw from the deal (leading to states 9 and 6 respectively). B can also declare that the task is finished (state 4), which A may or may not accept (moving to state 5 or 3, respectively). The conversation is considered ended either at successful conclusion (state 5) or at one of the withdrawal states (6, 7, 8, and 9).

Whew. Does this seem like real life to you? It was hotly debated at the time.[230][231] Other business processes were developed to accompany Conversation for Action, and Winograd and Flores launched software based on the approach. This was used by a number of large companies for a few years, until it was found too restrictive for effective business operations.[232] People don't really move from state to state of a process like the one above. In fact, even prairie dogs don't communicate in the narrow way that Maturana and Varela proposed — it turns out that they have a richly descriptive language, which they use to describe the colour of clothes that humans are wearing, their size and shape, and even whether they are carrying a gun. In a few years, prairie dog may appear in the dropdown list at the top of Google Translate.[233]

Let's not throw the baby out with the bathwater, though. Humans definitely negotiate with each other in standard ways, and we all know from daily experience that what people say isn't quite what they mean — or rather, it isn't what they intend. Conversations can go badly wrong if the people involved have different intentions. Have you ever been in a meeting where people seem to be talking at cross-purposes? One person may be explaining their new design, while others are talking about the kinds of products that people want right now in certain countries. Some people are focusing on a specific risk, asking what we should do about it, while others are trying to work out the remit of the group as a whole, and the funding available. People stand up one by one and deliver reports, gaining no interest from the senior people in the room until a particular item catches their attention.

This can also apply to personal relationships, of course. The classic example might be two people having dinner together, unsure whether the occasion is romantic or platonic. There are many kinds of intention. Whether you're out on a date that might not be a date, or trying to do some form of productive work together, you can classify all conversations into one of four kinds — Context, Possibility, Disclosure, and Action. Doing so turns out to be very helpful. In a work context, it avoids long pointless meetings where people are talking at cross-purposes, and enables you all to work towards the goals you committed to when you took on your roles. Classifying conversations can be useful in personal life, but here I'll only discuss conversations held for work purposes. I'll illustrate it by considering a community that wants to do something about local wellness.

First, you have a conversation for Context. Before people can even think about working together, they need to establish what it is all about. In our example, this might be a meeting including government agencies, third sector organisations such as charities, and community organisations of various kinds, to discuss approaches to community wellness. Rather than focusing on particular services or individuals, the meeting is to review local wellness issues and the different ways in which the community might address them. What problems are we trying to solve, and what sort of solutions are available? This could result in a draft vision statement, such as "by 2030, our town will offer local employment to young people and local residents will live in safe, inclusive neighbourhoods". It might also be possible to start drawing up a vision statement, setting out the sort of industries that will be developed and ways in which neighbourhoods will be improved.

After this meeting, the participants would separately read up on the topics covered, think them through, and discuss them with colleagues. Then a second meeting might be held — a conversation for Possibility. At this second meeting, participants might draw up an outline wellness wheel showing a breakdown of key issues affecting local people. They might also agree more specific ways forward — for example, to set up physical wellness hubs in some types of location, such as supermarkets and train stations (we'll return to this later). A list might be put together of major local institutions to approach as partners. Participants might also discuss ways that local people could create a wellness plan and put together a personal support network, which might mean making new digital tools and devices available locally, as well as bringing together local volunteering efforts that currently work in isolation.

After this second meeting, emails will be sent, phone calls made, smaller meetings held, and documents drawn up that help to refine the mission statement. It will then be possible to hold a third meeting, for Disclosure. Here everyone starts to get down to the nitty gritty, and work out the art of the possible — the terms and conditions under which each partner could be involved, the blockers that need to be removed, any prior commitments that need to be adjusted or taken into account, and so on. It is essential to get all these details out in the open as early as possible, or the work could be undone at any time.

The third meeting will produce something closer to a mission statement, describing what will actually be done. It will also give rise to a further flurry of activity, to iron out details that couldn't be sorted out during a meeting. This will take time and effort, and once all concerned are reasonably happy that they have got as far as possible for now, a fourth meeting can be held — for Action. This is not the standard Conversation for Action of Winograd and Flores, but a way of planning future work that can take any form. At this meeting, a draft plan of action is hammered out, outlining the steps that will be taken, and assigning each one to an owner. The owner must be an individual, not an organisation, to make it fully clear where responsibility lies. The owner may delegate responsibility for parts of the work to others, of course, but they retain accountability — the buck stops with them, at least until they pass ownership on to another person.

This is not a one-off exercise, but should be thought of more as a template for cycles of activity that repeat, overlap, and nest inside each other. Each phrase in the vision statement, each line in the mission statement, and each step of the plan may give rise to its own set of conversations for Context, Possibility, Disclosure, and Action. It is the pattern that is important, and that avoids a lot of people wasting a lot of time and energy.

It is also a helpful way to think about diverse interactions you have in life. When you interact with a group of people, or an individual, what type of conversation are you really having? For several years after my first book was published, a large part of my working life was as a keynote speaker, travelling to conferences around the world to present the ideas and sometimes run workshops. If someone came up after a talk to ask for my card, or signed up for one of my workshops, it didn't necessarily mean they intended to put the ideas they were learning into practice straight away, or ever. For them, it was a conversation for Context. Any implementation would have to align with organizational strategy, plans, and budget, so they would get in touch later if they wanted a conversation for Possibility. Even this might not lead anywhere, since there would then have to be conversations for Disclosure, internal to their own organisation and with facilitators such as me. Only after all this would it be possible to set up a conversation for Action. Again, this is not the Winograd and Flores process called "Conversation for Action", but a discussion aimed at creating a plan — sorry, I know it's a bit confusing.

There is a similar path for wellness planning. At the first meeting between a person with low wellness and an agency or community organisation, they need to establish what the person's wellness issues are, and some of their key goals — this is Context. Then there is Possibility — where should they focus, what sort of resources are available, and who might be able to help support them? After this, a conversation for Disclosure will result in a better idea of suitable organisations, individuals, and resources (funding, training, places, spaces, tools, and so on), in some cases under terms and conditions that govern usage. Finally, it is possible to hold a conversation for Action to put together the person's wellness plan and personal support network.

With all types of activity and all types of conversation, it is vitally important to keep a balance between physical and digital interactions. In other words, meet in person as often as you can. A key part of the decline in American

civic life chronicled by Robert Putman is how citizens'
groups founded recently tend to be for mass-market sub-
scription rather than local membership: "membership in the
newer groups means moving a pen, not making a meeting".
I discussed above how we evolved to be social animals.
"Humans are remarkably effective at sensing nonverbal
messages from one another, particularly about emotions,
cooperation, and trustworthiness." Our encounters with
others rely at least as much on facial and vocal expressions,
postures, movements and gestures as on words, and losing
this information risks losing crucial elements of trust and
compassion that we build from "eye contact, gestures (both
intentional and unintentional), nods, a faint furrowing of
the brow, body language, seating arrangements, even hesita-
tion measured in milliseconds".[234]

With whatever mixture of personal and long-distance
interaction you hold a conversation, it might happen in a
single meeting, at four separate meetings, or spread across
ten meetings. The important thing is to understand the sort
of conversation you are currently having, so that you don't
jump ahead and omit key stages. This lets you all build a
house on rock rather than sand, knowing that the wellness
plan you make is what the person needs and wants, that it
can be carried out, and that everyone has what they require
in order to contribute as expected.

As this shows, it's important to understand the purpose of a meeting. It's just as important to understand the
purpose of an email or telephone call, which can be even
more confusing. Emails are particularly subject to confu-
sion, since the content often doesn't correspond to the subject. An email may cover many topics at once. People may
use an email thread to introduce new topics, only partially

related or totally unrelated to the original message, some of which may be social rather than work-related. An email conversation may start out by raising a social care issue and end up debating last night's football or arranging to meet up for a curry, with new people being copied in along the way. Even if everyone manages to stay on topic, when an email it is addressed or copied to many people it's hard to know who is supposed to do what as a result of the message. The intention of an email often gets lost amongst all this noise. The shriek of a prairie dog instantly results in the pack diving for cover, but emails are usually about as effective in generating action as waving a white flag in a blizzard.

People who work regularly in teams often try to address this by using an app or Web tool that lets you create focused chat threads. However, after the initial burst of enthusiasm, people often end up using exactly the same behaviour as they did with email — mixing up all sorts of things in a single thread, with a semi-random group of people involved. Another way around the problem is to arrange a conference or video call. However, this loses the convenient asynchrony of email or chat — everyone has to be available at the same time, which can be hard if not impossible to arrange, and generally introduces an unwelcome delay.

A better solution is to use whatever tool you prefer — email, instant messaging, project management system, whatever — but write to people in a structured way. First, choose a subject or topic that describes the purpose of the message. The natural topic for a message is a specific goal of the endeavor you are all involved in. Make this the subject. Then address the message to everyone who has that goal among their list of responsibilities. Try not to leave anyone out, and if you do need to add someone as you go along, keep the message limited to people who are interested in that goal. Finally, stay on topic. If you want to talk about something else as well, whether it's another shared goal or to arrange a curry, do it in a different email or chat thread.

Suppose you're involved in setting up a wellness initiative for your community, the conversations for Context and Possibility have just taken place, and you all went away to refine the details of the mission statement. A natural topic for an email would be a line in the mission statement, such as "Set up wellness hubs in supermarkets". The people addressed would include appropriate representatives from organisations that would need to be involved in this, along with anyone who might have advice to offer, such as on legal or ethical issues. If the discussion starts to veer towards setting up hubs in train stations, start a new thread, letting people in the first thread know that you have done so.

Or suppose Sarah is worried about her children's safety on the school bus. She might email the ex-teacher in your personal support network, copying in her social worker who is interested in anything relating to her family's safety. She will use as subject, "Safety on the school bus". If Sarah's social worker then becomes aware that her ex-partner has not been attending their alcohol dependency clinic, they won't reply to this email to let Sarah know, they will start a new email. This will have subject "Ex-partner visitation" and be copied to other people in Sarah's personal support network that have accepted a responsibility to help safeguard her.

This requires some discipline, so it's best to introduce

this way of working with a short workshop where people practice communicating with each other in a range of made-up situations. Then it will take time to bed in. People will need reminding. Even then, they might not always find it easy to adopt a structured approach to email and chat. What then — give up? Carrot? Stick? This brings us to the third principle of Human Interaction Management, Contribute.

Contributions and recognition

In order to engage with their work, people need recognition and appreciation. Praise should be personalized, heartfelt, and timely. Volunteering has huge benefits, most of which accrue to the volunteers themselves.

How do people choose what they do for a living? Conventionally, it comes down to money. In a survey of over 230,000 workers from 31 countries, including three generations and a multitude of industries and occupations, 84 percent said that salary, benefits and financial incentives would influence them to choose one job over another.[235]

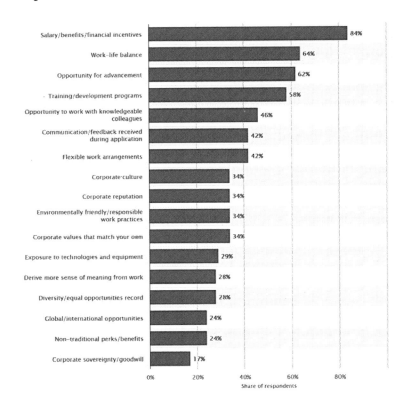

Figure 36: Most important employment factors when choosing jobs worldwide 2014

This may be changing. Research in 2017 showed that "Jobs are increasingly perceived as core to one's self-identity ... For many employees, a job is not only a paycheck: employees put considerable thought and effort into deciding where to work and why ... many employees seek meaning as much as, or even more than money."[236] Meaning rather than money is especially important to millennials and to Generation Z, who care more than older workers about intangibles such as social connections and company purpose, and "strive to work where they feel that their input makes a difference to customers, colleagues, peers, and supervisors".

Global unemployment is at its lowest level for a decade,[237] allowing people more choice in their careers, and more and more of them are becoming motivated by meaning rather than money. Meaning is closely related to what is called employee engagement. This term emerged in 1990, and gained widespread adoption at about the same time as positive psychology. It means the degree to which people associate their personal selves with the roles they play at work: "in engagement, people employ and express themselves physically, cognitively, and emotionally during role performances."[238] Self-employment in your role underpins and drives other factors that increase your productivity, such as effort, involvement, flow, mindfulness, and motivation. In other words, you work better if you feel personally connected to what you are doing.

The advantages of being engaged with your work are demonstrable even if you choose your job purely for financial reasons, since you work better if you feel personally connected to what you are doing. On top of that, paying you extra won't make you feel more connected.[239] Organizations who try to motivate employees through "tangible cash and cash-like rewards" are wasting their money. They would do more to help employees achieve a sense of meaning and purpose at work by "increasing recognition and appreciation as part of their total reward strategies."[240] Paying you more money isn't without effect, but the best way to make you feel more engaged is a regular pat on the back from colleagues.

Unfortunately, this message has not yet been taken on

board by the employers of over 80 percent of American workers, who say they do not feel recognized or rewarded.[241] This not only reduces productivity, but dramatically increases the odds of a syndrome called burnout.[242] The World Health Organization describe burnout as related to chronic workplace stress that has not been successfully managed, manifesting itself in "feelings of energy depletion or exhaustion; increased mental distance from one's job, or feelings of negativism or cynicism related to one's job; and reduced professional efficacy."[243] Lack of recognition also causes what human resources people call churn, or staff turnover, which is an expensive problem for employers. When people leave their jobs voluntarily, 80% of the time it is because they feel under-appreciated.[244]

This brings to mind the discussion above on the huge difference that positive parental and other influences have on child development. Human beings work harder and achieve more if they receive encouragement and praise, whether in school or in the workplace. All of us, even senior managers, were children at one time, so why is constant encouragement and praise not the norm in every office, shop, and factory floor? Evidence suggests that a simple, heartfelt thank you from a manager is enough for employees to feel like their contribution is valued.

Possibly this is because although a thank you does not have to be made face to face — a video or even an email seems to work just as well — it does require some effort. Giving recognition "requires an understanding of the specifics of the workplace, including contextual and cultural factors as well as the distinctive quality of the individual contributor's work … recognition should be accurate and specific, highlighting the recipient's unique contributions."[245] In other words, praise needs to be personalized, heartfelt, and timely. A canned message sent to the whole team or department on a regular basis won't do the trick.

The third principle of Human Interaction Management, Contribute, is about recognizing and rewarding contributions of all kinds. It is as important to thank people for coming up with, or helping develop, an idea as for staying late to get a product out of the door. In a wellness context, you should thank both the friend who suggests a new fitness technique and the trainer who gives the classes at your local community centre. Some people's contributions are even subtler — they may provide value by helping build and maintain a social network, making useful introductions and connecting people at vital times. Sarah was struggling to ensure the safety of her children on the school bus until the ex-teacher in her personal support network said a word in the right ear. Then there are enablers — people who contribute indirectly, such as the council worker who reminds community organisations to update details of their activities in the local digital hub. Administrators are often particularly bereft of appreciation, being singled out only when things go wrong. No-one thinks about the work that goes in to ensure event listings are accurate, but if you turn up at 8pm on a rainy evening to find only a dark, locked building because no-one let you know a club was cancelled, you might look for someone to blame.

The positive effects of being appreciated are visible in recent research into the wellness benefits of volunteering. In 2008, a systematic review of evidence on the links between volunteering and health by Volunteering England found a wide range of positive health outcomes not only to the people that volunteers help but also to volunteers themselves. Volunteering increases your self-esteem and confidence. Volunteers have more social interaction, experiencing better integration and support from the community. Giving time to others helps you manage any illnesses you experience, reduces depression, and leads to a less intense response to grief.[246]

Just as employers often may recognise and reward their employees by financial means, so are some communities providing volunteers with benefits that are cashable or that represent a cost saving. A popular way of doing this is timebanking. "Timebanking is a way of spending one hour of time helping someone out and earning one-time credit in return, which can be spent on receiving an hour of someone else's time. For example, Sam helps Lee with gardening, and then spends the time earned by receiving help from Jo, who teaches Sam basic IT skills. No money is exchanged."[247]

Time banks are sometimes used by institutions as a way of encouraging people to participate in volunteering activities. "For example, a hospital might wish to provide a home-care service for patients who have left the acute care setting but are still in need of support — somebody with a broken leg, for example. The hospital would organize the informal support needed, such as help with cooking meals, doing shopping or running basic errands, using the local time bank to provide help rather than paying professionals in the traditional manner." They can also be used by organisations as a way to trade with one another without use of money. "Organisations such as local businesses or public sector agencies might give the local time bank access to some of their resources. This might be the use of a minibus or sports hall, or skills such as graphic design or legal advice."

Many people find time banking a valuable as a way of acquiring services that they cannot afford to pay for directly. For example, the council may offer time in the local leisure centre swimming pool time in return for helping out with gardening in the local park. This enables households on a low, fixed income to gain access to facilities they could not otherwise afford. However, they are working for the privilege, not volunteering, so this advantage should not be confused with the wellness benefits that accrue from giving up your time for free. Time banking may well generate social capital through building "networks of people who give and receive support, enabling people from different backgrounds, who may not otherwise meet, to form meaningful and fruitful connections and friendships". However, it only does this in the way that any other paid work would, if that work had a social benefit — and people who give up their time in return for swimming pool credits still benefit from being thanked, just like people who do any other job.

As society has learned more about the wellness benefits that come from reward and recognition, thought leaders have also come to see the critical importance of volunteering in delivering these benefits. The United Nations has sponsored a long-term international effort over the last two decades to measure the value of what the International Labour Organization defines as "Unpaid, non-compulsory work; that is, time individuals give without pay to activities performed either through an organisation or directly for others outside their own household".[248] In 2001, the UN General Assembly passed a resolution calling on governments to establish the economic value of volunteering.[249] In 2005, a UN resolution following the International Year of

Volunteers called for "Governments, with the support of civil society, to build up a knowledge base on the subject, to disseminate data and to expand research on other volunteer-related issues, including in developing countries".[250]

The International Labour Organization's "Manual on the measurement of volunteer work" recommends measuring it via labour force surveys, although it acknowledges that this approach "limits the range of issues that can be explored." It does indeed! In a 2014 speech, Chief Economist of the Bank of England Andrew Haldane reported on research into the true impact of volunteering in the UK by the charity Pro Bono Economics, which "helps charities measure performance, improve their services and better track outcomes."[251] Their findings are startling. The outputs and outcomes of volunteering are far greater than you might expect, which leads us to the fourth principle of Human Interaction Management — Calculate.

Outputs and outcomes

To achieve great impact for low effort, make interventions local and personal, focus on outcomes not outputs, and ensure that organisations work together. Depending on the scale, use Agile techniques or value maps.

"We have a volunteer army, the full-time equivalent of 1.25 million people, diverse in age, gender, background and ethnicity and potentially growing in number. They create each year economic value of at least £50 billion and potentially higher. They create private value for individual volunteers of maybe as much again. And although the confidence intervals are large, it would not be unreasonable to apply a social multiplier of upwards of two to these estimates.

However you cut this onion, it is clear that the value it creates is eye-watering. And this is value, let's remember, much of which is not captured or visible from official statistics."[252]

Haldane is trying to make it clear just how dramatic the impact the impact of volunteering could be in the UK if only it was properly integrated into the functioning of society. The onion he refers to is a picture showing how the economic, private, and social impacts of volunteering are nested.

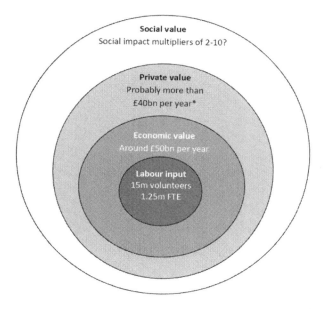

Source: Bank and Pro Bono Economics calculations.

Note: The estimate of private value shown is an estimate of the benefits to an individual's well-being, not including health benefits or improvements to an individual's skills or employability.

Figure 37: The Volunteering Onion, a summary of the estimated contribution from volunteering activities in the UK

At the heart of the onion lies economic impact — the outputs that volunteers generate by giving their time for free, which would otherwise have to be paid for. Making some assumptions about the relationship between labour costs and output value, as well as about the competency of volunteers compared to paid professionals, Haldane declares that the economic output of volunteering "could exceed £50 billion per year, or around 3.5% of annual UK GDP. This would place the volunteering sector on a level pegging with the UK energy sector (both extraction and utilities). Very few sectors add more value. Clearly, the inner layer of the volunteering onion — economic value — is a very significant one."

This is only the start. The next layer of the onion is the private value of volunteering — benefits to the volunteers themselves. Haldane divides these into three categories: enhanced well-being, health benefits, and increased skills and employability. The first two of these categories relate to the research discussed above, from 2008, on the personal wellness benefits that accrue to volunteers. In the third category, Haldane finds only weak evidence that volunteering helps you find a job, but stronger evidence for it making you more productive. While he emphasizes that it is hard to put a precise figure on this, he stresses "how big a potential benefit that could be. If the UK's 15 million volunteers were each 5% more productive, that would deliver a boost to national income of £23 billion each year." He puts the private value of volunteering at £40 billion per year.

Let's put these numbers into context. The total so far, from layers one and two, is £90 billion per year in the UK. If we equate this to UK government spending, only the Department of Health and Social Care receives more, with a budget of £132 billion in 2019-20.[253] The next largest budget, for the Department for Education, was a mere £64 billion in 2019-20, about two-thirds of the economic and private benefits from volunteering. But even this is still only the start.

Haldane then considers the social value of volunteering, the third and outer layer of the onion. He sees this as a multiple of the cost of the labour input to volunteering, since it delivers a social return on investment. For example, reducing homelessness saves society money by getting young people into employment or training, preventing them from re-offending, treating their mental health issues, and reducing their substance misuse. Every £1 spent by the homeless charity Centrepoint delivers a social benefit of at least £2.40. Similarly, helping exploited children results in fewer missing person calls to the police, lowers the probability of them becoming classified as Not in Employment, Education or Training, reduces substance misuse, and delivers a number of benefits from their being in secure accommodation. In this case, the social return on investment is somewhere between six and twelve pounds for every pound spent.

Haldane is clear that "the precise social multipliers are likely to vary, charity by charity" but stresses that "the lowest multiplier we have found … is around 2.5, while the highest runs into double figures." Let's be as pessimistic as possible, and assume that volunteering delivers an average return of 2.5, the lowest figure they found for any charity. Our 90 billion pounds becomes 225 billion pounds. This is far higher than any single government department, approaching twice the budget allotted to health and social care.

These numbers confirm the research summarized by Volunteering England in 2008.[254] In communities where people volunteer, carers have less of a burden, and anxiety is generally lower. Hospice patients survive longer. Children show improved cognitive function, with more mothers breastfeeding and fir longer. Children are more often immunized and have better mental health, while adults show better parenting skills. People in such communities have better physical health — they exercise more, eat better, and manage their own health more effectively. There are fewer hospital visits, and patients have more productive relationships with health professionals.

Calculations such as those by Pro Bono Economics reveal that, in community life, the impacts can be wildly disproportionate to the amount of effort put in, and not just when it comes to volunteering. A Policy Exchange report in 2014 showed how targeted interventions driven by dedicated individuals, including government agency staff as well as community volunteers, can make an enormous difference to crime, unemployment, gangs, and violence on deprived housing estates in the UK. "In Taunton, the Halcon Estate was turned around by one dedicated police officer and his team. In South London, gang activity on the Stockwell Park Estate was curtailed by a job fair. On the Pengegon Estate in Cornwall, one Neighbourhood Manager revitalized the community. In Castlemilk, Glasgow, the work of one progressive nursery has saved lives."[255] The report highlights how none of these interventions required large amounts of additional funding — many costs were met within existing local government budgets, simply by working better with people on the ground. This meant doing making hyperlocal interventions, and collaborating with residents to introduce them.

Those leading interventions must live in or near the area, and have genuine, in-depth knowledge of the problems faced by residents. Detective Constable Andy Murphy was appointed Beat Manager of Halcon Estate in Taunton, dominated by organized crime families, because he was a local. "I was one of the most hated cops in the town," Murphy says, "because I had arrested most of them and locked them up." Knowing first hand that this hadn't reduced crime levels, Murphy sat down to talk to the residents who were reporting crimes like burglary, theft and intimidation. He asked them what was wrong, and their feedback was clear. They felt no one cared about them — not the police, not the council, not social services. Whenever they rang, the police would turn up, but they seemed disinterested when they did arrive. They could never get through to speak to someone when they rang the council or social services. Children's social services were renowned for doing the "silent knock": they would call in at the address, pretend to ring the doorbell but never enter the property. That address would then be ticked off their list. It was clear that Murphy would need to find a way to get the community to trust the authorities again, but it was also clear that the authorities would need to become worthy of the community's trust.

The first challenge was to break the wall of silence and increase the reporting of crime. Murphy struck a deal with the local supermarket to put a police base in the heart of Halcon. The symbolism was deliberate: through creating a permanent, visible presence, Murphy was making a statement that the police were interested in the area and would be there for the long haul. In the supermarket's car park, they installed a Policing Pod, a portacabin covered in police insignia, funded by the supermarket. An informant could say they were going shopping and use that as an opportunity to give their statement. Residents could report matters and make statements without having to go to the main police station in Taunton, and thus avoiding intimidation and threats. As a result, prosecution and detection numbers started to rise. Criminals were arrested, raided, convicted then evicted. At the time of the report, only one criminal household remained.

Greater reporting also helped support early intervention and access to support services, but Murphy recognized that agencies work in silos, without cooperating. To address this, he developed a "One Team" Approach based on regular cross-agency meetings to share information and form partnerships, similar to the MARAC approach to dealing with domestic violence discussed above. Further, interventions were traditionally too high-level and strategic, so Murphy also brought in a community mapping approach, using data to examine each household in the community and ensure that interventions were specific, targeted and effective.

Local people should be involved in making the interventions happen, and the interventions should be based in or near the estate so people don't have to travel in order to take part. In Stockwell Park, the idea for a job fair came from a gang member called Snipes, after he and Sergeant Jack Rowlands struck up a friendship when they met on neutral ground in a community centre. Rowlands had chased Snipes frequently, but could see that his hustle was just a masquerade and challenged his life choices. Snipes challenged Rowlands in return, saying "Get me a job,

Sarge." Knowing that other gang members would prefer work to a life of crime, which was not even very profitable, Rowlands liaised with Lambeth Council and voluntary organisations to organize a job fair on the estate. The first one was attended by 21 gang members, and 18 got jobs. Subsequent job fairs went from strength to strength, and the model became adopted across London.

Collaboration is vital, both between different government agencies and with locals. The Pengegon Estate, in Camborne, Cornwall, is among the country's most deprived areas, with high levels of unemployment, drug and alcohol abuse, domestic violence, child poverty and low educational attainment. It is only a few miles from the coast, but many children have never been to the beach. Over half of under-16s live in poverty, the highest level for the whole of Cornwall, which is itself one of the poorest parts of England. A number of serious crimes have blighted the area. In 2008, a group of children fell victim to a paedophile ring that included two men from Camborne.

Much like in Halcon, the major catalyst for change on the Pengegon Estate was one committed individual. Claire Arymar, Cornwall Council's Neighbourhood Manager for Pengegon and the surrounding area, started working out of a house on the estate in 2008. This house quickly became a formal neighbourhood office — a physical presence for the council on the estate. From her office, Arymar helps develop good relationships between residents and agencies such as the local health authorities, Devon and Cornwall Police, and Cornwall Council. In particular, she encourages agencies to operate drop-in sessions from the office. Arymar has also helped residents apply for funding to benefit the local area, set up resident associations and organized community events. She now tours the areas under her responsibility on a converted children's bus.

At the time of the report, Arymar was struggling to achieve the same level of agency buy-in as the One Team in Halcon. "The statutory agencies have been shocking. They don't want to move out of their little silos because people are chaotic, sweary, and don't turn up. The workers at the agencies are the problem. They sit in meetings and say they want to work with the hard to-reach, but they don't want to get stuck in because it is messy. I haven't seen a teenage pregnancy adviser, employment, non-smoking adviser in 5 years. They must be aware we have a drop-in surgery. Everything is so target-driven." Arymar tries to make up for this by acting as a champion for local residents, a bridge between them and the services they need. "We got rid of arson by engaging the local fire brigade, Blackwatch. They will come and play football and are on first name terms with the local lads. The boys don't set fires anymore because they are scared that Blackwatch will clip them round the ear or will stop playing football with them."

As well as addressing issues, Arymar tries to improve opportunities. "I keep on offering activities that they haven't done before, go to the Eden project, I make sure that you do fruit kebabs because kids don't know what a peach is," Arymar says. "We have a fishing club which the EA funds and we have a fishing tackle library. There is a group of men who would normally fish illegally, now I take them in a minibus. They are taught how to fish properly. They are taught not to swear. Two local coaches are paid for by the EA. The outreach worker from Addaction has engaged. All this has been done through building relationships."

Everyone must feel part of the solution, especially

women and children, who are often particularly at risk. At the heart of Castlemilk, an area in Glasgow rated as being in the top 15% of the most deprived communities in Scotland, is the Jeely Piece Club Nursery. It is a children's centre catering to preschoolers, but also provides an extensive offering to parents, ranging from addiction rehabilitation programmes to adult education, and has a variety of programmes for primary school children. The Jeely, as it is known locally, has served its area for over two decades, making a sustainable and long-term contribution to the community, not least through the network of older children who attend the nursery.

I'll discuss the notion of a community asset below, and the different forms they can take. The Jeely was founded by a small group of mothers who applied for a grant to create a nursery. It an example of how assets within a community can revive the area. Maureen Douglas, one of the mothers, is a driving force. Karyn McCluskey, the Director of the Scottish Violence Reduction Unit says, "What difference do assets make? Maureen is an asset. She is wonderful. I can't tell you how much I like her. They had loads of gang fights. She looked at the problem. These women at that nursery deal with thousands of kids who come from the worst of backgrounds. They go out and challenge the gang members — don't you be fighting here. They absolutely changed it. They call them the Jeely Weans now. They are 17 and 18. She is really measured, incredibly thoughtful. The difference that they have made in Castlemilk, which used to be a really tough area, is an absolute testament. She'll make you smile. She loves kids. She believes in the dandelion children, who make it despite growing up in hostile environments. Despite the worst background they make you think that if you invest in them it will make a difference." Jeely Weans grow up to become mentors and role models within the community.

Hyperlocal interventions place the community front and centre — they are done with, rather than to, local people. By being locally-minded, a few determined and creative individuals can introduce small-scale, simple, inexpensive changes that make a real difference. The challenge is how to scale this up.

If you equate a community to an organisation, the problem becomes apparent. Even a small town may have tens of thousands of residents. An organisation with this many staff would be a major player, probably with a global presence. Introducing change into such organisations is a complex, lengthy, and time-consuming business. It may well be spearheaded by a few determined and creative individuals, like the community interventions above, but in order to be effective will require large-scale planning. The resulting plans typically contain hundreds or thousands of tasks. The people assigned these tasks find it difficult to see the context of their work. Day to day, they often end up working through a personal task list without any sense of what impact their actions are having, if any, and with no idea how they could use their working time better.

Management consultants have known for a long time that this is a problem. Legendary management guru Peter Drucker observed that "Effective knowledge workers, in my observation, do not start with their tasks. They start with their time. And they do not start out with planning. They start by finding out where their time actually goes. Then they attempt to manage their time and to cut back unproductive demands on their time." Drucker went on to observe how effective people consolidate their "discretionary" time into the largest possible blocks, in which they have the best chance of getting something done.[256]

That's fine if you are a senior executive in a company, or in a community context, a powerful local figure such as a councillor or agency head — you have the ability to see where your time goes, and the authority to decide how to use your working day. Most people, however, aren't in this fortunate position. In the last two decades, organisations have tried to address the time management challenge by introducing change in an Agile way. Instead of planning change over a long period, they break it into small chunks — often called Stories, since they describe a new state of affairs that is desirable. Then they plan only a short distance ahead, for a short period called a Sprint, which might last two weeks. A few days before the start of each Sprint, everyone involved sits down together to agree on the most urgent Stories, and assess how many of these could fit into the next Sprint. They also review how the current Sprint is going, and whether any lessons learned could be applied to improve the way everyone is working together.

In a community context, an Agile approach works really well for personal wellness planning, although there may be no need to adopt jargon such as Stories and Sprints. Sarah cannot deal with all her wellness issues at once. To avoid feeling overwhelmed, she needs to focus on one or two at a time. The people in her personal support network can and should help her do this, by meeting and talking regularly to work out what her current top priorities are, address these, and review progress. As some of her goals are met, or partially met, Sarah and the people that support her can go around this loop to adjust priorities and focus on new goals. Initially, Sarah might be most concerned about the safety of her children on the school bus, and about any risk to the family from her ex-partner. Once these concerns are addressed, other goals such as safety of sockets and shelves in the home may come to the fore. At each meeting, everyone takes a few minutes to discuss how they are working together, and whether they could be doing anything better.

An Agile approach may or may not work as well for collaborative work on a larger scale, such as introducing change into communities to improve wellness. It can be ideal for small-scale interventions such as those discussed in the Policy Exchange report. When the community size is a few hundred people, people often take an Agile approach naturally, working collaboratively to introduce small changes one after another. However, with a community such as a parliamentary ward in a city, which may contain a hundred thousand people, it is not so easy to make change in an Agile way. There are too many different agencies, services, places, spaces, groups, activities, issues, risks, agendas, vested interests, stakeholders, sources of funding, and sinks of cost.

Large organisations, whether a company or a community, cannot make change effectively without a long-term strategic vision that ensures all their moving are joined up parts properly. If you're only ever thinking two weeks ahead, and about a few small chunks at a time, it's easy to lose direction. It's like navigating out of a bog by following the paths that seem most solid rather than using a compass. You might end up on the edge of an impassable body of water, whereas getting your feet wet for a while would have taken you to dry land.

One way to bring together a strategic vision with an Agile approach is value mapping, sometimes called Wardley mapping after their originator Simon Wardley.[257] A value map shows the needs that a programme of change will address, with each need underpinned by the mechanisms that will be adopted or introduced to meet it. It also shows how both needs and mechanisms will evolve as the change programme continues, grouping them to show how the work can be split among teams. An example value map is shown below, for an initiative to help communities build a local ecosystem for social trading (I'll say more about social trading later on).

An example value map is shown below. Don't worry if you can't read the text – the image is shown only to illustrate the approach. The map can be read vertically, going from needs at the top down through connecting lines to the mechanisms that meet them — visible mechanisms are near the top and underpinning mechanisms near the bottom. It can also be read horizontally, going from now to the future. Early needs and accompanying mechanisms are on the left, switching over to future versions as you move to the right.

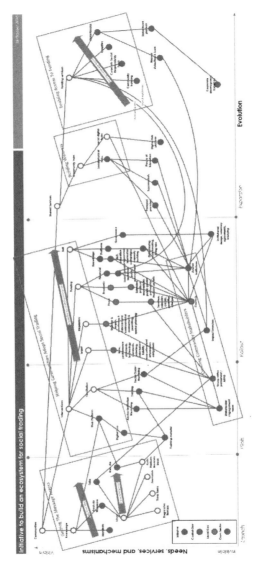

Figure 38: Value map for initiative to build an ecosystem for social trading

In the value map above, the very top on the left shows the customer that the programme serves — communities. This doesn't change over time. Underneath this are what a community needs in order to develop a social trading eco-system, and this changes as the programme moves through stages. In the initial Genesis stage, the programme is focused on developing and promoting its core ideas, so it will meet a need for Knowledge through publications, talks, and interaction with thought leaders.

The project then moves into its Custom Built stage, where staff will hand craft products and services to offer communities. Here it addresses needs for Interventions by working with pilot communities, offering them a digital platform, gathering and evaluating innovative approaches via Idea Boxes, assembling these into out-of-the-box ("turnkey") solutions, and working with different stakeholders to introduce measures that supports social trading.

There is then a Product stage. This isn't about meeting new needs, but about refining and standardizing the help provided to pilot communities in the previous stage, so that the project can extend their offer to communities world-wide. Finally, in the Commodity stage the solution becomes available to all communities as a common underpinning enabler for local life. At this point, the project will focus on introducing economies of scale, by bundling its offerings into shared services that are available off the shelf at low cost. As it becomes normal for communities to set up well-ness hubs and operate social businesses, they will adopt these underpinning mechanisms in the same way as they purchase other utilities such as energy, water, and waste.

Under each of these needs are the services that the initiative will build to meet it, with underpinning mechanisms below each service. There is an outline around related services, which has two purposes. First, it shows how communities will get better support in a particular area as time goes on. Second, it lets the programme divide the work up unto teams. Each of these teams can then use an Agile approach to manage the work, while remaining in line with an overall strategic direction. They may develop lower-level value maps of their own, and divide up the work still further.

A value map also shows which types of organisation provide each part of the solution, by colouring the services and mechanisms differently. You will see that the initiative sits at the heart of the map but does not try to do everything itself. As with the small-scale interventions documented by Policy Exchange, much of the work is done (and must be done) locally, by people based in each community.

The value map shown here is for an international project to serve communities worldwide, but any community can use a value map to plan how it will introduce and harmonize local wellness and social trading initiatives. This top-level value map can then be extended with lower-level value maps showing how the community will support specific issues (such as transport or safety), neighbourhoods (such as a deprived housing estate or parliamentary ward), or interest groups (such as new migrants or homeless people). Value maps allow communities of any size to bring together the outputs of individual teams with the outcomes of a large-scale change programme. No matter how large scale the community, or how grand its vision for change, they can create a value map to divide up the work. Then, small teams can work in an Agile way in order to produce outputs effectively, while staying aligned to the overall goals of the community.

However, a big programme of change takes years, and in that time, all sorts of things will happen. New issues may emerge for a community and current issues become less important. External events may affect the economy in a good or bad way. There may be an influx of new people that face new challenges. There may be a natural disaster locally, such as a flood. A new government policy may change things for people in an unforeseen way. Any of these things will have an impact on the overall needs of the community, and hence on its value map.

Value maps can be updated and new ones created, but the community must ensure that it stays aware of external events that may have an impact on the community, and then it must respond to such events. It is often far from obvious how to respond. An event such as a natural disaster or complex change to regulations may have a ripple effect that affects multiple stakeholders. They will each need to understand the impacts of this on their own interests, and arrive at joint decisions in a coordinated way. To see how this can be managed, let's look at the fifth and last principle of Human Interaction Management — Change.

Awareness and responsiveness

To notice events and respond, use Research-Evaluate-Analyze-Constrain-Task (REACT). To conduct Research, use Access-Identify-Memorize (AIM). Separate leadership into Strategic, Executive, and Management Control.

We all love acronyms. Or do we just put up with them? Either way, they pop up everywhere, and were doing so long before texting. Some even become words — think of laser (Light Amplification by Stimulated Emission of Radiation), radar (RAdio Detection And Ranging), and scuba (Self-Contained Underwater Breathing Apparatus). Even taser is not in fact an homage to Star Trek phasers — sorry, trekkies — but stands for "Thomas A Swift Electric Rifle" (named after Tom Swift, hero of over 100 books between 1910 and 2007, a teenage genius tinkerer who consistently anticipates real world inventions such as the videophone, electric locomotive, and house trailer). My favourite acronym is the www prefix to website addresses, which at nine syllables takes far longer to say than the three syllables of "world wide web".

So far, this book has avoided acronyms, but there's no use in delaying the inevitable. In order to apply the fifth principle of Human Interaction Management and deal with Change, we must introduce REACT and AIM. Taken together, these patterns describe how to notice events and plan corresponding actions. In a community context, a structured approach like this is most useful when thinking about interventions in community life as a whole. It may sometimes be helpful to a personal support network, if the person they are helping has particularly complex and wide-ranging wellness issues, and it is hard to see the wood for the trees. However, here I will illustrate it by looking at actions taken by stakeholders in a community to improve life for their members, since this kind of large-scale work is often where it makes the most difference to manage change using a structured approach.

To Calculate local needs and how they will meet them, a community can make a value map. To deal with the resulting Change, they can then start to make a plan of action. Since noticing and responding to events is critical to any plan of action, it must always be included, which (as per the first principle of Human Interaction Management, Commit) means assigning such a responsibility to some roles as a goal. The people who play these roles will then be charged with keeping an eye on things, both inside the community and in the outside world, and sharing recommendations with other roles when action is required. Before diving into REACT and AIM, though, do we really need new acronyms? Let's look at standard approaches to structured noticing and responding, to see if any might fit the bill.

The first well-known approach emerged from manufacturing, where there is a strong financial incentive to notice process faults that result in defective items, and fix the processes so as to reduce costs. In the 1920s, the American statistician Walter Shewhart applied himself to this challenge. Until Shewhart's time, quality control in factories was based on inspecting products as they came off the assembly line, and making informal attempts to reduce the number of defects by adjusting manufacturing processes. The lack of control over process adjustment meant that factory managers might make many diverse interventions in succession, which was directionless, often ineffective, and could lead to changes that undid each other or were counter-productive. Shewhart adopted a technique that he derived from the scientific method, in which you make a hypothesis, carry out experiments to test it, then evaluate the findings and possibly revise your hypothesis. His approach turned quality control into a virtuous circle in which information about defective items is measured against a statistical norm, then used to make graduated interventions. These build on one other to reduce variation from the expected standard to an acceptable level.[258]

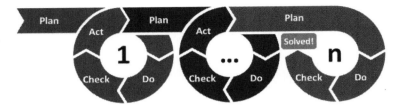

Figure 39: The Shewhart cycle

The Shewhart cycle is also known as the Deming cycle, since it was championed by physicist W. Edwards Deming, who created the acronym for it, PDSA (Plan, Do, Study, Act).[259] Deming's lectures in the 1950s to Japanese engineers are often credited with helping power the subsequent success and expansion of the Japanese economy. Japanese manufacturing practices based on PDSA became known as kaizen, from the Japanese characters kai meaning "change" and zen meaning "continuous improvement". In the 1980s, kaizen was popularized as Lean management, a widely used technique for eliminating the wasteful aspects of business operations.

An alternative approach to noticing and responding emerged in the 1980s, with an aim that might be thought of as an evolution of Shewhart's. DMAIC (Define, Measure, Analyze, Improve and Control) adopts a highly structured approach to measurement and analysis of data focusing on the identification of root causes for variation. DMAIC became the basis for a management method called Six Sigma that aims to reduce the number of defective items to just a few per million of those produced.

Another alternative to PDSA from around the same time is known as the OODA loop (Observe, Orient, Decide, Act). This was developed by US Air Force Colonel John Boyd for running military campaigns. OODA describes how we gather raw information about the evolving situation (Observe), then filter out some aspects (Orient) in order to Decide and then Act. "The second O, orientation—as the repository of our genetic heritage, cultural tradition, and previous experiences—is the most important part of the OODA loop since it shapes the way we observe, the way we decide, the way we act."[260] OODA didn't come out of manufacturing, but has since been applied to it, for example in helping structure the way that artificially intelligent machines make use of data captured from automated sensors.

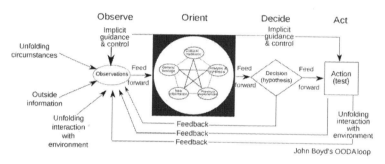

Figure 40: John Boyd's OODA loop

PDSA, DMAIC, and OODA were all developed to help people adjust and refine their response to an ongoing situation with a concrete aim: factory production to manufacture items (PDSA and DMAIC) or a military operation to win a battle (OODA). In the factory, the assembly line goes around and around every day, and you use PDSA or DMAIC to devise interventions that make it more efficient — less wasteful, as in Lean, or more consistent, as in Six Sigma. On a battlefield, you and your enemy are engaged in a game of move and counter-move, with each side reconnoitering the other for intelligence, probing the other for weaknesses, and looking for the decisive move than will enable them to control the territory. In both cases, there is a standard aim — for the factory, to consistently produce outputs for a minimal cost, and for the army, to claim the field for their own.

None of this bears much resemblance to the challenge faced by communities — to notice and respond to external events as they crop up, so that they can adjust their value maps and plans. Communities are not seeking to go around a loop until a specific aim is achieved. They might do the opposite, and change their aims entirely on the basis of an internal or external event, since this event might change local needs. New government regulations might make it unnecessary to provide certain services locally, or introduce a need for hitherto unexpected types of service. The creation of a university in the area might open new possibilities for employment, or local flooding might make it necessary temporarily to focus all efforts on disaster relief.

REACT is similar to OODA, but provides more detail in the first and second Os, Observe and Orient. Boyd left this deliberately vague and open, since a battle unit commander in the field needs to trust their own judgment based on the information to hand. There is no time to conduct extensive investigations, explore all the available options in detail, and make objective comparisons. Boyd recognized that decision making in an operational situation draws on "the repository of our genetic heritage, cultural tradition, and previous experiences" to devise an appropriate response to information as it emerges. However, this doesn't offer enough guidance for people who have responsibility to safeguard their community's welfare over an extended period of time. To help them feel confident that they are fully able to notice and respond to complex environmental changes on behalf of their community, they need a structured approach that breaks the work down into more manageable pieces.

So, REACT renames the first O of OODA, Observe, to Research, and expands it to a sub-pattern AIM (Access, Identify, Memorize) that shows how to go about it. REACT also splits the second O of OODA, Orient, into Evaluate and Analyze. Put together, this provides the structured approach to noticing and responding to events that community leaders need. Let's work through the elements of the pattern.

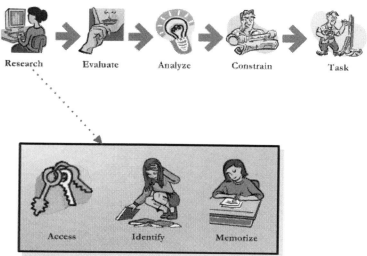

Figure 41: The REACT pattern, with Research broken down into the AIM sub-pattern

The first step in noticing and responding is to keep an eye on what is happening. Sometimes this is called horizon scanning. In practice, this is a form of **Research**, requiring you to gain information from sources and turn it into personal knowledge. We'll look at the details of Research below under the sub-pattern AIM. Broadly, it involves reading, listening to, and watching news stories, talks, discussions, studies, papers, books, and other material on economic, financial, legal, political, environmental, and social matters. It may also mean talking to people in the know to find out more about how emerging ideas, trends, and issues relate to your own community. Suppose you are aware that flooding is a risk to your community. Research will inform you of how likely this is, what form it might take, what the impacts might be, what means are possible to counter it, the experiences of other communities, the sort of costs involved, what funding mechanisms are available, and how much time it may take to put in place mechanisms for prevention and harm reduction. For example, what kinds of flood barriers are available, who produces them, how much do they cost, how long is it between order and delivery, how long do they take to install, and what sorts of firms are qualified?

There is a lot going on in the first stage of REACT. So, I break Research into a sub-pattern, AIM (Access, Identify, Memorize), to show how there are three different types of activity underpinning it.

Before you can even start researching, you need a way to do it — **Access** to services that point you at information sources. This might be a helpful librarian, an information website that lets you search environmental or civic news articles or journal papers, or events such as talks and conferences on climate change or flood control. To do your own horizon scanning, you need to decide where you will obtain information from, and obtain access. This might involve contacting someone, registering for a website, or buying event tickets and travel.

Then you need to **Identify** which resources you are interested in. If you are meeting someone for a discussion, what particular issues will you ask them about, and will you try to cover it all in the first meeting? If you are using a website, you need to decide what to search for. It might be better to search via the most well-known hashtags, which means finding out what they are. If you are attending a conference, you may have to choose a track to follow and workshops to attend.

The third and final aspect of Research is to **Memorize** the information you have obtained. This doesn't mean you need to commit to memory whole books or articles! But you do need to make notes on the key points you want to follow up, and have a way of keeping these in your mind. Otherwise, you won't be able to move on to the next stage of REACT, Evaluate. You cannot synthesize ideas unless you know what they are. You may decide that the three things you need to follow up are dredging, rewilding, and flood barriers, and keep some key points about each in mind.

The second step in the top-level pattern REACT is to **Evaluate** the information you have gathered — step back and consider the knowledge you have acquired. Once you have discovered the general lay of the land, you then need to familiarize yourself with it. You may need to carefully read a pile of papers on your desk, or to mull over some advice that you don't yet understand. This stage may take significant time, but it is crucial — there is no point going any further unless you have taken on board the information you researched. Gaining real understanding of information means internalizing it, by making connections between different opinions or facts. Evaluating the information that you have gathered about flooding will make you a local expert on the issue, giving you a way of categorizing the issues and options available, with an understanding of the different advantages and disadvantages. Does dredging work or is it counter-productive? Where is rewilding practical and what form could it take? What types of flood barrier would best suit the local area?

On the basis of your new-found understanding, you can then decide on whether action is needed, and if so, of what kind — **Analyze** the situation. You may apply try and chop up what seem to be complex challenges into more manageable chunks, about each of which you feel more confident to make a judgment. By whatever means you arrive at conclusions, the important thing is to make decisions that provide a way forward for now, and have enough confidence about those decisions to advise the other people you are working with. Sometimes it is hard to be sure whether you are doing the right thing, so you might choose a way forward that hedges bets — follows multiple paths at the same time, in the hope that at least one will work — or decide only that exploratory action is needed to gather more information. But you have to make some kind of decision at this point, at least on how to start. You may decide to install flood barriers in the lowest lying parts of the community, issue sand bags and advice to others, and start working on long term measures to increase tree cover and restore flood plains.

Then you **Constrain** the actions required by putting some boundaries around them. This might be as simple as putting tasks in order and agreeing how long to spend on each one. Alternatively, you might think a response to the challenge requires a professional level of project planning, including risk, issue, and dependency analysis, critical path definition, budgeting, resource planning, contingency planning, and so on. Each challenge will be different. You may have personal preferences for how to approach different types of action, and may prefer certain techniques that you feel comfortable with. You may have specific tools available, such as apps or websites that your community colleagues prefer to use. Whether you decide to use a to do list on paper, or an app, or a work breakdown structure, that's fine — the aim at this point is to have some kind of plan of action. This could divide into two main stages, where you focus for now on protection and then start working on prevention.

Finally, in the **Task** stage you get the work going. You have decided how to break the work into pieces, so it's now a matter of handing out these pieces to appropriate people (including yourself), and encouraging all those concerned can get on with the tasks at hand. For a small job there might only be a few chunks, and you might do most of them yourself. For a large one, this stage may involve many different people and organizations working together to provide a new community resource, or change a product or service so as to address a new challenge. This brings us round in a circle, to the first principle of Human Interaction Management, Commit. To carry out work, people need to accept roles with goals. In this case, the roles and goals are determined by the plan of action you settled on, collaboratively or alone, in the Constrain stage of REACT. Government agencies, local institutions, companies, community organisations, and others will all have a part to play, so they need to understand and accept their responsibilities in order to work well together.

Joining up work by so many different organisations can be very difficult. One challenge is getting everybody to buy into the solution. People will only engage with, review, evolve, and endorse a plan of action if they understand and accept its benefits to them and the interests they represent. They also need to believe that that any work carried out will deliver those benefits, or new benefits that supersede the ones originally planned for. I showed above how you can use Wardley maps to illustrate what needs you will meet, how you will do it, and how this will change over time. This is only the start, though. To reassure the stakeholders in your community that work will succeed, and ensure that they participate, every programme of change — whether to address flood risk, switch school canteens to using only organic suppliers, or get people to do more physical activity — must demonstrate that it has an effective way of working.

The first principle of Human Interaction Management, Commit, refers to the importance of having the right people and organisations accept the right responsibilities, so that everyone can work together effectively. Any plan you make for change must take a very wide view of who these people and organisations are. You must identify all your stakeholders, both internal and external, and make sure they understand what you trying to do, and why. Talk to them about their needs, and the needs they represent, then make sure these needs are taken into account in your plans. Stakeholders might include all the local organisations, businesses, and households at risk from flooding, and they might have a range of needs from being able to access their buildings to avoiding damage to equipment and furniture.

Then you need to make sure that your plan allows for these needs to be met while change is in progress, at least as far as possible. In particular, you need to think about any disruption that might be caused by the change you are planning. If you are putting in flood barriers, how will you ensure that people can access their properties while work is going on?

Once you have incorporated their needs into your plans, doing as much as possible to avoid disruption, you need to think about how to communicate the benefits to each stakeholder. If they don't understand how their needs will be met in a new and better way due to your work, or don't feel confident that the work actually makes this possible (or makes possible new benefits that turn out to be better than the ones originally planned), they won't support it. Remember that they are the experts. If an aim of flood barriers is to protect equipment and furniture, could exceptionally heavy rain back up behind them on the riverside and make paths impassable in a different way? Ask local residents what they think. They will have seen heavy rain on the riverside for years so can help you judge.

Finally, everyone will realize that the work will fail if you run out of time or money to do it properly, and this could cause lasting problems, affecting other areas of daily life. Which of your outcomes depend on one another, and what risks are there to each outcome? Asking these questions will let you plan how to prevent these risks turning into real issues. Despite your best efforts, it might happen anyway, in which case you will need to have a way of managing any ripple effect when issues crop up. Plan you will manage risks, and make this a key part of your communications with local stakeholders.

Planning and executing change in a community is not a simple matter. I mentioned above how most projects in the world fail to some degree, and community projects are particularly at risk since the work has many stakeholders, varied outputs, and complex outcomes for which it can be hard to assess benefits and ensure they are delivered. Demonstrating that you have an effective way of working can be simplified by breaking the challenge into what I call levels of control, and assigning the responsibilities in each level to different roles as goals (this is the first principle of Human Interaction Management again, Commit).

First, there is Strategic Control. This focuses on setting the scope of the work, working out who stakeholders are, getting them on board, and agreeing with them the key benefits to work towards. It is best if the people charged with this are well connected in the community and are widely regarded with respect. This gives credibility to the whole project and makes it much easier to arrange the right meetings and form strategic agreements. In the discussion of personality characteristics above, people suited to this may be in the social group, as well as being strategists in the leadership group.

Then there is Executive Control, which is about planning. Responsibilities here include to ensure that the needs of stakeholders are fully understood, including their need for minimal disruption to life while change is put in place. It is vital to identify risks take their mitigation into account as part of planning. It is also necessary to think about how to communicate the changes to people in the community, so that they make best use of its outputs — only in this way will the real outcomes, benefits to local wellness, be delivered. In the discussion of personality characteristics above, people suited to this may be in the action group, as well as being executors in the leadership group.

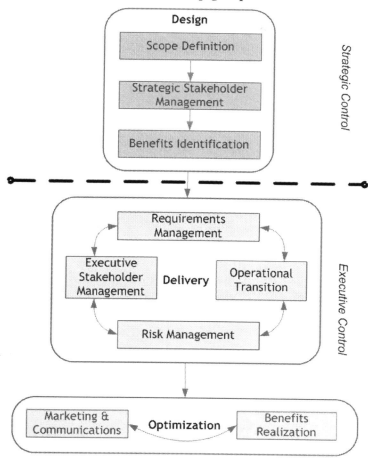

Figure 42: Strategic and Executive Control

Last, there is Management Control. Once work has been defined and planned, it must be carried out, and this requires supervision — to monitor progress, deal with blockers as they arise, report back, and create a good working atmosphere in which teams knit together and feel positive about their work. In the discussion of personality characteristics above, people suited to this may be in both the social and action groups, as well as being team leaders in the leadership group.

REACT (Research, Evaluate, Analyze, Constrain, Task) shows how to notice and respond to internal and external events — find out what you need to know, understand it, make decisions, plan a course of action, and put it into play. AIM (Access, Identify, Memorize) shows how to carry out the first part, Research — access sources of information, choose what to investigate, and fix the key points in your mind for evaluation. Thinking about control of the work as split into three different levels (Strategic, Executive, Management), and assigning responsibilities in each level to different roles as goals, helps ensure that you stay on top of needs, benefits, risks, and communications. Together, these patterns enable communities to address what might seem to be impossibly complex and confusing situations.

It may not be clear exactly who are we talking about here, though. When communities take action to address local wellness challenges, which organisations and individuals are taking the action? This is about communities helping themselves, so this is about action from within, not changes imposed from above. In other words, we're talking about communities taking ownership of their wellness. Let's look at who is involved in ownership, the different forms that ownership can take, how transformative it can be for a community, and different ways to participate.

Ownership

Taking ownership

Building a strong community requires years of civic engagement at grass roots, which must be multi-faceted and inclusive. It can be sustained or destroyed by municipal efforts towards regeneration.

For a few years, people in my local town of Frome, in the UK county of Somerset, took pleasure in sharing, on social media, clippings from national newspapers and magazines that declared what a great place it was to live. In May 2014, The Times called Frome the "sixth coolest town" in Britain. In 2016, it was a finalist in the 2016 Urbanism awards. In March 2018, the Sunday Times listed it as the best place to live in the South West. In April 2019, Frome made Time Out's list of the best weekend breaks from London. Eventually the accolades became too commonplace to attract much interest, so now people focus more on sharing news of celebrities who have moved to the area, or been seen in the street.

For a long time, though, Frome was a bit of a rough diamond. An ancient market town, preservation efforts by the local civic society meant it was still architecturally interesting, and while the light industrial base of its modern economy didn't lead to much local wealth in the twentieth century, community groups such as the carnival club kept going and enough artistic types were attracted to the cheap, characterful property to create a buzzy atmosphere and run a few independent shops. Everything changed up a gear for

Frome at the turn of the century, due to a number of community initiatives.

In 2000, former Royal Shakespeare Company actor Martin Bax started Frome Festival. From the start, its ten-day span at the start of July included as many as 200 events, mixing up many different types of entertainment, and featuring local alongside international names in the programme. By providing a cultural focal point, the festival inspired and regenerated cultural activities across the town, in which groups, clubs, venues, and events have since proliferated. Now led by another actor (also a musician and Green county councillor) Martin Dimery, the festival is celebrating its twentieth anniversary — and throughout the year, there is often as much going on in Frome, home to 27,000 people, as you might find in a London borough with ten times the population.

In 2003, floundering efforts by the town council to regenerate the market hall in the centre of town were transferred to an independent charitable trust. A new team of staff led by seasoned fundraiser Steve Macarthur took over, and started making careful investments into the future of the building. Frome Cheese and Grain is now a thriving community hub that supports local meetings and events by hosting touring headline acts (including iconic bands of yesteryear such as Jefferson Starship, Lee Scratch Perry, and Grandmaster Flash) in its concert space, running weekend festivals ranging from tattooing to veganism, and operating its own recording studio where locals get special rates.

The Frome Independent Market started in 2009 as St Catherine's Artisan Market, a not-for-profit company founded by entrepreneur Gavin Eddie, starting his second career after a first one in investment banking. The initial aim was to bring footfall to the independent shops in a picturesque cobbled street leading up a hill out of the town centre. Now the market takes over the whole town on the first Sunday of the month, bringing 80,000 visitors into the town each year and helping to generate £2.5 million for local traders as well as money for local charities. Great Western Railway puts on extra trains specially. Roads are closed and there are almost more stalls than it is possible to visit in a day.

Last but by no means least — in 2011 a coalition of politically engaged local people energized by the ideas of charity worker and green undertaker Peter Macfadyen, and guided by the longtime council leadership experience of Mel Usher, formed a non-partisan collective they called Independents for Frome and took over the town council, winning 10 out of 17 seats. A few years later, they won 17 out of 17. Frustrated by the inertia of party-led town councils, their mission is simply to make good things happen in the town. The new council borrowed money at the low interest rates available to all local government bodies, dispensed with the Victorian formality of traditional council meetings, and started investing in a bewildering variety of projects from green spaces to an energy cooperative to a car club to a share shop. The council works closely with local people and local organizations such as the credit union, medical centre, and poverty charity Fair Frome — a hands on initiative that delivers "real projects which make a real difference for real people". The model of Independents for Frome has been inspirational to other communities. Macfadyen outlined their methods in a pamphlet on what he calls flatpack democracy, and other towns across Europe are now following in their footsteps.

There are tensions, of course. Despite a general focus
on widespread engagement, not everyone feels equally included in activities, supported by others, or appreciated for
their efforts. For some, these headline initiatives have a
negative effect on their daily life, work, or aspirations.
Moves by one initiative may run counter to the interests or
beliefs of another, or of other parties in the town. Social
problems have not been eliminated and progress has not
been one way only — part of the town is still deprived, and
it is now harder to find affordable accommodation. At
times, the very idea of regeneration has attracted local
mockery, as when a London-based artist engaged to work
with schoolchildren hired a light aircraft to fly above Frome
trailing a banner with the town's new "motto", Something
Wonderful Will Happen. However, few people would really
wish success on the jokey grass roots campaign that followed, to "Make Frome Sh*t Again". In and around the
town, local people have worked together to create a boom
in social capital that has led to corresponding booms in
natural and financial capitals. Green spaces have been protected, much of the riverside area is being developed in a
sympathetic way, and Frome aims to become carbon neutral. The climate is easier for shops, there are many new
local businesses, and property prices have increased dramatically.

Could any town do these things, and achieve a similar
level of regeneration? Frome may simply be fortunate in
having the right local residents at the right time — or there
may be more to it than that. Some of the town's success
could be due to natural advantages and a legacy of industry.
The river Frome winds through the centre of town, with
hills leading up out of it in all directions, which creates a

sense of the town being its own little world. People like to say (with no justification that I've been able to discover) that the town lies at a confluence of ley lines — the term coined by Alfred Watkins in his 1925 book for what he believed were prehistoric trading routes, "old straight tracks" between sighting points on the landscape that he noticed from hilltop viewpoints during his travels as a beer salesman.[261] Historically, at one time, Frome was a thriving centre of cloth trading. In the 1720s, Daniel Defoe estimated that "Frome is now reckoned to have more people in it, than the city of Bath, and some say, than even Salisbury itself...... likely to be one of the greatest and wealthiest inland towns in England".[262] Even in its dog days, the town retained a measure of the resulting civic pride and energy. However, it seems unlikely that these factors are enough to account for such a sudden change in the town's fortunes after a century of decline.

I always remember the old gardener tending his immaculate lawn, who when asked by passers-by what his secret was, would respond "start forty years ago." Every professional sportsperson or musician knows from experience that it takes 10,000 hours of practice to achieve mastery — around 20 hours per week, every week for ten years. Similarly, the home-grown initiatives that began in 2000 with Frome Festival were sown on well-prepared soil. There were a host of cultural, charitable, business, and social activities that paved the way beforehand. Local artists and musicians were already active in town life, the local school encouraged arts and music, and there were regular cultural events both in the town and in nearby villages. Many local people were engaged in charity work, for both local and national causes, and collaborated closely with performers to spread the word – not just in the town, but also in the surrounding villages, such as at the Nunney Jazz Café which raised money for good causes by featuring well-known musicians alongside local players, art exhibitions, street theatre, and children's workshops. The cobbled street of Catherine Hill was well-known for its independent shops of all kinds, whose struggles to stay afloat were supported by the town council with cheap rates. The town has lively pubs, two theatres both with strong community leadership, and many clubs including football, boxing, tennis, and a long-running carnival club — the processional night-time carnivals across Somerset throughout November are a little-known wonder of the world, rivalling Rio in the splendour of their floats (created by local clubs in fierce rivalry, with details closely protected throughout the year) and the ear-shattering volume of their music.

These activities and activists inspired and became central to the town festival, market hall, and street market, and key people also went on to take part in its independent politics. Each of the recent headline initiatives has faced numerous challenges over the years, ranging from financial to regulatory, and new problems emerge continually. They are sustained by close-knit teams that can not only draw on individuals with relevant experience and strong local connections but ongoing heroic efforts from the wider community. Not everything or everyone gets the same level of attention, including as usual in society some of the activities led by women (the national recognition given to Health Connections Mendip, described above, being a welcome exception), but the projects that make the papers would not have been possible without a decade or more of community engagement beforehand.

Heritage is about more than places and spaces, isn't it — there are many intangibles, which can be sustained or destroyed by municipal efforts towards regeneration. In 2016, I spoke at the INTBAU World Congress on behalf of the Royal Society of Arts. INTBAU, the International Network for Traditional Building, Architecture & Urbanism, is a global network dedicated to creating better places to live through traditional building, architecture, and urbanism.[263] The World Congress was held at the Royal Institute of British Architects in London, sponsored by the Prince's Foundation, and the session in which I spoke was run by the International National Trusts Organisation. There were receptions beforehand at the House of Lords and afterwards at Clarendon House. With such high status organisations involved, it was fair to say that the event reflected the outlook and concerns of the worldwide architectural establishment — the organisations and individuals who are bringing the built environment in which we live and work into the twenty-first century.

My presentation was on the use of heritage places and spaces for community wellness. I showed how community, heritage, and tradition are overlapping social constructs. I discussed how the co-option of enduring, familiar, and reassuring heritage places and spaces for use by a privileged elite drives a wedge into the heart of communities, whereas their co-development with communities for use by all is a powerful force for social good. I asked how architects and town planners could use the built environment to empower personal change at scale — for example, could they reinvent parts of iconic buildings as holistic wellness hubs, where people could access a variety of local services in high value, well maintained settings rather than crumbling community centres? I argued that the responsibilities of architects and town planners went beyond helping to restore community cohesion and broad-based civic pride, to designing dedicated facilities where people can improve their personal wellness and build social cohesion.

At follow-up meetings, the general view was that, while this might be a laudable aim in principle, it went beyond the remit of architects and town planners. A recent report by the Prince's Foundation illustrates how those responsible for the built environment are contributing to social cohesion, and where they see their influence ending. The report discusses how sustainable urban developments in Poundbury and Fairford Leys have generated higher residential property values per hectare, retained throughout market cycles, attributing this to the perceived community value arising from a walkable, mixed-use environment. "People like to live in an area where they feel connected and have convenient ease of access to services and amenities. Walkability is important, as are good transport links. Attractive building design and layout, with a village feel that incorporates a good mix of homes and types of buildings, and encompasses a clean, tidy and well-maintained local area, is of importance to residents. ... A real sense of community is evident in the settlements, which contributes to a friendly, safe and welcoming atmosphere."[264]

The report highlights the role that the built environment can play in increasing the social value of community, showing its potential but also its limitations. Appendix A is a review of the relevant literature. "The concept of social value helps to make the case for better building and improving the sustainability of the built environment in the UK. Developers, contractors and supply chains contribute to social value in various ways (e.g. through responsible design; local procurement; local employment; ethical business practices; minimising noise and disturbance; work experience and educational engagement), and the impacts of a proposed development (on the lives and circumstances of people and communities) are evaluated in terms of net productivity gains, net job creation and changes in demographics across the operational life of the asset."

Builders build. They can enable social capital by creating a more human-friendly built environment, but it's not their job to create that capital. The report states that "there is room for improvement by creating options for all age ranges, as well as broader interaction across all demographics and tenure types particularly during evenings and weekends." It does not go on to suggest, or quote recommendations from literature, that architects and town planners should intervene. If residents of Poundbury and Fairford Leys want inclusive activities at evenings and weekends, it's up to them to make it happen. Each community needs to take ownership of their social life. In an age when cash-strapped governments are cutting back on postwar aspirations to provide nurturing wraparound care from cradle to grave, this applies also to local wellness, so like it or not, communities may have to step up and take ownership of the situation.

Ownership is a loaded word, though. What does it mean?

Forms of ownership

Ownership takes many forms. Useful ways to think about it are stewardship and stakeholding. Opening up control over activity typically increases its success, both economically and by more holistic measures.

In his introduction to Thomas Hanna's recent exploration of public ownership in the US, Andrew Cumbers takes the long view of ownership.[265] "Political-economic systems can to a large extent be defined by the dominant property relations. Karl Marx famously viewed human history through the lens of the differing forms of ownership of the means of production. In tribal societies, for example, communal ownership and cooperative labour was widespread. Ancient societies, by contrast, were characterized by patrician ownership, with slave labour — while not necessarily numerically predominant — serving as the critical source from which the propertied classes extracted their surplus. In the feudal societies of the Middle Ages, agriculture owned by landed elites served as the primary economic driver, with labour provided by a peasant class tied to the land. Under industrial (and financial) capitalism, on the other hand, the means of production has largely been in the hands of capitalists, to whom the working class sell their labor for wages. Due in part to Marx's intervention, and to the resulting titanic twentieth-century ideological, political, and military struggle between capitalism and communism, much popular understanding of ownership in the economy has been reduced to a simplistic dichotomy — complete private ownership, on the one hand, and full public ownership, on the other."

Cumbers' point is that a binary understanding of ownership is unhelpful. "Modern political economies are much more complex than such a dualism allows, and many encompass a variety of ownership forms and arrangements." Between the extremes of an unregulated private enterprise and a business run as an ordinary government department, a wide variety of arrangements are possible. Labelling all forms of public ownership as Soviet-style centralized planning, repressive and doomed to failure, is throwing out the baby with the bathwater. Hanna's short but carefully researched study illustrates that ownership of all industries and community resources, including the many forms of activity related to wellness, can adopt highly variable patterns — and often the more widely that control is opened up, the more successful the activity becomes, both economically and by other more holistic measures.

Discussion of ownership can be highly charged. E.F. Schumacher observed in 1973 how "those with a strong bias in favour of private ownership almost invariably tend to argue that non-private ownership inevitably and necessarily entails 'planning' and 'totalitarianism', while 'freedom' is unthinkable except on the basis of private ownership and the market economy. Similarly, those in favour of various forms of collectivised ownership tend to argue, although not so dogmatically, that this necessarily demands central planning; freedom, they claim, can only be achieved by socialised ownership and planning, while the alleged freedom of private ownership and the market economy is nothing more than 'freedom to dine at the Ritz and to sleep under the bridges of the Thames'. In other words, everybody claims to achieve freedom by his own 'system' and accuses every other 'system' as inevitably entailing tyranny, totalitarianism, or anarchy leading to both. The arguments along these lines generally generate more heat than light, as happens with all arguments which derive 'reality' from a conceptual framework, instead of deriving a conceptual framework from reality."[266]

A way to generate more light than heat might be to focus attention on identifying, by industry and locality, which forms of ownership most closely match the needs of a specific community and the wider public of which it is a part, which approaches are most efficient and effective in the local case, and which are most antifragile (thriving rather than failing on external change). A sensible starting point is to ask local people what they want, which can produce surprising results. I discussed above the sweeping extent of privatization in the UK. Four decades in, a poll commissioned by a free-enterprise think tank in October 2017 found to their horror that 83 percent of respondents favored nationalizing the water sector, followed by 77 percent for gas and electricity, 76 percent for trains, 66 percent for defense and aerospace, and 50 percent for banks.[267] Nearly a quarter were even in favor of nationalizing travel agents. This suggests that people may like to see some form of public ownership for the industries, services, and activities available to their communities.

Then there is efficiency and effectiveness. A plethora of studies by leading economists over the decades demonstrate that hybrid forms of public ownership are no less efficient or effective than privately held companies. In recent years alone, a 2007 report for the UN by Ha-Joon Chang found that, when it comes to performance, there is no clear case against state owned enterprises, and when such a case is made, it is often under "stringent" and "unrealistic" conditions.[268] In 2008, political economist Germá Bel and city and regional planning professor Mildred Warner analyzed 35 studies from the water and sewage sectors and found that in the majority there was "no difference between public production and private production."[269]

Writing in the Harvard International Journal in 2009, Francisco Flores-Macias and Aldo Musacchio maintained that "the world has changed" and certain modern public enterprises can be "efficient, even in comparison to their private counterparts."[270] And in 2014, the Organisation for Economic Co-operation and Development summarized a number of studies of publicly owned German banks by writing that "savings banks appear to be at least as efficient as commercial banks."[271] Different forms of ownership deliver optimal results in different settings and circumstances.

A commonly quoted example of hybrid public ownership is the German town of Wolfhagen, which won a federal government award for energy efficiency after the council bought back the grid from EON Mitte in 2006. Despite having a population of only 14,000, the town's strategy to promote renewables led to being self-sufficient in renewables by the end of 2015, which it did by building five wind turbines and a 42,000-panel solar park. Wolfhagen demonstrates a new approach to public ownership that combines citizen involvement with state support. The municipal company set up a community cooperative in order to give local residents a 25 percent stake in the business, a profit-sharing arrangement that not only distributes revenue but also fosters greater civic engagement.

Particularly relevant to wellness are community hospitals, small local hospitals that provide a diverse range of services to their community — beds, maternity, clinics, minor injuries units, X ray departments, and so on. In the UK, there are over 500 community hospitals, which have "been part of our health care system for over 150 years and offer a strong tradition of care that local populations have known over generations ... Originally established as converted cottages offering inpatient beds, they have developed into hubs of services that have developed to meet changing needs. These services range from health promotion, diagnostics, treatments, rehabilitation and end of life care. The community hospital plays a particular role in intermediate care, and is a focus for integration for many staff and services in both health and social care. Community hospitals vary considerably, as they have adapted to the needs of their local populations. They are typically highly valued by local people, and this support is shown through actions such as volunteering, fundraising, promoting and campaigning."[272]

Healthcare organisations in the UK are still owned mostly by the state, but even in the US around 20 percent of community hospitals are publicly owned (and another 58 percent are non-profit). Denver Health is an example that operates similarly to community hospitals in the UK — "a highly successful community-benefiting institution structured as an innovative blend of state-level public ownership and direct municipal accountability. As a subdivision of the state of Colorado, the Denver Health and Hospital Authority now has relative autonomy over decision-making, yet is subject to the state's open-meetings law (allowing for public involvement) and has a board that is appointed by the city's mayor."[273]

Hanna illustrates how it is important to get the full picture for each example by considering the Bank of North Dakota. Formed after the first World War, this publicly owned institution enabled its state to weather the 2008 financial crisis and recession unscathed, contributing to the state's budget, providing liquidity to local banks, and making loans to consumers while private banks were freezing credit. Nevertheless, "it has hardly been an engine for social justice and the development of alternative economic institutions. Recently, the [Bank of North Dakota] was widely — and rightly — criticized for lending the state as much as S10 million to cover the costs of policing the American Indian-led Standing Rock protests against the Dakota Access Pipeline (although it is unclear whether or not the bank could have legally refused the state's order even if it had wanted to). But its operating record as an instrument of state economic development is impressive nonetheless." We'll return to forms of community-based financing below.

There is evidence that businesses with some form of public ownership can be strengthened by competition, but markets are not always a sensible way to deliver the services most needed by communities. Utilities and transport provision, for example, are natural monopolies, with a large and lumpy sunk cost. Their outputs cannot be stored or traded, and they are strongly interdependent. These conditions lead to what economists call market failure, which an element of public ownership can rectify by cutting the Gordian knot and removing the element of competition. However, one size does not fit all. Finding and implementing the right solution for each industry in each community requires a nuanced set of judgements that also take into account economic and financial measures such as the development of regional employment and employability, as well as wider issues such as decentralization, democratic participation, transparency, accountability, sustainability, long term social benefit, and the complex of all — antifragility. Which forms of ownership seem likely to thrive in the face of unpredictable events? A model is emerging from examples such as the US city of Cleveland and the UK city of Preston, which took an approach based on working closely with "anchor institutions" — large employers with strong local connections, such as universities and hospitals, for whom moving location would be unrealistic or impracticably expensive. The approach is becoming known as community wealth building or the Preston model.

In Cleveland, progressive thinkers from local and national organisations convinced hospitals and universities to use their purchasing power not only to support existing traders in the local economy but also to collaborate in developing new suppliers that train and support disadvantaged people. The Evergreen network of worker cooperatives is linked via a community-wide neighbourhood corporation, to which anchor institutions have been able to make a long-term commitment that would not be possible for enterprises working in isolation. Anchor institutions have stable, large-scale public financial support, so this arrangement enables the community as a whole to plan economically for the future without losing the agility and independence enjoyed by small scale enterprises.

In Preston, leader of the city council Matthew Brown convinced the council, police, colleges and the university to buy goods and services from local businesses wherever possible. As a result, the unemployment rate halved between 2014 and 2017, and the city saw improvements above the national average for health, transport, work-life balance, and skills in both youth and adult populations. Research carried out by the accountancy firm PricewaterhouseCoopers and the thinktank Demos, which used a range of measures including employment, workers' pay, house prices, transport, the environment, work-life-balance and inequality to rank 42 UK cities, found that Preston had improved the most in its 2018 Good Growth for Cities index.[274]

Over the past 10 years, the UK think tank Centre for Local Economic Strategies has amassed a body of work around community wealth building in Preston, Greater Manchester, Birmingham and 11 other cities across Europe. In order to build an economy where wealth, including the spend of local anchor organisations, is recirculated locally for the benefit of local communities, they identify five central principles.[275]

First, plural ownership of the economy — deepening the relationship between the production of wealth and those who benefit from it. This means returning public services to direct democratic control by insourcing public goods and services. It's also about developing cooperatives and locally owned or socially focused enterprises in the public and commercial economy.

Second, making financial power work for local places — increasing flows of investment within local economies by, for example, directing the funds from local authority pensions away from global markets and towards local schemes and community-owned banks and credit unions.

Third, fair employment and just labour markets — working within large anchor institutions and their human resource departments to pay the living wage, adopt inclusive employment practices, recruit from lower income areas, build secure progression routes for workers and ensure union recognition.

Fourth, progressive procurement of goods and services — developing a dense local supply chain of local enterprises, employee-owned businesses, social enterprises, cooperatives and other forms of social ownership that can provide goods and services to large local anchor organisations.

Fifth and finally, socially productive use of land and property — ensuring that local assets including those held by anchor organisations are owned, managed and developed equitably, so that local communities can harness any financial gain from these assets.

Is community wealth building a form of protectionism? Yes, and that's a thoughtful nurturing tactic, not the demonic enemy of virtuous free trade depicted by mainstream economists. Successful economies have always safeguarded their interests while developing through careful management of financial flows. The US was the most protectionist country in the world during most of its phase of ascendancy, from the 1830s to the 1940s. Similarly, Britain was one of the world's most protectionist countries during much of its own economic rise, from the 1720s to the 1850s. Nearly all of today's rich countries used protectionism and subsidies to promote their infant industries. Many of them also severely restricted foreign investment, especially Japan, Finland and Korea. Between the 1930s and the 1980s, Finland used to classify all enterprises with more than 20 per cent foreign owner-ship officially as 'dangerous enterprises'. Several countries used state-owned enterprises to promote key industries, especially France, Austria, Finland, Singapore and Taiwan. Singapore is now famous for its free-trade policies and welcoming attitudes towards foreign investors, but produces over 20 per cent of its output through state-owned enterprises, twice the international average of around 10 per cent. Nor did today's rich countries protect foreigners' intellectual property rights very well, if at all – in many of them it was legal to patent someone else's invention as long as that someone else was a foreigner.[276]

There are three reasons why protectionism is vital

during the early stages of growth. First, young economies need to protect and nurture their producers until they acquire the capabilities to compete unassisted in a global market. Second, young markets do not function very well due to poor transport, poor flow of information, the ease of manipulation by big actors, and other reasons, so they need to be regulated actively and sometimes even deliberately created. Third, until there are enough private or third sector firms capable of running large-scale, high-risk projects, many things have to be done through government intervention, including setting up publicly-owned enterprises.

Protectionism can be, and often is, implemented at any level of community, although below state level it is usually in the form of discounts and other privileges for locals rather than tariffs for outsiders. Shops and businesses on Salisbury plain offer lower prices to members of the armed forces, which in the army towns includes much of the population. Local shops have always extended credit to local people and delivered to their houses without charge, usually on an informal basis and often without advertising that these services are available. Tickets for local events may be available earlier to local people through word of mouth, who may also get advance notice from shops when small deliveries of popular goods are likely to arrive. These privileges differ from tariffs not only in being beneficial to locals rather than punitive of outsiders, but also in being more flexible – each business can decide what and how to offer – and in that any higher prices paid by outsiders go straight to businesses rather than to government. The latter effect reduces the capability of local government to intervene in the ways described above, but has the advantage of avoiding red tape. Another difference is that privileges may stay in place even once a local economy has matured, and can trade widely without need of protectionism to safeguard it, both as a form of social cohesion and to continue the long-term project of community wealth building.

It's still early days for community wealth building, but success to date suggests that the model is replicable, and it is already spreading. More generally, the re-municipalization of public services has been gaining support throughout the world in recent years, often as a way to address pressing economic and ecological concerns while establishing local democratic control over the economy. A 2017 study identified 835 municipalizations and re-municipalizations involving some 1,600 cities in 45 countries. Re-municipalizations were most prevalent in the energy and water sectors, but also occurred in other industries such as transportation, education, housing, and healthcare. "These (re)municipalizations generally succeeded in bringing down costs and tariffs, improving conditions for workers and boosting service quality, while ensuring greater transparency and accountability".[277]

It's worth observing that community wealth building does not mean, or intend, that everyone in a community will magically become a high net worth individual. Such ambition would not only be unrealistic but beside the point. Evidence clearly shows that once a basic standard of living is achieved, further gains in wellness are related to increases in equality and community cohesion rather than income.[278] The way to make people happy is to help their communities become inclusive, close-knit, and caring. The purpose of community ownership is to increase local wellness, and the means may include anything from sharing equity in a community hospital to members of the community having a say in how social care or education are delivered. There are many new models emerging, bringing together elements of community and worker self-management with various forms of public ownership at local, regional, and central level. These models unite ownership in the sense of owning property or the means of production with more nuanced concepts such as stewardship, in which organisations take responsibility for safeguarding the community capitals they have control over, and stakeholding, in which organisations give a voice to parties affected by the community capitals they have control over.

Stewardship and stakeholding are ways in which communities can think about which models might suit their own community, but stewardship and stakeholding of what? In order to influence decision-making, and become decision-makers, local people need to understand what their community capitals are, along with the issues involved in managing these enablers of value over the long term. We've encountered community capitals in one form or another throughout this book, and it's time to set out a workable definition.

Community assets

Community capitals are enablers of community assets and can be separated into natural, human, and industrial. Community members can map assets in an online database, and plan their maintenance using visual models.

The collective noun for academics is a faculty, but surely it should be a disagreement. There certainly is little consensus when it comes to community capitals. The Center for SDIs and Land Administration, University of Melbourne breaks community capitals into 4 categories – Human, Financial, Environmental, and Manufactured.[279] The Forum for the Future, an international sustainability non-profit organisation, distinguishes 5 - Natural, Human, Social, Manufactured, and Financial.[280] The SFU Centre for Sustainable Development & Telos Sustainability Institute of Tilburg University identifies 6 - Natural, Physical, Economic, Human, Social, and Cultural.[281] The K-State Research and Extension River Valley District project uses 7 categories - Natural, Cultural, Human, Social, Political, Financial, and Built.[282]

My favourite breakdown is the simplest, from a training course devised by Maureen Hart,[283] now the Executive Director of the International Society of Sustainability Professionals. Hart distinguishes only 3 kinds of capital in a community: natural capital, human capital (which includes social capital as discussed above), and a third which I will call industrial capital. "Natural capital is all the things that nature provides for us, such as raw materials to make clothing, buildings, and food. It also includes the services that nature provides such as air to breathe, protection from UV light, rain to water our crops, and wetlands to filter water and prevent flooding. Human and social capital are the people that make up a community: friends, neighbors, coworkers. An important part of human capital is the connections among people, the way people work together to solve problems or run a community. It includes volunteer efforts and the community's governing structure. Other parts of human capital are the skills and education of the community members and their health. Financial and built [what I call Industrial] capital are the built structures like roads, bridges, and buildings in the community. It also includes the manufactured goods, the information resources, and the credit and debt in the community."

Hart's description is also more accurate than some, since it focuses on how community capitals are enablers, rather than assets in themselves. Consider a natural capital such as a river. It may empower an agricultural community to deliver value by providing a habitat for food, a source of water for crops, and a spiritual uplift for local people, but it won't do any of these things on its own. The value to the community is actually delivered by fishing, farming, and contemplative activities. Community capitals are necessary rather than sufficient, and their value is released by using them to make community assets. There is often a feedback loop between community capitals and community assets, which can be positive or negative. An agricultural community may plant trees alongside the riverbank that reduce erosion, and dam the river to create pools where fish can breed. Alternatively, it may deplete fish stocks by overfishing, and pollute the river with waste. A factory that makes use of local waterways for distribution, local skills for workforce, and local buildings for warehousing may benefit the community by raising living standards, degrade local infrastructure through lack of maintenance, do both, or do neither.

Community capitals can be used to build community assets that help improve local wellness, and a key focus for communities who start to engage with social issues is to map their community assets. One way to create a community asset map is to annotate Google Maps for your local area[284], adding markers for local places and landmarks markers that describe how they are used. This may focus on assets of specific types, as in the example below from the

University of Ottawa Heart Institute.[285] Google Maps is a powerful tool, but has limitations for many types of asset – groups and activities are often diffused across locations, and assets that provide financial or emotional support may not be easily located on a geographical map at all.

Figure 43: Example community asset map as a Google Map

Another approach is to make an infographic – an explanatory picture. The example infographic below is from a guide to Community Engagement produced in 2018 by the North American Association for Environmental Education.[286] If well designed, which can be a challenge, infographics are a powerful communication tool. However, the effort required to produce an infographic means they tend to remain static, which renders them obsolete after only a short time. Further, the amount and detail of information that can be shown is limited, making them too hard to use as a practical tool.

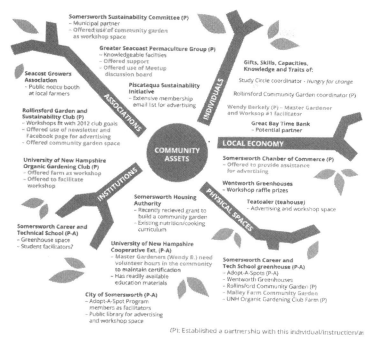

Figure 44: Example community asset map as an infographic

A third approach to documenting community assets is to write them up as text in a spreadsheet or other document, although this suffers from the same update problem as an infographic while being harder to use. These issues can be partially resolved by creating an online list and making it available through a website. An example from Health Connections Mendip is shown below.[287] However, it is very time-consuming to maintain such a list, and the content is prone to inconsistency and inaccuracy. As more and more assets are recorded, ensuring that addresses, dates, times, and contact details stay up to date for the various services provided by community organisations from different locations becomes an almost impossible task, and one that consumes a great deal of effort from link workers that they could spend more usefully on helping local people with their wellness. It also becomes more and more likely that people will turn up to a locked building at 7pm on a dark rainy evening because the advertised club is now on a different night, or in a different place.

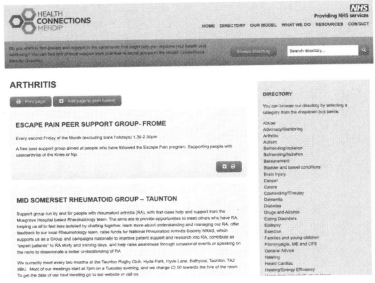

Figure 45: Example community asset map in an online list

The ideal solution to mapping community assets is an online database that is maintained by the community, rather than a single team. We've met the notion of digital hubs before. A digital hub for the community is an online tool where each local organisation and service is responsible for keeping their own details up to date. This is important as an enabler not only for community ownership of assets but also for the antifragility that results from empowered usage of those assets. In times of emergency, such as a pandemic, the resources available locally change fast, requests for service must be handled, there needs to be a way for people to leave feedback then use it to ensure reliability, and the people who normally keep track of things for the community may become unavailable at short notice. Communities everywhere responded to the coronavirus crisis by self-organizing to support vulnerable members, with groups forming to deliver food and prescriptions, shops and eateries providing home service, supermarkets opening at special hours for NHS staff and the elderly, and more. However, in communities without a digital hub, many vulnerable people found it hard to know what was available, and community services struggled to liaise both with each other and with local government bodies in order to manage capacity.

A digital hub where the community can distribute the workload of updating asset information is a basic mechanism that empowers communities to take control of their wellness at all times. However, when things are normal, people need motivation to come together around it. An incentive can be provided by making the local digital hub a platform for community organisations to promote and provide their services. People can then use it not only to find out what is available, but also manage which community assets are in their wellness plan, book appointments and tickets, liaise with members of their personal support network to ensure their use of assets is effective, and provide feedback to community organisations on how their services are helping them achieve personal wellness goals (or not). Some of this feedback can be shared with the community, to help others understand what might be useful to them, using guidelines to ensure that discussion is always polite and positive. A digital hub makes use of Google Maps and other freely available apps and websites to show people information in various helpful forms.

The example screenshots below are taken from digital hubs commissioned in the UK town of Frome and city of Birmingham.[288] Digital hubs can be nested within one another to avoid duplication, or overlap if they are non-geographic, and used to cover all areas of community life. I'll explore below how a digital hub can also help measure local wellness.

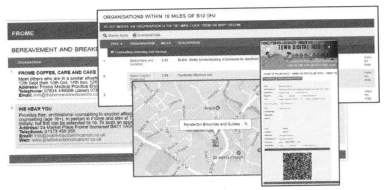

Figure 46: Example community asset map as a digital hub

Comprehensive asset mapping is critical to community wealth building – especially if done using a digital hub, since then it is possible to see how people are using local assets, how effective they are finding them, and where there are gaps and overlaps. These analyses enable a streamlining of local investment, both from government and from community members. I discussed above how, since the 1970s, financializing strategies for maximizing shareholder value have led to companies extracting profits into the hands of managers and shareholders rather than re-investing them into their own capitals in the traditional way. As a result, apparent economic growth over the last few decades as measured by income has obscured a weakening of the global industrial base. Communities can avoid this by creating financial flows that bolster their natural, human, and industrial infrastructure by reinvesting savings and revenues from community initiatives back into local assets. This becomes a virtuous circle, in which the initiatives that release greater value from community capitals results in a further strengthening of those capitals, and thus even greater potential for future benefit.

Mapping assets is generally done as an early step in forming a local strategy to releasing greater value from community capitals. An element of such strategy can be councils transferring major community assets such as central buildings into community control. The UK government is encouraging this, describing in a 2016 paper how "Many Parish and Town Councils have been working in partnership with their principal authorities in this way and councils have been collaborating with residents, businesses and community-based originations to transform assets for some time, as demonstrated by the many successful [Community Asset Transfers] across England. However, this new drive to increase power and responsibility at the local level provides an even greater role for [Community Asset Transfer] as an opportunity for councils as they assess the best possible use of land and property in their area and as a means to give people the power to improve where they live."[289]

The paper gives as an example a leisure centre in Nottingham, UK. Since 1979, the Lenton Community Association has been working and providing community services. In 2004 a decision was made by Nottingham City Council to close the Lenton Leisure Centre, which occupied part of their building. In response, the Association formed itself into a Trust, The Lenton Centre, which has come a long way since then. After much hard work, and embracing a community enterprise approach, the reopening of the swimming pool and complex took place two years later, and continues to operate as a sustainable community organisation.

As discussed above, community ownership can be beneficial since it tends to bring a more holistic approach based on stewardship and stakeholding. These attitudes can play a role in supporting the delivery of policies and priorities, enhancing local services, more effective community engagement, a stronger and more enterprising community and voluntary sector, enhanced partnership working including with councils and businesses, improved management of buildings, revenue and capital savings, and attracting additional investment. However, taking ownership of high-value local assets such as leisure centres, libraries, market halls, and so on is not to be taken lightly – if the process goes wrong it can lead to wasted resources, mistrust and a breakdown of communications between community organisations and councils.

It is worth understanding the difference between transfer of a building (or other physical assets) to community ownership, for example via a long-term lease, and transfer of a service, when the council commissions delivery from a community organisation rather than running the service itself. Both forms of agreement may carry terms and conditions, but transfer of building ownership is a more radical step. While it is likely to grant greater freedom to the community in deciding how to use the asset, and is more likely to engage volunteer support and community-based investment, it may cut the community organisation off from low-cost shared services that were available when the asset was owned by local government, such for managing the upkeep of the building, operational staffing, information and communications infrastructure, security, and administration. A mixture of both models is sometimes possible, but can bring complications of its own.

An interesting type of community asset is a library, since it sets some of the issues about ownership into relief. Grassington Hub & Community Library, a volunteer led community hub in Grassington, North Yorkshire won the Duke of York's Community Initiative Award 2019 and North Yorkshire County Council Library of the Year 2019. The Hub provides a wide range of services to residents and businesses; including the promotion of local events and the production/sales of tickets for community groups in the locality. They host a range of services from their outreach room which is hired by different agencies and local residents.[290] A library is a traditional centre of education and social engagement that has powerful resonance to the community, making it a natural physical hub for local services of many kinds.

However, there is also strong feeling among professional librarians about the deprofessionalization of libraries. A survey of postgraduate library students in 2018 revealed not only excitement about changing possibilities for libraries – "Who would have thought that public librarians would be running workshops on coding, stop motion, and 3D printing 10 years ago? Now it's fairly common to walk into a public library and sign up to any of those workshops and more" – but also concerns about deprofessionalization, which could kill the sector entirely through lack of under-standing of what librarians actually do. "There is a common perception that libraries and the library sector is dead. Why do we need libraries when we have Google and Amazon? This needs to be addressed effectively to a broad range of people, not just an educated elite".[291]

A community library can still employ professional li-brarians, but enabling this needs careful planning. General-ly, if communities are to take ownership, in whatever form, of their assets then they need a way to formulate a strategic approach, deciding where to put their energy and how to ensure that the assets are managed sustainably. Value maps, discussed above under **Outputs and outcomes**, can be very helpful here.

Value maps help to formulate and communicate the strategic needs of a community, the evolution of these needs over time, and the changing mechanisms the com-munity will adopt to meet these needs. Value maps can also be nested, to drive out details of strategy down to the level of individual assets. However, value maps do not provide a way of comparing options and making decisions for how to deal with assets. This can be very complicated, since there are so many factors that affect each asset, the value it ena-bles, and how to sustain it. One way of approaching this is to think about value as flowing between different "stocks" that the community holds, since then you can see how community capitals enable processes to produce more out-puts. Let's take as an example an archetypal community whose economy depends in part on fishing.

A fishing economy has capitals including the local wa-ter quality (natural), the average amount of time people that make available for fishing (human), the average level of skill in fishing (human again), fishing equipment held within the community (industrial), and the revenue sharing arrangement that distributes money from catch sales back to the community (industrial again). We can also visualize the process of commercial fishing as a flow between stocks of fish. It starts with a flow from breeding fish into fish population, some of which become new breeding fish. There is a flow from this into the number of fish caught by the community, which in turn creates a flow into fish sold by the community. Visualizing this graphically shows how value flows between different stocks (blue rectangles), along with the community capitals that affect the flow (orange ovals). Stocks must always be of the same type – you cannot have a flow between different things such as hours per week and money received.

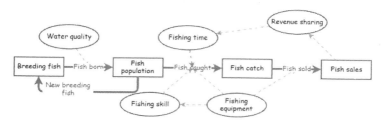

Figure 47: Fishing economy stocks (blue rectangles) and capitals (orange ovals)

You may feel some things are missing from the picture above. For example, we might want to add natural and industrial capitals reflecting pollution level, since these affect the water quality, which in turn affects fish breeding. The fishing equipment available to the community affects not only how much fish is caught, but also the type of fish caught and hence the total sales, so it might be worth including investment into equipment (industrial) and something about its maintenance (a combination of industrial and human, depending on how this is managed). There is a clear dependency on people and their skills, so we could add the training given to young people (a combination of industrial and human, depending on how it is provided) which would increase the number of people with fishing skills. Cost and quality of bait (natural or industrial, depending how it is procured) might also be worth including. To keep it simple, though, let's stick with the stocks and capitals shown and ask how we could intervene.

One way is to identify dependencies between capitals. The line from fishing equipment to fishing skill level represents the influence that equipment has on ability to fish – higher quality equipment could increase or decrease fishing skill, depending on the equipment in question. Another way is to identify feedback loops. The lines to and from revenue sharing show how it affects the amount of time people are inclined, or able, to devote to fishing. The nature of the revenue sharing arrangement could increase or decrease the time people devote to fishing, depending on the amount they receive. A loop such as this is called **reinforcing** if stocks increase as you go around it, and **balancing** if stocks decrease. In this case, the loop could be either reinforcing or balancing, depending on the revenue sharing mechanism chosen. Taking these factors together, the diagram shows the community that they could increase catch sales per week either by investing in equipment which increased the average skill level or by devising a fairer revenue sharing scheme. If we had included pollution, investment into equipment, equipment maintenance, training for young people, and bait in the diagram, there would be more dependencies, more loops, and more intervention opportunities.

To explore the possible impact of interventions, you can use diagrams like this to see how stock levels rise and fall under different conditions — for example, to explore ways of achieving higher catch levels at minimum cost without reducing fish population by overfishing. First, you enter numbers representing the starting value of each capital and each stock. You then write a formula for each flow shown on the diagram per unit of time — in our case, we could interpret this as fish per week. For example, there will be a certain weight of new fish from breeding each week before taking into account water quality, and another weight of fish might be caught per week before taking into account the effect of fishing time, fishing skill, and fishing equipment. You then adjust these formulas to take the missing factors into account — for example, if you express water quality as a percentage of purity, this might adjust the number of new fish from breeding by a corresponding amount.

Then you press a button and watch how the stocks rise and fall over time. Shown below is an example of how fish population, catch, and total sales change over 2 years. You can see that the fish population is periodically exhausted, causing catch to drop and total sales to flatline accordingly. Each time the recovery is less effective, until eventually there are no more fish at all. An exercise such as this could help a fishing economy predict overfishing and take steps to avert it.

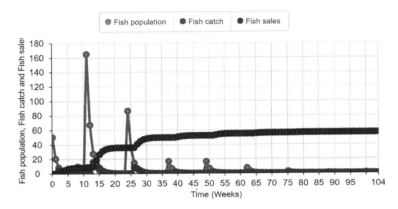

Figure 48: Fishing economy over 2 years

You can do this yourself using simple online tools, such as the free one I used to prepare the diagrams above.[292] Please feel free to experiment for yourself with the example. You can watch the values change over time then adjust the values or formulae, possibly add new capitals along the lines suggested above, and run it again to see how the stocks behave differently as a result.

Drawing a diagram like this is called modelling, and watching the stocks rise and fall over time is called simulation. These techniques help investigate options and make decisions. The fishing economy is an example of how a community can use simulation to predict, and thus hopefully avoid, exhausting a resource on which it depends. In the case of a community library, simulation could help show how investment in a professional librarian, even if only part-time, could help local people to gain acceptance on training or university courses, and improve employability by developing skills valuable in the marketplace, thus contributing to economic regeneration as well as bringing the wider wellness advantages that accrue from learning. The diagram could be used to explore options for diverting some of the revenue from regeneration, and cost savings from improvements to health, towards the cost of the librarian.

This particular approach to modelling and simulation is known as system dynamics. We've met systems before during the discussion of autopoiesis, the way in which some organisms demonstrate emergent behaviour as they reinvent their internal structures to deal with external challenges. A biological organism is just one example of a system — other examples include communities, companies, cities, and economies. Any collection of things that affect each other in some way can be viewed as a system, such as the fishing economy above. Systems have a physical boundary and may only exist for specific periods of time. Their parts are influenced both by each other and by their external environment. If a system expresses synergy or (as in autopoiesis) emergent behavior, it is effectively more than the sum of its parts.

System dynamics has a venerable if controversial history. In 1971, the theory's originator Jay Forrester created a model of the world as a whole, World3, with the aim of showing the environmental impact of economic growth.[293] This became famous in 1972 when a team of researchers published simulations of World3 that forecasted economic collapse during the 21st century under a wide variety of growth scenarios.[294] The forecasts have stood the test of time surprisingly well for such a large model, and updates have been published regularly.

You can learn a lot from models. For example, a system seems likely to be more antifragile if there is more going on inside it. A diverse system with multiple pathways and redundancies, is more stable and less vulnerable to external shock than a, uniform system with little diversity – it may exhibit adaptive, dynamic, goal seeking, self-preserving, and sometimes, evolutionary behavior.[295] In other words, a community is more likely to thrive in the face of external change if it is closely-knit and cohesive, with many ways of accomplishing the thriving side by side.

This sounds very like a market. Does that mean it makes sense for communities to operate like markets? Well, yes, in fact it does, but we must take care to create markets that are human, personal, and ethical. Replicating neoliberal principles in which value is all and only about relative price would be to make the same mistake at local level that the world has made globally. Let's look at how a new form of business is taking a more holistic approach to business, by returning to an ancient model.

Social trading

Local economies can build social cohesion and access specialist finance via social trading, which has ethical as well as commercial aims. Social traders must act cooperatively. They think differently about opportunity cost.

Matt Ridley concludes his study of the way in which evolution embedded cooperative instincts in the human brain with an homage to trade as the foundation of a better society. "For St Augustine the source of social order lay in the teachings of Christ. For Hobbes it lay in the sovereign. For Rousseau it lay in solitude. For Lenin it lay in the party. They were all wrong. The roots of social order are in our heads, where we possess the instinctive capacities for creating not a perfectly harmonious and virtuous society, but a better one than we have at present. We must build our institutions in such a way that they draw out those instincts. Pre-eminently this means the encouragement of exchange between equals. Just as trade between countries is the best recipe for friendship between them, so exchange between enfranchised and empowered individuals is the best recipe for cooperation. We must encourage social and material exchange between equals for that is the raw material of trust, and trust is the foundation of virtue."[296]

Unfortunately, the neoliberal vision of free markets leading to harmonious cooperation has not come to pass. One only needs to look at high profile economic relations in the world today to see how free markets are leading to conflict rather than trust. The main trading partner of the US is China, which never saw any benefit in entering the Trans-Pacific Partnership free trade deal, from which the US has itself now withdrawn, and the two countries are currently engaged in an escalating spiral of tariff raising alongside military posturing in the South China Sea. After years of bitter wrangling that failed to produce a deal acceptable to both sides, the UK left the European Union and may well end up leaving its common market as a result. The Commonwealth of Independent States free trade area that includes Russia and Ukraine did nothing to stop the former invading the latter. For a market to deliver human cooperation, there has to be more to it than buying and selling — it has also to build human relationships. One way forward is social trading, in which people earn their living by buying and selling but also have an ethical purpose.

Social enterprises are often locally based, providing products and services that reflect a strong commitment to a neighbourhood or group of people with specific needs. As you can see from the online social trading resource Social

Echoes,[297] social enterprises are practical, competitive businesses that do more than make money – and part of the reason they are so competitive is that people are starting to understand that there is more to choosing a product and service than how it much it costs. Both your community and you personally benefit from buying clothes made by a social enterprise that works with charities to bring new people into the workforce, and that belongs to a mutually supportive local trading ecosystem. Social trader prices may not be quite so startlingly low as on Amazon or at Primark, but they strengthen the community you live in economically, help improve your natural environment, and offer you a form of participation that in itself enhances your own wellness.

There are also commercial advantages to businesses in operating as social enterprises, since governments may offer tax reductions and other financial or economic benefits. For example, in 2005 the UK introduced a form of incorporation known as a Community Interest Company, intended as a more streamlined option than incorporation as a charity. In the next ten years, over ten thousand of these were registered. Any surpluses such businesses make are not distributed to shareholders as dividends, or to employees as bonuses, but reinvested for the purpose of the business or to the advantage of the community. Their assets are also locked, which means that there are restrictions on the transfer of company assets that ensure that they can only be used for community benefit. In return, Community Interest Companies can access forms of finance traditionally open only to charities, such as grants and low-cost loans. In other words, staff can pay themselves fairly and control their operations without being burdened by the formalities that come with charitable status, while enjoying the financial boost and community goodwill that comes from committing to a social purpose.

Many other models exist for community enterprises. In the UK, other choices include Company Limited by Guarantee, Community Benefit Society, and Charitable Incorporated Organisation. Elsewhere, a similar variety of new corporate structures is emerging. It is possible to apply for certification that your business is a genuine social enterprise. The Social Enterprise Mark and Social Enterprise Gold Mark are internationally recognized, and there are over 200 organisations that hold such accreditation currently.[298] Another form of certification is B Corporation (the B stands for Benefit), an international standard that can apply to both non-profit and for-profit enterprises who operate responsibly with respect to social and environmental issues. The detailed and thorough certification process requires companies to meet social sustainability and environmental performance standards, meet accountability standards, and be transparent to the public according to the score they receive on the assessment.[299]

In some ways, social enterprise is a return to ancient ways of trading, which throughout history has typically been what we now call social — local, and thus keen to be perceived as ethical. Until recently, many business people didn't have much choice! Thinking back to Kate, the depressive baker in the updated version of my Dad's joke, her business wasn't a Community Interest Company, and her oven wasn't under an asset lock, but modern mechanisms like these weren't necessary then – they were assumed. The fact that we have had to introduce them in recent years says something in itself. From ancient Mesopotamia through to nineteenth and even twentieth century Europe, most businesses were small, run by people who lived in and so were part of their community. There was no real separation between work and life. Their business activities, like all their activities, were embedded into a closely-knit social fabric, which brought them responsibilities as well as rewards. Successful business people who didn't contribute to their community were likely to be ostracized socially, and in practice, most people observed a religious obligation to give away ten percent or more of their revenue. Of course, there have always been grand enterprises, operating at the level of nations and empires, but it's only in the twentieth century that businesses of all sizes adopted what we now call a corporate mindset, focused on profit and separated from the life of the local community. This separation, of business practices and everyday life, has had such a dramatic impact on society that we now tend to forget it was not always thus.

Small-scale socially-integrated enterprise is the daily reality of people in developing countries, who are forced by circumstances to be far more entrepreneurial than their counterparts in developed economies, but who lack the societal infrastructure that would allow them to develop businesses at anything beyond community scale. As Ha-Joon Chang observes, "people are far more entrepreneurial in the developing countries than in the developed countries … in most developing countries 30-50 per cent of the non-agricultural workforce is self-employed (the ratio tends to be even higher in agriculture). In some of the poorest countries the ratio of people working as one-person entrepreneurs can be way above that: 66.9 per cent in Ghana, 75.4 per cent in Bangladesh and a staggering 88.7 per cent in

Benin. In contrast, only 12.8 per cent of the non-agricultural workforce in developed countries is self-employed. In some countries the ratio does not even reach one in ten: 6.7 per cent in Norway, 7.5 per cent in the US and 8.6 per cent in France ... So, even excluding the farmers (which would make the ratio even higher), the chance of an average developing-country person being an entrepreneur is more than twice that for a developed-country person (30 per cent vs. 12.8 per cent)."[300]

Developing countries also tend to be more religious,[301] which can mean that religious traditions supporting entre-preneurship are preserved. For example, mandatory chari-table giving is embedded in Judaism as tzedakah and in Is-lam as zakat. Traditional Jews commonly practice ma'sar kesafim, tithing 10 per cent of their income to support those in need, and sharia law requires each Muslim to give 2.5 per cent of their net wealth to benefit the needy. Tzedekah and zakat each have eight similar categories, the first of which is described by Maimonides as "Giving an interest-free loan to a person in need; forming a partnership with a person in need; giving a grant to a person in need; finding a job for a person in need, so long as that loan, grant, partnership, or job results in the person no longer living by relying upon others."[302] An analysis of recent zakat activity in Malaysia asserts the importance of giving not just fish but also a fishing rod: "the allocation of zakat propor-tion for zakat recipients must not only suffice to cater for their basic necessities but it must also be enough to help the recipients expand their zakat fund. Otherwise, the zakat recipient will carry on receiving zakat in the following years."[303] The Christian tradition of tithing a tenth of the fruits of one's labor and justly acquired profits, still prevalent among people with Evangelical beliefs,[304] is related to these practices, although it replaces the eight categories of tzedakah and zakat with giving to one's religious institution, which may then distribute some of it philanthropically in whatever manner it sees fit (and the Catholic Church now asks the faithful only to give whatever they can "to assist with the needs of the Church"[305]).

The challenge faced by young economies is how to develop the infrastructure that players need in order to go beyond operating at a subsistence level. Chang also points out that a characteristic of richer countries is how their businesses have learned to collaborate, both with each other and with government at various levels, in order to build this infrastructure for themselves. "in the rich countries, enterprises cooperate with each other a lot more than do their counterparts in poor countries, even if they operate in similar industries. For example, the dairy sectors in countries such as Denmark, the Netherlands and Germany have become what they are today only because their farmers organized themselves, with state help, into cooperatives and jointly invested in processing facilities (e.g., creaming machines) and overseas marketing. In contrast, the dairy sectors in the Balkan countries have failed to develop despite quite a large amount of microcredit channeled into them, because all their dairy farmers tried to make it on their own. For another example, many small firms in Italy and Germany jointly invest in R&D and export marketing, which are beyond their individual means, through industry associations (helped by government subsidies), whereas typical developing country firms do not invest in these areas because they do not have such a collective mechanism."

Social enterprise is critical to community wealth building, but requires social enterprises to go beyond producing goods or offering services on a small scale as isolated ventures, and become major players in their local economy, linked by cohesive networks in order to provide high quality, large scale products and services – including and especially services critical to wellness that fill the gaps left by government, and on which local people depend. This may mean navigating a course that encroaches on specialist areas such as health, education, and crime prevention as well as personal life issues such as disability, addiction, safety, finance, housing, employability, and more. It may require engaging with volunteers as well as employees. There can be complex cultural narratives at play and regulatory issues to contend with. Handling all this requires a high level of sensitivity, commitment, communications skill, willingness to learn, and personal resilience.

Social trading also requires a business understanding that in some ways is more developed than one might find in a typical corporate environment. Since the nineteenth century, businesses have been guided by the principle of comparative advantage set out by David Ricardo in 1817.[306] Comparative advantage means you can produce goods and services at a lower opportunity cost than your competitors. Understanding opportunity cost means thinking about trade-offs. Let's see how this works using a simplified example.

Suppose you are a professional trainer who has skills in CV writing and Web design. Training in CV writing pays £300 per day, whereas training in Web design pays £500 per day. The opportunity cost of giving a CV writing course is £200 per day, since you could earn that much more money giving a Web design course. Naturally, you choose to specialize in Web design training, since for you this has zero opportunity cost.

Now, suppose your friend is also a professional trainer, with the same skills as you plus also skills in corporate leadership, which pays £1000 per day. For your friend, the opportunity cost of giving a Web design course is £500, since they could earn that much more giving a corporate leadership course. Of course, they choose to specialize in corporate leadership training. Even if your friend is better at teaching Web design than you, more appreciated by students and getting them better grades in exams, there is no competition between the two of you in the market for Web design training, since your friend can use their time more profitably giving corporate leadership courses.

A more realistic description of opportunity cost would also include your expenses per day of training, as well as your fixed overheads, and taking this into account shows how opportunity cost is often more about how much it costs you to do business than how much customers are willing to pay you. Keeping it simple, we can see this by reframing the above example to be about the location of the courses. Suppose all three courses pay £500 per day to the trainer, but you live near a Web design training centre, your friend lives near the headquarters of the corporation that needs leadership training, and each of you would have to drive to different places each day to give the CV writing course. Taking into account your travel and accommodation costs, your opportunity cost is zero for the Web design course and your friend's opportunity cost is zero for the corporate leadership course. Just as above, your more highly skilled friend won't compete with you.

Having a lower opportunity cost than your competitors

allows you to offer lower prices than they could, and sometimes still gain more profit than they could possibly make. Businesses know this, so they usually spend their resources – including the time of their employees – on producing the products and services that have the lowest opportunity cost. However, this may not be true for social enterprises. Their motive for trading is more than profit, also including ethical priorities and concerns about specific issues, which may lead them to take other things than opportunity cost into account.

Let's return to the example above, and suppose that you and your friend are both social traders. To help the people you train in Web design get decent jobs afterwards, you might decide to spend some of your time giving CV writing courses. Your friend, motivated like you to improve employability, might then decide to spend some of their time giving Web design courses, to fill in while you are training people in CV writing. Being fair-minded people, perhaps you would then collaborate, and agree that on balance it was fairer for your friend to do the CV writing courses, since their highly paid corporate leadership courses make it easier for them to make up the opportunity cost of giving relatively low-paid training.

This shows how social traders have more complicated calculations to make than normal businesses. Since they are not in it for the money alone, the strategic reasoning they must do is harder to reduce to spreadsheet form. In some cases, it is possible to turn ethical and social issues into numbers, which then help social traders (and other interested parties) reason about strategy. However, to do this you often have to make assumptions that are hard to validate, so in the end social traders need to make business decisions that are based more on making enough money to stay in business than on making the maximum amount of money possible. This comes naturally for many people, since they have a stake in the outcomes they affect, and get a non-financial reward for helping improve those outcomes. What is more, demonstrating that they have a stake in community capitals can lead to community members doing the same for them – taking a stake. This opens up sources of investment unique to social enterprises, and some of these sources are worth hundreds of billions each year.

Having a stake

Some social traders cannot access traditional community finance or impact investment. They can access global capital markets at low cost via stakeitbacks – a new way to fund good things, see the impact, and get a return.

Mervyn King, Governor of the Bank of England throughout the worldwide financial crisis of 2008 – 2009, tells of asking a Chinese central banker over dinner in 2011 what importance he now attached to the Industrial Revolution in Britain in the second half of the eighteenth century.[307] His Chinese friend thought hard, then replied, "We in China have learned a great deal from the West about how competition and a market economy support industrialization and create higher living standards. We want to emulate that." Then came the sting in the tail. "But I don't think you've quite got the hand of money and banking yet." King adds wryly in an endnote, "There was no need for him to add that neither has China."

The erudition that King demonstrates throughout his description of modern central banking's failings make it all the more surprising that he makes no mention of how ancient societies solved the problem. He acknowledges that the recovery since the 2008 crisis has been "neither strong, nor sustainable, nor balanced" but proposes only that central banks change their approach to providing liquidity, from the current "lender of last resort" model to "pawnbroker for all seasons", which makes assessment and protection for collateral more measured. King acknowledges that this is nowhere near enough to deal with radical uncertainty, but his claim that a "new approach" is needed takes no account of how the Bronze Age kingdoms of Mesopotamia delivered social stability lasting thousands of years.[308] We may not wish to replace parliamentary democracy with autocratic despotism, but there is still much to learn from early societies.

In the ancient Near East, palaces managed economies using an institution that intermediated between state, merchants, and populace to deliver a combination of tax revenues, low but consistent economic growth, and social protection. The temple stored grain, distributing it to the populace as needed. It collected taxes, but wiped out tax debt in years of bad harvest or other hardship. It provided and recompensed work to the destitute – what we might now call workfare as opposed to welfare. Raw materials for the goods produced by temple workers were supplied by merchants, who also exported the finished products, in return for interest charged at a fixed rate. The interest rate was equivalent to 20 percent per annum, which is high by modern standards, but loans were annulled if a trading venture failed due to piracy, shipwreck, or other external causes.

The temple of ancient times was a nuanced, sophisticated mechanism for which there is no equivalent in modern economies. The economy that it enabled was based on a mixture of state and private enterprise far more fluid than the current distinction between nationalized and privatized industries. The era ended with the Bronze Age Collapse, after which economic power passed into the hands of oligarchic private interests and an age of turmoil began. The Collapse may have been triggered by a combination of climate change[309] and new military technologies against which state armies were defenseless[310]. The end of the Bronze Age is both a lesson and a warning for the present day.

Despite the disaster caused by modern banking practices, the financial establishment has not yet recognized the need for root and branch reform, or the popular demand for this to happen. Urbane dinner table anecdotes by bankers do not capture the strength of feeling amongst ordinary people in the West about their profession. It's perfectly clear to us that the financial sector is taking taxpayers for a ride. Even after demonstrating levels of greed and incompetence that very nearly destroyed the world economy, bankers used the vast sums that government had to contribute in order to save the day to award themselves bonuses. Nine of the US financial firms that were among the largest recipients of federal bailout money paid about 5,000 of their traders and bankers bonuses of more than $1 million apiece for 2008. At Goldman Sachs, for example, bonuses of more than $1 million went to 953 traders and bankers, and Morgan Stanley awarded seven-figure bonuses to 428 employees. Even at weaker banks like Citigroup and Bank of America, million-dollar awards were distributed to hundreds of workers.[311]

This is enough to make anyone's blood boil, but it is still only the tip of the iceberg. The deeper problem is a fundamental change in the aims of corporations. Mariana Mazzucato illustrates the shift in priorities not only with data but also by contrasting two statements from business leaders of different periods. While Samuel Palmisano (IBM President from 2000 to 2011, and CEO from 2002 to 2011) argued that IBM's main aim was to double earnings per share over the next five years, half a century earlier in 1968 Tom Watson Jr (IBM President from 1952 to 1971) argued that IBM's three core priorities were (1) respect for individual employees, (2) a commitment to customer service and (3) achieving excellence. [312] This may be only anecdotal evidence, but the two pronouncements by two different CEOs of IBM at two different times illustrate how priorities have evolved. It's not surprising that a 2017 survey of more than 33,000 people in 28 countries found that most people do not trust business, media, government, and NGOs to do what is right, with people in 13 out of 28 countries eager for greater business reform, including policies hostile to businesses' license to operate.[313]

The shift to maximizing shareholder value since the 1970s means that, rather than re-investing profits in production of goods and services, businesses now adopt financializing strategies such as investing in complex financial products and share buy backs. Financial institutions maximize return on investment via mechanisms such as derivatives, and their apparent success leads to pressure on managers of non-financial firms to deliver comparable levels of return for their shareholders, using similar investment strategies. This leads in turn to a narrow concern for short-term profit in corporations that decades ago would have been focused on developing their industrial base. Similarly, use of profits to buy back a company's own shares, often from senior managers as a form of bonus, increases share price but does nothing to strengthen the industrial base of the economy. In fact, it may well weaken the financial position of companies, since buy backs are often done regardless of share price, or even when the price is at a peak in order to increase the reward to the employees who own them.

Economist like Mazzucato now argue that corporations should focus less on delivering value to shareholders and more on creating as much value as possible for all stakeholders and seeing any decision as a balance of interests and trade-offs to achieve that goal. "In sharp contrast to Friedman and Michael Jensen, who advocated strongly that a company succeeds simply through profit maximization, a stakeholder view emphasizes the social relationships between management and employees, between the company and the community, the quality of the products produced, and so on. These relationships give the company social goals as well as financial ones. Together they can create more sustainable 'competitive advantage'. And because value is created collectively, through investments of resources by a multitude of actors, it should also be distributed more collectively -not just to the shareholders. In contrast to Maximizing Shareholder Value and its goal of short-term profit maximization and its marginalization of human capital and R&D, stakeholder value sees people not just as inputs but as essential contributors who need to be nurtured. Trust – critical for any enterprise – is then built between workers and managers, in a process that acknowledges the vital role of workers in value creation. Investing in people is an admission that workers add value."

Stakeholder theory maintains that the pursuit of gains for shareholders at the expense of other stakeholders is a pursuit which ultimately destroys both shareholder and stakeholder value.[314] Building stakeholder value is more far-sighted, requiring a patient form of finance that supports long-term investments. Such a form of finance is starting to emerge at community level.

Community finance is the provision of affordable financial services, including loans and savings and general financial management support, to businesses, civil society organisations, individuals and homeowners unable to secure mainstream finance to deliver economic and social benefit. Community finance also encompasses the principles of the social finance sector – mobilizing private capital to invest in the double bottom line, in order to deliver a social dividend and an economic return.[315] Community finance institutions provide services to businesses and entrepreneurs, especially in disadvantaged communities, who cannot secure finance from banks or other mainstream commercial institutions. They work with civil society organisations such as social enterprises, charities, and voluntary organisations who emphasize social, environmental and stakeholder as well as financial objectives. They may support individuals unable to access short-term, low value credit and other financial services who must deal with sometimes abrupt fluctuations in income, as well as homeowners who are unable to access a loan from a commercial lender (or a grant) to carry out essential repairs, adaptations and improvements to their property. A variety of new institutions are emerging, and old ones are re-emerging.

A Community Development Finance (or Financial) Institution is a relatively new form of private financial provider, dedicated to delivering responsible, affordable lending in order to help low-income, low-wealth, and other disadvantaged people and communities join the economic main-stream. They provide loans, advice, training and mentoring to businesses (profit and non-profit) as well as to individuals. Such a provider may operate as a bank, a loan fund, a venture capital fund, a microenterprise development loan fund, a community development corporation, or under other new models adapted for social needs from modern mainstream finance.

By contrast, credit unions, mutual building societies, and mutual banks are longstanding models of community self-help, whose heyday was in the nineteenth century and which are now coming back into prominence. They have a mutual structure, which means they are owned by their customers, policyholders, or other members – they are financial cooperatives that, like other forms of club, offer services only to members. Mutual companies don't maximize profits in pursuit of shareholder value. Instead, they put their profits back into customer service, better products, competitive mortgage rates and fairer pricing for their members. They may also distribute profits to members in dividends. By whatever means a mutual company makes and allocates its money, it stays in the community.

Then there are attempts to utilize the vast resources of capital markets for social purposes. A capital market channels investment from all sources towards long-term productive use. There are two types of capital market. Stock, also known as equity, markets are based on the trading of shares in companies, either directly or in derivative forms such as options and futures – rights and obligations, respectively, to buy or sell shares at a fixed price on a future date. Stock markets are typically higher risk and higher reward than the other type of capital market, bonds. Governments and companies issue bonds when they need money to extend their operations, build new infrastructure, or pay off debts – bonds are a form of loan, paying interest at a fixed rate to the purchaser until a maturity date when the purchase price is returned. In 2018, the size of the global equity market was $74.7 trillion, and the global bond market $102.9 trillion.[316]

Out of this total global investment of $177.6 trillion, estimates vary dramatically of how much is made with the intention to generate positive, measurable social and environmental impact alongside a financial return. Global Sustainable Investing Alliance reports sustainable investing assets of $30 trillion globally, or 16.9%.[317] By contrast, the Global Impact Investing Network estimate in 2019 was $502 billion – only 0.28%.[318] The huge difference between these two estimates comes from the difficulty of defining "environmental, social and governance" investments. Whether a company or fund manager is honestly committed to improving their environmental, social and governance dynamics, and how crucial those elements are to ultimate financial success and sustainability, can be difficult to determine.[319] Much, perhaps most, such investment is in fact greenwashing – sham or exaggerated policy, or an environmental, social or governance project that has no meaningful impact except positive public relations. There is a big difference between actively doing some good (what social investment is meant to be for) and not provably doing any harm (what it often amounts to in reality).

In 2010, a form of social investing designed to eliminate greenwashing emerged from the UK – impact bonds (known variously as Social Impact Bonds, Development Impact Bonds, Social Benefit Bonds, and Pay for Success

Projects). An impact bond is a means of funding public services when government bodies struggle with the necessary innovations, collaborations, or long-term budget commitment – a public-private partnership that funds social services through a contract that measures performance and pays the provider accordingly. Organisations that are capable of delivering high quality services can obtain private investment to develop, coordinate, or expand those services via impact bonds that create a partnership with federal, state, and local governments prepared to pay for outcomes. If, following measurement and evaluation, the program achieves predetermined outcomes and performance metrics, then the outcomes payor repays the original investor accordingly. However, if the program does not achieve all its expected results, the payor does not pay for unmet metrics and outcomes.[320] The total amount invested in impact bonds is vanishingly small by comparison with other forms of investment – $370 million, or 0.002% of the global capital market.[321] What is more, this amount is decreasing. 24 new impact bonds were signed in 2018, down from 34 in 2017, a decrease of almost a third in one year.[322]

Impact bonds are the latest manifestation of a vision that emerged from the progressive movements of the 1960s. In the 1970s it was called socially responsible investing, and since that time it has taken various different forms.[323] Over the last fifty years, the challenge of assessing environmental and social value has crystallized into a triangular relationship between the government bodies who require new services and are willing to pay for outcomes, the third or private sector providers who deliver those services to members of the public, and managers of impact investment funds who channel funds into those services from corporations or wealthy individuals seeking an ethical investment. The government bodies are willing to pay for outcomes since they know that if the services are not provided, then people's lives will fall apart, resulting in a knock-on cost for them in policing, justice, healthcare, social care, housing, welfare, reduced tax revenues, and so on. They calculate these costs, and fund the impact bond from their expected future savings, as well as from more positive benefits such as increased revenues from taxes and rates.

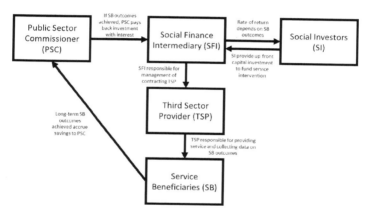

Figure 49: The typical structure of an impact bond[324]

Impact bonds address greenwashing in a clever way, but the solution comes at a high price. Impact bonds are extremely complex to set up and monitor, which means skilled people need to devote large amounts of time to project management and outcomes measurement. Either these people work for the delivery provider, in which case they spend their time on administration rather than on providing a service to the public, or they are consultants, in which case they charge fees for their time. Either way, the need to track service delivery in detail leads to it becoming entangled in bureaucracy. "The additional oversight that private social investment brought to bear on service operations had a number of unintended effects. Whilst intensive, real-time performance measurement and management introduced a heightened degree of 'responsiveness', 'discipline' and 'rigor' to contracts, it also detracted resources from front-line service provision and reduced the autonomy of some front-line practitioners. The requirement to measure social outcomes, but also record and seek approval for service processes in real-time, demanded a change in the way third sector organisations planned, revised and executed their operational strategy ... there was an excessive focus on ways of measuring outcomes, rather than ways of working and incentivizing innovation."[325]

Impact bonds are not only expensive but make services less effective – by restricting the autonomy of third sector organisations, they run the risk of reducing the impact of outcome-based commissioning that aims to help those most vulnerable to social exclusion. As a result, criticism of impact bonds is widespread, and some people feel that they take social investing in the wrong direction altogether. "The inevitably complex contracting arrangements ... transform the nature of policy accountability, with governance and reporting systems geared toward the needs of private funders rather than elected officials. [Impact bonds] exemplify the financialization and privatization of social and public policy; they reduce the rights of citizens both as service users and as a polity."[326]

After ten years, the future of impact bonds is uncertain – and more generally, it's been fifty years since the concept of socially responsible investing emerged, but widespread greenwashing means the current good publicity attached to social investing does not correspond to equivalent real benefits on the ground. Might there be other mechanisms, simpler and more robust, through which people could invest into good things, see the impact, and get a return?

The fundamental problem with impact bonds is they are financial products. First, the return received by the investor is not fixed, but depends on which of the outcomes are achieved, and to what extent – the more outcomes that a project or service delivers, and the more successful each outcome is, the more money that investors get back. This means that, like a share or conventional bond, the value of an impact bond may rise or fall at any time. To help manage such fluctuations, impact bonds are provided by intermediaries – impact bond fund managers, who may do a lot more than act as brokers. They often work closely with community organisations to help establish services and advise them on operations, which increases their chances of success but also creates a close relationship that, to protect investors, must be regulated. It is regulation that generates the layers of red tape around everything, since impact bonds then have to implement complex measurement and assurance mechanisms designed for global capital markets in which billions of dollars are traded every day. This hinders large projects, and renders small projects simply impossible. It also makes large projects very difficult to get off the ground, since from the very start they are burdened with administration designed for large-scale commercial investment, so are forced to run before they can walk.

Let's look back to how the institutions of ancient Mesopotamia helped fund foreign trade. Loans to merchants by temples of antiquity to fund foreign trading ventures were void if the venture failed due to an event such as shipwreck or piracy, rather than being inherited as a liability by their families or resulting in confiscation of collateral such as a home. Also, interest was fixed — both sides agreed the total cost of the loan at the start. It was a pay for success model, like impact bonds, but much simpler and without intermediaries. If community initiatives are framed as small individual investments with a specific purpose, rather than bundled into large complex projects with multiple aims, this ancient model is ideal.

Suppose your community wishes to build a new classroom, dig a well, put up a flood barrier, equip a community centre with computers, create a cycle path, set up a community shop or pub, open a community market garden, train young people, offer community transport, or do any other small-scale project that enhances community capitals. Most of these can potentially save money for government, and the others can generate revenue from some source. A new classroom will bring additional children and hence funds into the school, a well will reduce healthcare costs, a flood barrier will eliminate the expenses of emergency relocation, computers in the community centre will create local businesses that pay rents and taxes, a cycle path will reduce pollution and thus the cost of treating respiratory disorders, a community shop or pub can put money aside from earnings to pay for the setup cost over time, young people who receive training can contribute back to their community once they get jobs, community transport services are much cheaper for government than ambulances and taxis, and so on.

Such potential monetary gains make it possible to create a mechanism that I call a stakeitback. To fund a community project, the organisation that will deliver it first works out where the financial return will come from, then divides the cost up into affordable chunks which it offers to the community for a proportion of the total return. For example, suppose a town would like to reduce pollution by convincing all its taxi drivers — the main users of town centre roads — to switch to electric vehicles. Such vehicles are too expensive for taxi drivers to purchase or lease, so a community organisation proposes to buy the vehicles itself and rent them cheaply to drivers by the day. They work out that, if drivers share some of the vehicles by using them at different hours, 10 electric vehicles will be needed. Each vehicle has a total cost of ownership (including servicing and repair) over 5 years of £50,000, giving a total cost of ownership over 5 years of £500,000 for all 10 electric taxis in the town.

The community organisation also works out an hourly rental price that is attractive to drivers, taking into account their savings on fuel and maintenance. Doing the sums, they calculate that at 80% usage, rental income will amount to £60,000 after 3 years — 20 percent more than the total cost of ownership. They talk to taxi drivers, who quickly see that the deal is a win-win — both they and the community will benefit. So, the taxi drivers agree that if the organisation buys the electric taxis, they will switch to renting them. The community organisation also talks to a local supermarket with a large, secure car park, who agree that it's fine for the taxis to be parked there for free when not in use. The supermarket also offers use of its electricity supply for charging — the cost is minimal compared to its overall electricity usage, especially as most charging will be at off-peak times, and this helps satisfy the supermarket's obligation to give something back to the community (its corporate social responsibility, which may be legally mandated).

With these agreements in place, the organisation divides up the £500,000 they need into 500 stakeitbacks of £1000 each, and offers them to the community with the promise of a 20 percent return when the rental income reaches £600,000, which will probably be in about three years. This is a better return than most people are getting on their savings over three years, so 420 of the stakeitbacks are immediately purchased. The remaining 80 stakeitbacks are offered to a wider market and sell fast.

The community organisation now has the funds to put its plan into motion. The taxis are purchased, the taxi drivers start using them, and the pollution level in the town starts dropping. A little over three years later, rental income reaches £600,000 and the stakeitback holders are informed that they can now redeem their holdings for the agreed £1200 per stakeitback, a return of £200 on the £1000 they invested. Rental income will continue to flow into the community organisation, which it can use to invest into other community capitals. Several aspects of this are worth looking at in detail.

First, there will also be some form of financial return to local healthcare services from reduced pollution. Respiratory ailments will decrease, meaning fewer medical appointments and lower prescription costs – as well as, of course, increased quality of life for those that would have been affected. It would be possible to negotiate with the local health service to add their cost saving to rental as a source of revenue from the electric taxis. Some of the people who might have been affected will now take less time off work, so there will also be an economic saving, although this is harder to allocate since it's spread over many employers.

Second, people are more likely to use the taxis. Not only are they greener, but stakeitback owners will see their taxi fares as contributing to their eventual return. Investing gives them a stake in the success of local taxis, which motivates them to engage with the service and make the most of it. Stakeitbacks create a virtuous circle of community engagement and cohesion.

Third, the total rental income so far can be made public by the community organisation, for example on the Web or in an app, showing everyone how close the stakeitbacks are to being ready for redemption. This makes it possible to calculate, objectively, a current market value for the stakeitbacks, based on what proportion of the threshold income for redemption has been taken so far. In other words, people can trade stakeitbacks at any time amongst themselves, in an open way, without having to wait for the community organisation to take the full £600,000 and the stakeitbacks to be redeemable. This creates what is called a secondary market for social investment. This is very important, since it opens up social investment to people unwilling to tie up their savings indefinitely. If they suddenly need funds in an emergency, they can liquidate their stakeitbacks easily, quickly, and for a fair price. The objective way of calculating current market value for stakeitbacks also means that the secondary market cannot be derailed by speculators.

Fourth, much of the measurement required to keep stakeitback holders informed could be automated – not just rental income but also usage of the taxis, in terms of which routes are taken and when. This is important data for the community. Local people will be able to see the progress of their investment and analyze its impacts in various ways, for example, to understand how traffic flows, where there is congestion, and how local transport could be made more efficient. In fact, stakeitbacks themselves can be automated using open-source technology,[327] which opens up community initiatives to worldwide investment on a huge and transformative scale, unlocking the vast resources of global capital markets to power good things at local level.

Fifth and finally, like temple loans to merchants in antiquity, stakeitbacks deliver a fixed return without setting a specific date and without need for an intermediary. This means that they are not subject to the conventional regulations applied to financial products, freeing them from the red tape that strangles projects funded via impact bonds and prevents new projects from getting off the ground. Let's explore why this is true by looking at the regulation applicable in the UK – the Financial Services and Markets Act 2000 (Regulated Activities) Order 2001.[328]

The only section of this act relevant to stakeitbacks is section 84 (Futures) of Part III (Specified Investments), which defines its topic in paragraph 1, "Subject to paragraph (2), rights under a contract for the sale of a commodity or property of any other description under which delivery is to be made at a future date and at a price agreed on when the contract is made." Paragraph 2 goes on to exclude from regulation "rights under any contract which is made for commercial and not investment purposes." Such commercial arrangements are defined in paragraph 6, as being specific to the deal, with prices that are not set by market competition, and with no fixed redemption date: "It is an indication that a contract is made for commercial purposes that the prices, the lot, the delivery date or other terms are determined by the parties for the purposes of the particular contract and not by reference (or not solely by reference) to regularly published prices, to standard lots or delivery dates or to standard terms."

All this means that stakeitbacks are commercial arrangements rather than specified investments, and hence not subject to regulation by the UK Financial Conduct Authority. Without going through financial market regulations for every country in the world, similar arguments are likely to apply in many if not all other regions. It is worth noting that, for the same reason, exclusion is likely also to apply to stakeitbacks automated as cryptoassets. Guidance issued by the UK Financial Conduct Authority in July 2019[329] defines 3 types of token: exchange, utility, and security. Stakeitbacks are neither exchange nor utility tokens — they are closest to security tokens, but page 16 of the guidance excludes from regulation security tokens that are not specified investments.

Legalese aside, stakeitbacks are simple and direct, which means that people can understand them, believe in them, and use them. They are attractive not only to local people seeking an ethical, local destination for their savings but also to the global capital markets, where traditional safe sources of investment are no longer delivering respectable returns. At the time of writing, the European Central Bank deposit rate is -0.5 percent, the lowest on record, and the rates in some national banks are even lower. The current Danish deposit rate is -075%, for example. Two-year bonds are returning (if that is the right word) 0.22% in Japan, -0.78% in France, and 0.91% in Germany. Higher returns are available in some countries, such as Indonesia and India, but risk-averse investors will be wary of volatility in these economies. Meanwhile, investment banking is in a slump since trading revenue, especially in fixed income, has been declining for years – activity has been slow, and technological advances have slimmed margins. The US market is still strong, but it is threatened by a possible tariff war with its biggest trading partner China, and American manufacturers reported a steady decline in new orders in 2019, a recession red flag.[330] Taking administration fees into account, institutional investors may soon find low risk deposits and bonds actually lose them money, while stocks do not return enough to justify the higher risk.

Were stakeitbacks to become available on a large scale, they would represent an intermediate destination for global capital markets – higher risk than bonds but lower risk than stocks, with returns that may well be higher even than the latter. This could divert hundreds of billions of dollars of investment into good things at community level. However, creating a stakeitback means that community organisations must work out what to measure about a project or service, and how to equate these measurements to money returned or saved. In the next section, I'll unpick this as we look at the difference between outputs and outcomes, and how to capture both without measuring at all.

Measurement

The impact of change

To ensure that outputs lead to desirable outcomes, benefits must be managed. This can be hindered by cognitive biases of various types, and helped by application of REACT and AIM to create virtuous loops.

Outputs are often confused with outcomes. The outputs of a community service, project, or initiative may not in themselves represent an improvement to community capitals or anyone's personal wellness. For example, the outputs of a service for employability training could be the number of people who attended courses, the number of them that complete the courses, their grades in associated exams or tests, and any feedback they provide. None of this may make any difference to anybody. It is the outcomes that really matter - the employment they obtain as a result, improvements in their personal finances, decrease in their use of health and social care services, and any increase in subjective wellness that they report – and outputs do not automatically lead to outcomes. On the contrary, they don't, unless someone ensures that they do.

In the business world, ensuring that outputs deliver outcomes is called benefits management. A benefit is a measurable improvement from change that is perceived as positive by stakeholders, and which contributes to their strategic goals. Benefits can be financial, such as increased income or lower costs. Benefits can also be many other things that relate more broadly to quality of life and community capitals. In particular, a benefit can be to make a community more antifragile, for example by increasing the skills and confidence of its members, or the breadth and depth of resources available to them. A benefit may directly improve the life of community members, or indirectly empower them to improve their own lives by increasing the capitals available to their community, or both.

Benefits management is the identification, quantification, analysis, planning, tracking, realization, and optimization of benefits. It is generally thought of as a loop, which starts with identifying desired benefits, goes on to do work with the people generating outputs to ensure that outcomes are also achieved, continues with a lessons-learned exercise to review and analyze what could have been done better, then starts all over again by looking again at what benefits are desired the next time round. An effective way to do this is by applying the REACT and AIM patterns discussed above. A single turn around the loop requires key stakeholders to Research the benefits needed by the community (which means they need to Access, Identify, and Memorize the necessary information, including lessons learned from previous exercises), Evaluate these benefits to ensure they understand them fully, Analyze the findings to put them in priority order, Constrain local projects and initiatives to work towards achieving these benefits as a result of outcomes, then Task people with the associated actions. This isn't simple, however. Managing benefits can be hard for a number of reasons.

First, outputs do not generate outcomes automatically – the outputs must be used, either as intended or in an alternative manner that is equivalently effective. Suppose a community invests in physical and digital wellness hubs.

No-one's wellness will improve unless people visit the physical hub, use the equipment there to access the digital hub, make effective wellness plans online, form personal support networks, get to know the people who are supporting them, and work with them to carry out their wellness plans. There are many reasons why people may not be willing or able to do this – the hub may not be easily accessible by public transport or to disabled people, the opening hours may be inconvenient, it may be in an area perceived as unsafe by some people, there may not be enough staff to assist people who are digitally disadvantaged or need other forms of guidance, the staff may not speak the right languages or be trained to deal with people who have communications challenges, there may not be enough devices of a suitable type for people to use, the devices may not be functioning properly or be too slow, there may not be enough community assets of the right kind for people to put in their wellness plans, people may struggle to assemble a personal support network, community organisations may not be able to cope with demand, and so on. As with wellness itself, providing a community service is a holistic challenge and any impediment can block it from delivering the intended value.

Second, people may be well aware that other communities face similar challenges to them, and even that some of these communities have overcome those challenges successfully, but still not make use of hard-won ideas and experience from other places. Many places and organisations have a strong "not invented here" culture that leads people to think their own situation is somehow unique, and that the specific needs of their own community mean they must develop their own ideas from scratch. This is usually not true – differences are almost always much more minor than they seem – and such an attitude leads to every community having to learn the same lessons for themselves, making the same mistakes along the way and wasting huge amounts of time and energy. In general, very little is new under the sun. If your community has a problem, the chances are very high that many other communities have also had it, that many will have tried to solve it, that some will have succeeded, and that you can save yourselves a lot of trouble simply by following in their footsteps with small adjustments to match your own situation. Don't reinvent the wheel! Searching the Web can often lead you to the information you need, and if not, solutions are emerging for structured re-use of community initiatives.[331]

Third, there is a natural tendency for busy people to focus on outputs, and treat as lower priority the overarching need to ensure that outputs actually turn into outcomes. It is very easy to get caught up in the day to day. If your community centre is always busy, with a constant flood of people in and out of the door, there may be so much to do all that time that it's hard to set aside the time and energy to ask whether the centre is really delivering the benefits for which it was intended. Yet unless this is done, it may turn out after a few years that, without anyone realizing it, the wellness resource into which stakeholders invested so much time and money became a subsidized coffee shop for the chattering classes and co-working hub for high end tech workers, from which disadvantaged and marginalized people in the community felt increasingly excluded. In such a case, the net effect of the intervention may in fact be to decrease community cohesion and increase inequality. It's critical to notice such trends before they become too evident to the wider community, and adjust how the community project or initiative is managed to ensure that it delivers the intended effects and people still believe in the original vision (or an updated but equally powerful one).

Fourth, when planning a project or initiative, it's easy to fall prey to what are called cognitive biases – habits of thinking that lead you to overestimate its potential benefits and likelihood of success, and underestimate the likely costs and challenges. People involved may want it to happen so much, and feel so strongly that it's the right thing to do, that they come to believe firmly in its eventual success without taking full account of the risks, and without allowing for the mistakes that people might make along the way. There are different forms of cognitive bias.

Expectation bias, also known as confirmation bias, is when you select evidence that aligns with your existing beliefs and assumptions, and discount or overlook evidence that tells a different story. The planning fallacy is knowing about similar things in other communities that have failed to realize the expected benefits but believing, for no good reason, that your case will be different. The framing effect, or loss aversion, is what happens when a project or initiative is described in terms of the bad things that would happen if you don't do it, rather than the good things that will happen if you do – psychologically, this makes people more likely to agree that it's necessary, since people find loss about twice as painful as the reward from an exactly equivalent gain.[332] Anchoring is what happens when you give undue weight to the first estimate made about chances of success, and fail to adjust it sufficiently in the light of information that comes to hand afterwards. Groupthink is what happens when a body of people make common assumptions, and the shared belief reinforces each person's tendency to overlook contradictory evidence.

All of these cognitive biases can lead to serious failures of planning, so it's vital to be aware of how typical human thought processes might be misleading you and others. This brings us to the final source of challenge to realizing benefits. It will often be in some people's interests that a certain project or initiative takes place, and that its delivery and resourcing is prioritized by the community. This might be because they stand to profit financially or in some other way from the project – for example, if an organisation with which they are associated will help deliver it – or it might be simply because it is a pet project of theirs, in which they believe very strongly, and have been working towards for a long time. Conversely, there will be other people who have an opposite attitude. A new resource might be exactly what the community needs, but make their own work, or something into which they have invested a great deal of time and money, obsolete. A digital hub makes many static websites unnecessary. A community centre offering subsidized food and drink might take away business from local cafes and restaurants. Skills training may challenge the business model of local agencies and training companies. Green gym equipment in a park might reduce attendance at local gyms and leisure centres. People in these situations will be strongly motivated to present evidence and arguments for and against (respectively) a new venture in a stronger light than would be completely fair. They may consciously or unconsciously represent data unfairly, focusing on certain elements and excluding others. They may use passionate arguments to convince people, and work behind the scenes to lobby others, using social networks and relationships to ensure that their preferred outcomes come to pass.

This is human nature, of course, and a problem as old as human society itself. To work around it, a first step is to recognize what is likely to happen as early as possible, identify which stakeholders are likely to behave in such ways, and liaise with them to minimize the impact. Ideally, it will be possible to adjust the outputs and outcomes so as to enable then to take a more dispassionate attitude to evidence and planning. For example, a digital hub could link to local websites, the produce of local cafes could be purchased by a community centre, trainers from commercial businesses could deliver classes for community organisations, and leisure centre staff could run fitness sessions in the park. To make such arrangements possible and effective, it is necessary to share openly and widely all the effects of a proposed solution on stakeholders, so that all people and organisations who influence decision-making are forced to acknowledge and declare their interests up front, then work together towards maximally positive outcomes.

This applies not just before a new project or initiative starts, during proposal and planning, but also when putting it in place and then during delivery of the resulting products and operation of the resulting services. Managing benefits means continuing to gather and update evidence over the long term, so if you're not careful the effects of cognitive bias and manipulation of perceptions are likely to be ongoing and cumulative. Measurement is a performative act, in the sense that what you seek to measure often determines the way you go about it and hence the results you obtain. Scientists doing experiments involving humans work around this using double-blind trials, in which the people participating are separated into groups that follow different pathways, but neither the researchers nor participants know which group each participant belongs to. Experimenting on people in such a controlled way is unlikely to be an option for community organisations, so in order to ensure fairness, it is necessary to take a different approach to measuring outcomes.

Measuring personal wellness

A community that aims to become antifragile needs its members to assess their own progress towards wellness. This can be enabled by providing diverse but standardized self-assessment tools in a digital hub.

This book started with a discussion of fragility, and how by 2050 half the world may be living close to personal disaster on a daily basis. We saw how the people on such a knife edge, who often have the lowest quality of life and generate the greatest costs to wider society, are not typically lazy, feckless, or criminal. Rather, they have low wellness in the broadest sense, which goes further than physical and mental health to include safety, employability, connectivity, and much more. For communities to become antifragile – to move beyond being resilient to being able to thrive in the face of unexpected events – it is essential to increase the wellness of their members. Individuals and organisations within a community can learn to treat external events as a source of opportunity rather than a source of threat, but this depends on their having two things. First, they need what psychologists call PsyCap – the positive psychological capital or HERO qualities that enable them to Hope for better outcomes, put the necessary actions in Effect, be Resilient against setbacks, and feel an underpinning Optimism that motivates them to take ownership of their life and locality, then move forwards come what may. Second, they need access to resources that allow them to put their plans into action, including not just products and services but also personal support from other people and organisations, which connects them to their community and provides a vital lifeline. We've seen how communities can create physical and digital wellness hubs where people facing life challenges can make wellness plans that draw on local resources (which in turn depend on human, social, and industrial community capitals) and form personal support networks that collaborate to help them execute these wellness plans. With all this in mind, what should communities seek to measure, and how?

The discussion of wellness wheels above showed how wellness is a holistic matter that takes into account almost every aspect of a person's life. The concerns and priorities of different people vary according to their own personal and cultural dynamics at each point in time, so it is very unlikely that there will ever be a single formula that defines how well a person is – and this isn't what we need anyway. Communities that aim to become antifragile must try to assess how capable local people and organisations are of turning crisis into opportunity, which means assessing the degree of PsyCap they possess, and to what extent they have access to the resources they need. These are personal, subjective judgements, and none the worse for it. PsyCap isn't about being fully psychologically healthy, or even about feeling happy all the time, but rather about feeling empowered to improve your own lot in life – and you can have the resources you need in order to do this without being wealthy or possessing an abundance of material goods.

Executing a wellness plan is an Agile way of going about things, in which you work by going around a short feedback loop many times in succession. Each time round the loop, you prioritize your challenges, take actions to address the main ones, then reflect on your own situation in order to see what has changed and what you should do on the next iteration. Physicians call this self-reflective, cyclical process "self-activation", and a key part of self-activation is continually assessing your own state of mind. There are many standard questionnaires for this purpose, which allow anyone to estimate their own level of depression, anxiety, and other mental issues. People can mix and match such question sets to obtain indicators that provide an overall picture of their state of mind. Different people may use different sets of questions, which is natural and something to encourage – choosing which measures to use is all part of self-activation.

For this reason, it is helpful to make these questions sets available in a digital hub, since this allows people to self-test at any time of day or night, at their own pace, and without external pressure. In particular, having free and uncontrolled access to self-testing reduces the likelihood of external influence on the choice of questionnaires, and on the answers given. Not only does such open self-testing reduce the burden of administration for health and social care organisations, both in the community and in government (who traditionally spend a lot of time asking people to fill in forms then processing the responses) but it also means that people are more likely to explore the different types of test to choose the ones that they find useful, and by giving them a convenient way of seeing their own progress, it enhances the HERO feeling that enables them to take back control of their lives. Shown below are some illustrative self-assessments from a digital hub.

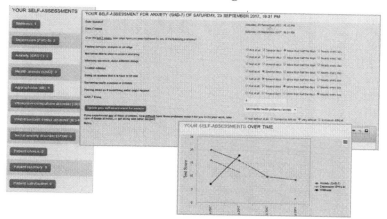

Figure 50: Self-assessments from a digital hub

In the example shown, 11 question sets are available, and the graph shows how the scores from each type of test vary over time. Each test type asks the user to respond to a set of statements or questions in simple plain language, offering the same small set of multiple-choice answers for each statement or question. The user can then add notes at the end to capture in free text anything else they would like to add. All the test types are taken from standard clinical tests. Let's look at a few in detail.

The Wellness test is based on the mental health recovery star discussed above. It prompts the user to respond to statements including "You are managing to look after your mental health", "You are managing to look after your physical health", "You manage practical matters fine day to day", "You feel included in social networks", "You have work that you find satisfying and that meets your financial needs", "All your important relationships are healthy", "You can control any addictive behaviour", "You are fulfilling your key responsibilities", "You know yourself and are OK with yourself", and "You know where you are going and believe that you will get there". The user can choose from answers including "I can manage without help", "I'm learning how to do this without help", "I need some help but my own efforts are making a difference", "I want someone else to sort things out for me", and "I don't want to think about this yet". A score is generated from these answers, but it is only indicative, and not of great use in itself. The real purpose of the test is to encourage the person taking it to think about how they are getting on in different areas of their life, so that they can decide where to focus as a top priority. Many other wellness tests could be used, and to an extent each of the 11 tests shown in the example could be considered as a form of wellness test.

The Depression test is known to medical professionals as Patient Health Questionnaire (PHQ) 9. Like the Anxiety test described below, it was developed by Drs Robert L. Spitzer, Janet B.W. Williams, Kurt Kroenke and colleagues. PHQ 9 asks the responder to indicate how often have they been bothered over the last 2 weeks by any of the following problems: "Little interest or pleasure in doing things", "Feeling down, depressed, or hopeless", "Trouble falling or staying asleep, or sleeping too much", "Feeling tired or having little energy", "Poor appetite or overeating", "Feeling bad about yourself — or that you are a failure or have let yourself or your family down", "Trouble concentrating on things, such as reading the newspaper or watching television", "Moving or speaking so slowly that other people could have noticed. Or the opposite — being so fidgety or restless that you have been moving around a lot more than usual", Thoughts that you would be better off dead or of hurting yourself in some way". The user responds to each question with "Not at all", "Several days", "More than half the days", or "Nearly every day". There is then a final question, "If you ticked any problems, how difficult have these problems made it for you to do your work, take care of things at home, or get along with other people?", to which the user can respond with "Not difficult at all", "Somewhat difficult", "Very difficult", or "Extremely difficult".

The Anxiety test, known as General Anxiety Disorder (GAD) 7, is very similar. It prompts the user to give the same responses to a different set of problems: "Feeling nervous, anxious or on edge", "Not being able to stop or control worrying", "Worrying too much about different things", "Having trouble relaxing", "Being so restless that it is hard to sit still", "Becoming easily annoyed or irritable", and "Feeling afraid, as if something awful might happen". Both PHQ 9 and GAD 7 are used by clinicians worldwide, but people rarely have the opportunity to take them at will and in their own time. More commonly, people are asked to complete one or both tests on paper or in an electronic form during an appointment with a health professional, who then notes the results on their patient record and uses the generated score as input when devising a treatment plan. The patient may not even be told their score, since it is indicative only and clinicians are wary of people becoming over-reliant on its accuracy.

The next few tests are also standard clinical question sets. The Agoraphobia Mobility Inventory (MI) questionnaire lists 27 places or situations, for each of which the user indicates the degree to which they would avoid it due to discomfort or anxiety. The Health Anxiety Inventory Short Week Scale (sHAI) measures anxiety about health by asking the user to what extent they experienced particular feelings during the past week, or think they are seriously ill. Similarly, the Obsessive Compulsive Inventory (OCI) tests for obsessive-compulsive disorder, the Impact of Event Scale – Revised (IES-R) tests for post-traumatic stress disorder, and the Social Phobia Inventory (SPIN) tests for social anxiety. The remaining 3 tests are standard measures of the success of the user's interactions with health and social care services, looking at the degree of choice they experienced as a patient, their recovery experience, and the overall satisfaction they feel with the care received.

It is possible to add any number of test types to a digital hub, and to an extent the more the merrier, since feeling empowered to measure your own progress and having the option to choose how are critical to self-activation. The process is more important than the mixture of tests that each person chooses as a personal navigational aid on their life journey. However, some care should be taken when setting up a new test type. Standard clinical tests each use a carefully designed means of producing a single score each time, based on rigorous research and extensive peer review to ensure that the indicators produced are reliable and useful. Any community could add its own tests, for example to evaluate how people feel able to cope with specific local issues, but the risk of cognitive bias must be kept in mind.

In particular, any community who needs a particular type of test should check to see whether something of the kind already exists, and if it does, assess its quality before inventing something for themselves. If there has already been a serious research effort into developing a test that might be suitable, it would make sense to adopt it if at all possible. Often a standard test can be adapted to local needs simply by translating or rewording the question so as to preserve the meaning but use more idiomatic and familiar language.

Each person in a community with a concern about their own wellness can choose a combination of tests to assess their own wellness, and take the tests as often as they wish. This generates a historical set of scores that can then be shown on a graph – the example above, "Your Self-Assessments Over Time", illustrates a person's depression and anxiety decreasing while their wellness increases. Flexible self-measuring in this way avoids the necessity for clinical and administrative staff to spend time and effort on the mechanics of testing. Not only does this reduce service costs but it enables professional time to be spent on personal interaction rather than on supervising form filling by the patient and updating their records correspondingly. In addition, a person can add health and social care professionals to their personal support network, which allows these professionals to see scores from all their tests over time – opening up to medical services a richer and more extensive set of data than could be obtained from tests completed only during consultations.

Self-measuring drastically improves both the efficiency and the effectiveness of evaluating wellness for individuals in the community. What about the wellness of the community as a whole, though – is there a corresponding mechanism for assessing wellness in the large?

Measuring community wellness

Assessing wellness of the community as a whole means identifying gaps and overlaps in provision of resources that support individual wellness. Data from wellness plans can be aggregated with data from other sources.

The wellness wheel shows that wellness of an individual is holistic. Being physically and mentally healthy is not enough if you are struggling financially. If you succeed in getting a good job, but still feel unsafe in your own home, your wellness journey continues. In a sense, it never stops. Part of having PsyCap is the sense that this lifelong journey is empowering and worthwhile in itself – even enjoyable, through bringing a constantly renewed sense of purpose. We can get a sense of the wellness of a community by considering how the individuals within it are responding to the challenges of this journey.

When someone in a community uses a digital hub to make a wellness plan, they consider each issue and goal they wish to address, and add to their plan corresponding community assets – places, spaces, groups, and activities they can make use of to improve that aspect of their own life. Then, as they visit an asset and take part in activities, they have the opportunity to record feedback. They can add private notes, shared only with their personal support network, on how they used the asset. They can also provide indicators that help others in the community understand how much that asset helped address the issue and goal for which they used it – its WellPower. They can offer polite, helpful, and constructive feedback to the organizers as well as to other local people – both as free text and by responding to standard questions. For example, they can indicate whether helpful information was provided, the atmosphere was positive, people listened to and respected each other, participation was encouraged, and whether they would recommend the asset to friends and family.

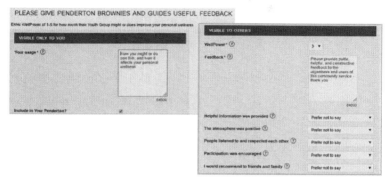

Figure 51: Recording feedback on a community asset in a digital hub

Taken together, this feedback gradually builds into big data – a set of information that can be analyzed in various ways by community organizers. A particularly useful analysis is of gaps and overlaps. For which issues and goals is there little or no provision at all, or multiple assets providing similar services? How does this vary geographically and according to various demographics? Once this understanding is available, organisations and individuals active in the community can liaise with local stakeholders to smooth out provision and identify where there are systemic problems.

For example, a community might have many assets that support health but little provision for employability or safety. Alternatively, people may be financially robust and safe but have little access to culture activities or nature. The mixture of needs will vary, since there is no one size fits all for community assets – it is unrealistic and unhelpful to assume that every community should have basic levels of natural, human, and industrial capital. Rather, each community needs to understand where and how the most pressing needs of local people are unmet, so it can focus the efforts and corresponding investment appropriately.

Analyses of unmet needs can be informed from other sources too. Government bodies maintain large data sets relating to health and social care among other areas, much of which is anonymized then made open. Anonymized summaries of client records may also be available from some organisations. Impact investment mechanisms such as impact bonds and stakeitbacks need to measure outcomes, which generates useful data, especially where automation is employed to capture, cleanse, and aggregate data.

Ongoing measurement is the bedrock on which efforts to maintain the wellness of both individuals and communities depend. It must be as comprehensive as possible, so that analyses and resulting actions are not one-sided but reflect a wide range of local needs. This can be expensive, especially over the long term, so efforts towards automation will generally produce a worthwhile return on investment. Open-source technologies and the goodwill of tech-savvy individuals and organisations based locally can and should be harnessed, including from schools where the production of local data analyses can be used as the basis of assignments and projects. More data is always useful, subject of course to it being reliable and robust.

I discussed in the Preface how the process of observing the world and turning those observations first into data, then into information, then into knowledge, and finally into wisdom, is fraught with difficulty and open to challenge at every stage. Statistical methods are not easily understood by the layman and can be used in arcane ways to create multiple versions of any truth, including versions that seem opposite to one another — they are like a lens, that sharpens your view of one point in a picture while blurring the rest of it. Despite this difficulty, every community that seriously wishes to improve local wellness must grasp the nettle. One of the key enablers of transformation is taking ownership of local data, so both communities as a whole and the individuals that step up to help the people around them must get to grips with the numbers. In the next section, we'll look at other enablers of transformation, and see how the process can be emotionally and spiritually draining but also restorative, rewarding, and quite possibly life-changing for those involved.

Transformation

Telling the story

Communities that use autopoiesis to become antifragile must tell their stories to inspire others. Community wealth building, grass roots regeneration, and social prescribing are a starting point but not yet fully holistic.

Robert Putman describes how in 1940 Tupelo, Mississippi, was one of the poorest counties in the poorest state in the nation. It had no exceptional natural resources, no great university or industrial concern to anchor its development, no major highways or population centers nearby. What was worse, in 1936 it had been ravaged by the fourth deadliest tornado in U.S. history, and the following year its only significant factory closed after a deeply divisive strike. A university-trained sociologist and native son, George McLean, returned home around this time to run the local newspaper. Through exceptional leadership he united Tupelo's business and civic leaders around the idea that the town and surrounding Lee County would never develop economically until they had developed as a community. Concerned about the dim prospects of the county's cotton economy, McLean initially persuaded local business leaders and farmers to pool their money to buy a siring bull. That move proved the start of a lucrative dairy industry that improved local incomes and therefore made businesses more prosperous. To create a less hierarchical social order, the town's elite Chamber of Commerce was disbanded and a Community Development Foundation open to everyone was started in its place. The foundation set to work improving local schools, starting community organizations, building a medical center, and establishing a vocational education center. At the same time, businesses were welcomed into town only if they paid high wages to all employees and shared this as a goal. Rural Development Councils were set up in outlying areas to encourage self-help collective action — from technical training to local cleanup campaigns in a setting in which cooperative action for shared goals had been countercultural.

Over the next fifty years under the leadership of McLean and his successors Tupelo became a national model of community and economic development, garnering numerous awards and attracting a constant stream of visitors eager to copy the town's success in their own communities. Since 1983 Lee County has added one thousand industrial jobs a year, garnered hundreds of millions of dollars of new investment, produced arguably the best school system in Mississippi, constructed a world-class hospital, and kept unemployment and poverty rates well below the state (and sometimes even the national) average. The community's success was based on its unwavering commitment to the idea that citizens would not benefit individually unless they pursued their goals collectively. Today it is unthinkable that one could enjoy social prominence in Tupelo without also getting involved in community leadership. Tupelo residents invested in social capital — networks of cooperation and mutual trust — and reaped tangible economic returns.

Another example from Putnam of the benefits of community cohesion is Roseto, Pennsylvania. This small Italian American community has been the subject of nearly forty years of in-depth study, beginning in the 1950s when medical researchers noticed a happy but puzzling phenomenon. Compared with residents of neigh-boring towns, Rosetans just didn't die of heart attacks. Their (age-adjusted) heart attack rate was less than half that of their neighbors; over a seven-year period not a single Roseto resident under forty-seven had died of a heart attack. The researchers looked for the usual explanations: diet, exercise, weight, smoking, genetic predisposition, and so forth. But none of these explanations held the answer — indeed, Rosetans were actually more likely to have some of these risk factors than were people in neighboring towns. The researchers then began to explore Roseto's social dynamics.

The town had been founded in the nineteenth century by people from the same southern Italian village. Through local leadership these immigrants had created a mutual aid society, churches, sports clubs, a labor union, a newspaper, Scout troops, and a park and athletic field. The residents had also developed a tight-knit community where conspicuous displays of wealth were scorned and family values and good behaviors reinforced. Rosetans learned to draw on one another for financial, emotional, and other forms of support. By day they congregated on front porches to watch the comings and goings, and by night they gravitated to local social clubs. In the 1960s the researchers began to suspect that social capital (though they didn't use the term) was the key to Rosetans' healthy hearts. And the researchers worried that as socially mobile young people began to reject the tight-knit Italian folkways, the heart attack rate would begin to rise. Sure enough, by the 1980s Roseto's new generation of adults hid a heart attack rate above that of their neighbors in a nearby and demographically similar town.

These are powerful examples of the benefits of community cohesion. For communities to follow in their footsteps, stories such as these are vital as inspiration and encouragement. However, in a world beset by economic inequality and climate change, where by 2050 half the planet may be living on some kind of knife edge, the measures these communities took and the results they obtained may not be enough — and the latter case shows how community capital can be lost as well as gained. Communities now must go further, to autopoiesis and antifragility, so there are different stories that need telling, of new possibilities. There are economic stories such as community wealth building in Cleveland and Preston. Social stories include regeneration and social prescribing in Frome, as well as community-led transformation of more deprived areas such as the Halcon Estate in Taunton, the Stockwell Park Estate in South London, the Pengegon Estate in Cornwall, and the progressive nursery in Castlemilk, Glasgow. Even these new stories, though, are illustrative of only a part of the journey ahead. The ideas described in this book are only just emerging so, as yet, there are no complete examples of how all the pieces can fit together – and when this starts to happen, the application of the ideas will be different in each community, so we will need many such stories to provide a well-rounded picture.

The stories we need may emerge from charitable initiatives working at community level, or from international bodies with a focus on community, such as the UN Habitat project. They may emerge from socially minded think tanks such as the Democracy Collaborative in the US or Centre for Local Economic Strategies in the UK. If community becomes a focus of public interest, we may see more stories about community in national and international media. In whatever way that narratives emerge, it will be important not to lose sight of the component elements of change described in this book.

Communities need to take a holistic vision of wellness, enable it using tools such as wellness wheels, and implement it via wellness plans and personal support networks. To put this in place, and make it work, they will need to collaborate effectively by adopting the five principles of Human Interaction Management. They will have to develop social enterprises that take ownership of community capitals, managing and sustaining these resources to create and maintain community assets that benefit local people, the wider public, and the planet. In order to fund the necessary social enterprises, communities will need not only to give local people a stake, but also to increase the total investment by diverting global financial flows into local good things. All stakeholders will wish to see the impact of their investments and get a return, which means communities must manage their activities efficiently — in particular, streamlining and lowering the cost of the necessary measurement via digital technologies. All this put together is shown graphically in the way of working shown below.

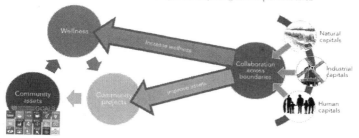

Figure 52: Way of working

Every transformation initiative helps pave a way for change. If you are on this route, share your story with me! Send an email to stories@supercommunities.info, explaining how your community is responding to the challenges of 21st century wellness, and I'll publish your story on www.supercommunities.info and in social media to inspire others.

It would be particularly helpful if you are able to explain not only your vision for the future of your community, but also how you are setting out on the mission to make it a reality. As with NHS GATHER, it is very helpful for others to know the stages that others went through to make a type of change happen. For each stage, write down what sort of people or organisations were involved, and the part each played in achieving the goals of that stage. For each activity carried out in a stage, say what the inputs and outputs were, who supplied the inputs, and who used the outputs for what. With this information, we can write up your story in standard format as a step-by-step plan, like an NHS GATHER Innovation Guide, and make it available to all through the stakeitback app. Others can then make a copy to follow in their own community, adapted of course to their specific local needs. The journey to becoming a super-community will be different for every community, but there is a lot we can learn from each other, and it makes no sense to reinvent the wheel time and again.

As examples of this kind appear, the ability to reuse knowledge hard-won in other places will make the path to becoming a supercommunity easier to follow. In the mean-time, there are already other ways to make it easier, which are open to all at zero cost.

Tools for change

To ensure that all community stakeholders play a posi-tive part in change, it is vital to be inclusive, ask open-ended questions that generate action, and use facilitation tech-niques to manage meetings effectively.

The basic challenge in creating community cohesion is for people to meet, converse, and work together in a posi-tive way. This can be very difficult to achieve. Some people will be anxious about the effects on change on their per-sonal or working life, which leads them to defend what they perceive as their own vested interests rather than cooperate with others in an open and socially-minded way. This can scupper attempts at change, and often does, quite unneces-sarily since community solutions typically benefit all con-cerned in the end. Others will be too nervous or intimidat-ed to speak up, or speak effectively, and end up unable to take the active part that they would like. This is a loss both to the community and to them personally. To ensure that all stakeholders play a positive part in change, it is vital to approach meetings in a sensitive way.

Peter Block gives examples of poor engagement styles within a community.[333] "Telling the history of how we got here. Giving explanations and opinions. Blaming and complaining. Making reports and descriptions. Carefully defining terms and conditions. Retelling your story again and again. Seeking quick action." By contrast, he sets out the characteristics of successful engagement. "An intimate and authentic relatedness is experienced. The world is shifted through invitation rather than mandate. The focus is on the communal possibility. There is a shift in ownership of this place, even though others are in charge. Diversity of thinking and dissent are given space. Commitments are made without barter. The gifts of each person and our community are acknowledged and valued."

To achieve successful engagement, Block suggests devising what he calls powerful questions, and setting up meetings so that people can respond in a constructive way. A powerful question is ambiguous, personal, and generates anxiety — in other words, it leads to a deeply considered reply. He gives examples of weak questions. "How do we get people to be more committed? How do we get others to be more responsible? How do we get people to come on board and to do the right things? How do we hold those people accountable? How do we get others to buy in to our vision? How do we get those people to change? How much will it cost, and where do we get the money? How do we negotiate for something better? What new policy or legislation will move our interests forward? Where is it working? Who has solved this elsewhere, and how do we import that knowledge? How do we find and develop better leaders? Why aren't those people in the room?"

Block's examples of powerful questions are designed to elicit a heartfelt response that leads to action. "What is the commitment you hold that brought you into this room? Why was it important for you to show up today? What is the price you or others pay for being here today? How valuable do you plan for this effort to be? What is the crossroads you face at this stage of the game? What is the story you keep telling about the problems of this community? What are the gifts you hold that have not been brought fully into the world? What is your contribution to the very thing you complain about? What is it about your group, team, or neighbourhood that no-one knows?"

So that people can respond to these questions effectively, Block identifies four tasks when introducing a meeting. Explain the questions when you ask them, focusing on key words such as "plan" to distinguish them from less action-generating notions such as "want" and "think". Make sure that people feel they can give unpopular answers. Don't tell people what they want or need locally, but invite them to query and discover community priorities for themselves. To build confidence in the room, start with the lower-risk questions — Block suggests opening with leading questions such as "How valuable an experience (or project or community) do you plan for this to be? How much risk are you willing to take? How participative do you plan to be? To what extent are you invested in the well-being of the whole?"

Meetings will fail unless the right people are in the room. One way to think about this is given by Martin Weisbord and Sandra Janoff: attendees should include decision-makers with authority to act, powerful people with resources such as contacts, time, or money, experts in the issues to be considered, those with specialist local knowledge, and those who need to be involved because they will be affected by the outcomes and can speak to the consequences.[334] You should be sure also to involve a mixture of age groups, interest groups, ethnic groups, and faith groups. Make sure marginalized elements of the community are represented and feel welcome. Bear in mind, too, the need for a mixture of personal characteristics as discussed above in **Goals and roles**.

Working out who the right people are is in itself a complex question that requires local engagement and preparatory meetings. Once you know who the necessary stakeholders are, it can be very hard to get them together in one place at one time, so plan meetings well in advance, offer a choice of dates, ask people to send a delegate if they cannot make it, and confirm regularly leading up to the meeting to build engagement and prevent drop-out. Don't just rely on email, but call or meet with key attendees personally if possible or at least call them to explain in conversation why it is important for them to be there.

Some meetings should be open the wider public – this needs to be decided on a case-by-case basis, balancing the capability of smaller meetings to generate agreement and action against the democratically engaging quality of larger meetings. When you hold a public meeting, make sure that everyone finds out about it well in advance, or people will feel aggrieved afterwards at being excluded. Promote the meeting via talks at existing groups, assemblies, and community events. Mention it on local radio and TV, and send press releases to newspapers and websites. Drop leaflets to local houses, shops, and public buildings. Use social media, engaging personally with people who are widely active so that they help spread the word. Set up an information stand in local libraries, supermarkets, train stations, and bus stations. Put up posters in local shop windows and at bus stops.

Motivating people to attend a meeting may require significant effort. An important step is writing an invitation to the meeting that is simple, clear, and challenging. It must set out the context for the meeting, the problems to be solved, why they are important, why action is required right now, and how the meeting will work. Here is an example. "The river Welling has flooded each winter for 5 years now, and each time it happens the effects are worse. If the floods get any more extreme, Wellingford town centre will be unusable for weeks or months each year, causing hardship and lowering property prices. The government has just announced a new flood relief fund for community projects, but applications close in two months so we must act now. This meeting is to agree a proposal for dealing with flooding that causes as little disruption as possible to life and work in Wellingford."

Meetings should be held in a convenient location, accessible by public transport and to the disabled. A high-status setting such as a town hall is ideal, since this lends credibility and reassures attendees that it is not a waste of their time. If this is not possible, find a venue that has other advantages, such as a local theatre or cinema with lots of comfortable seats available. In the example above, somewhere at risk from flooding might make sense, to reinforce the reality of the situation. If it's possible to have natural light in the room, do so. Arrange for microphones to be available, ideally wireless so they can be passed around easily, in order that people unaccustomed to public speaking or unable to speak loudly can be heard.

Refreshments should be available for free, which can be low cost but should be inclusive. Provide plain biscuits to keep people's blood sugar up, ideally gluten-free. Make sure there are jugs of water and, if you provide hot drinks, make vegan milk available. Have stewards to show people in, resolve any issues, and make everyone feel personally welcome, ensuring beforehand that enough people are available to do this. There should be informal gatherings at the start and end each meeting — during these times stewards should circulate, introducing people to one another and ensuring no-one feels isolated. Do not penalize late arrivals or early leavers, but thank them for coming and reassure them that it's ok. If people complain — and some always will — thank them for their input and ensure you act on it in some way, even if it is only to acknowledge it in a statement after the meeting.

If possible, arrange for the person who opens the meeting to be someone with a warm, friendly, personable presence that makes everyone feel included and welcome. If they can make people laugh, so much the better — and irreverence is something to aim for. Stuffiness and formality are enemies of engagement. The ideal opening is an inoffensive joke about something local, to which people respond by talking back from the floor.

Make a realistic agenda well before the meeting, distribute it in advance, and put it up during the meeting somewhere that everyone can see it, or as handouts on each chair. The agenda should include comfort breaks at least every 90 minutes, and the person who opens the meeting should tell everybody that it's fine to get up during the meeting at any time. During the meeting, avoid wasting time and going down rabbit holes by having a facilitator who steps in when the discussion goes off topic, and nips the digression in the bud by noting it on a list of issues to be addressed outside the meeting (this is called car parking). The facilitator is responsible generally for ensuring the meeting sticks to the agenda, car parking issues you do not have time to complete discussing.

Document the meeting in some way, by a combination of audio/video recording and nominating people to take notes. Afterwards, make the recordings and notes available publicly, not in a raw form but cleaned up and annotated so that they are easy to listen to, watch, or read and with some way for people to jump to the parts they are interested in. The obvious way to do this is publication to a website and posting the link to social media.

At the end of the meeting, put up on a screen, white-board, or flipchart the main conclusions and give everyone a chance to comment. Attendees should leave feeling that they have all understood and agreed practical next steps. This does not mean that everyone has to agree on a fixed plan of action in the wider sense, which is often impossible during a meeting (or ever), but rather that the meeting has drawn conclusions which document all the concerns voiced and assign clear responsibility for action. A poor conclusion might be, "Ask the council to look into putting sand bags around the river steps". A better conclusion would be, "Jane Taylor to work with Nadia Ahmed at the council to write up possible ways of preventing flooding at the river steps, and publish a cost benefit analysis by the end of June."

Each action such as this should be assigned to one person, so that there is clear accountability for doing something, but the action description should also identify who else is responsible for helping. If possible, all those involved should be represented at the meeting, and commit to their role during the meeting (see above under **Goals and roles**). If a group of people is required, it should have between 5 and 9 members, and work in an Agile way (see above under **Outputs and outcomes**). The outputs of the work should be made clear, and after they are produced, they must be thanked in subsequent meetings, with acknowledgement of challenges that they faced (see above under **Contributions and recognition**) — this should be done even if the work fails or is only partially successful. If along the way, it becomes clear that a better approach should be taken, this should be reviewed and endorsed by all stakeholders (see above under **Awareness and responsiveness**). During the work, people should communicate purposefully with one another, ensuring that relevant people are always included in messages and meetings (see above under **Communication, conversations, and purpose**).

Acting on these guidelines may require developing new skills, but they are useful life skills that will be of value not only to your community but also to you personally in the workplace. As described above in the discussion of volunteering, stepping up to support your community actually brings more benefit to you than to those you are helping. There is a final aspect to this, which is not just about social or working life, but about personal emotional, spiritual, and intellectual development.

Your personal journey

Engaging with community can be emotionally and spiritually draining. It can also be massively restorative, bring new and rewarding relationships, help you develop personally, and make you feel better about your life.

If this book has led you to feel that you'd like to get involved with your community, or communities, it is worth recognizing at the start that you may change as a result. In fact, you may need to change even to get started. This change will be mixed, but ultimately rewarding and possibly life-changing.

Engaging with community can be emotionally and spiritually draining. It can also be massively restorative. Some of the challenges you will learn about, and take part in facing, will be upsetting and stay with you. You may find yourself lending moral support to others to a degree you have not done before, and find this draining. You may also struggle with the accountability and responsibility you accept, finding it onerous and stressful. On the other hand, you will come to enjoy reciprocal affection and even love with new people, which will make a huge difference to you. You will engage with more people, more deeply, and more warmly than before. Every day when you walk down the street you will see new people that you share a connection with, and this will bring new richness and depth to your life.

Spiritually, there will be dark times but ultimately you will experience a new sense of connection, purpose, and meaning. Beforehand, you may have felt that the world was turning for the worse, and that there was little you could do about it. Perhaps you found that conventional ways of making your day brighter, such as the little boost that comes from shopping for bargains,[335] are no longer as effective as they once were – apparently, online advertisers are noticing a "drift towards negative engagement".[336] By contrast, working closely with others to build community, you will come to see how there are positive opportunities all around, with real visible outcomes that matter. You will gain an empowering sense of the world as full of ideas and possibilities, and you will feel closer to your social and natural environment from exploring them. You will build personal compassion and generosity, learning to deal more gently and sensitively with others as you come to engage with each situation individually rather than through generalized rules.

Finally, you will learn new things, and get into the habit of lifelong learning. The more that you understand the complexities of community life, the more you will come to understand about the world, and the more you will seek to know in order to deal with it effectively. The jazz pianist Thelonious Monk was an inspiration to his peers and much loved by them not just because of his eccentric style and offbeat tunes, but because of the deep, grounded confidence he showed in all his dealings with the world. His personal fortunes varied with musical fashions and record company foibles, but he always pursued a vision with dedication and without rancour, sharing his unique understanding of music generously with other players, and showing appreciation for their contributions. He wore a ring that read in one direction "Know" and in the other "Monk" — his motto, "Always know", sums up both his concern only for essential truth in music as in life, and his understanding that names are inspiring and important.

A rose by any other name might not, in fact, smell as sweet. The act of naming reifies something, giving it meaning, and meaning is always culturally dependent. Until the 1970s horse mackerel was sold to companies for cat food or thrown away. Renamed as tuna in the Western world, it became a staple food, and as toro (fat tuna) a fish that the samurai class refused to eat has become one of the most prized foods in Japanese cuisine. Similarly, British fishermen on the shore load dogfish for bait, but on the menu of fish and chip shops a hundred yards higher up on the seafront, it is called rock salmon. Less mundanely, no-one realized there was such a thing as a teenager before the word came into use in the twentieth century — now their natural history is studied by scientists.[337] William Melvin Kelley's legendary New York Times article of 1962, "If You're Woke You Dig It", shows how the significance of names can range from exclusion, secrecy, and protection to environment, security, and pride.[338] Since his article, the term woke has become a synonym for a progressive understanding and acceptance of minority concerns that previous generations may not have even known to exist. The fact that political correctness, like any social trend, can be a double-edged sword only illustrates the power of names.

Community and supercommunity are names that carry importance. A community, let alone a supercommunity, doesn't exist until you name it. People can live in an area, share an interest, have a common affiliation, or have anything else in common without being a community — until they declare that they are. This is an act of power. Power is hard to gain and easily lost. It can be used wisely or corrupt the holders. Communities of all kinds have the potential power to change their own world for the better. Realizing this potential as a supercommunity is a long road, but one that is well worth travelling. If this book has helped convince you to set out, and shown part of the way, it will have succeeded.

Afterword

Business will not save us from inequality, climate change, and new global crises. Government policies may help eventually, but when is unclear. Communities need to act now. The first step is to develop local social trading.

If the most powerful organisations are now corporations, why not just ask them to do more for the world? Couldn't representatives of local and national governments go to the boards of large corporations, and demand that they take more responsibility for the general welfare of the planet on which, after all, they also live?

One can imagine that such a move would receive a carefully worded response something like this.

"We appreciate and share your concerns. We too have families, care about the planet, and try always to act ethically. In particular, although corporate social responsibility legislation is voluntary, we comply with it and donate funds every year to worthy causes. We also aim to operate with minimal damage to people and the environment. However, we do not have any specialist expertise in charity work – and as board members and executives our duty is limited to ensuring the success of our company. Unless we focus on our duty, we personally risk legal action by shareholders. Even if we were somehow to avoid this, our shareholders (many of whom are institutions facing demands from their own shareholders) will simply sell their holdings, leading to a fall in share price that puts the company at a disadvantage to its competitors and may eventually drive it out of business."

This is a version of the prisoners' dilemma. It would be

better for all on the planet if each corporation was to recognise that their business depends on community capitals,
so its existing infrastructure such as accounting, marketing,
and quality is not enough – new skills and responsibilities
are required, that ensure profitable operations do not damage common natural, human, and industrial resources.
However, the system is set up to penalize the first organisations that do this. So, the first step towards better outcomes
for the world must be to change the rules of the game.

There are many ways to do this, and all are worth supporting. National governments are taking collective action
to change the principles of corporate taxation at international level and devise ways of enforcing them. New legislation is always being debated, at national and international
levels, to assess and penalize social or environmental damage by corporations. There is public pressure on large institutions such as pension funds to make more ethical investments, and on governments to be more open about the
influence of corporate interests on politicians. Progressive
thinkers are arguing for policies that facilitate the creation
of a stakeholder rather than shareholder economy, and for
government to assert its rightful place as a creator of value
by interacting more sustainability with industry.[339] Modern
Monetary Theory and growing popular support may, in due
course, empower governments to implement policies such
as Universal Basic Income and a Green New Deal.

Hopefully, all these moves will succeed, but right now
there is no reason to be particularly optimistic for systemic
change from the top any time soon. To counter transnational corporate power, countries will need to act together,
which means negotiating and funding large scale agreements. Such agreements are not only hard to put in place

but also vulnerable to the actions of nations that perceive their self-interest as lying elsewhere, and determine to continue (or begin) acting as tax and legislative havens. These challenges must be overcome by governments that were still reeling from the financial crisis of 2008 when a global pandemic hit a decade later.

This book argues that there is no reason to wait, since anyone can take part in making their own community or communities antifragile and autopoietic — able to thrive in the face of new challenges. Following the rules here, it's eminently possible, and since helping others will improve your own wellness, there's little to lose. We can all change the rules of the game without waiting for action by the powers that be, and doing this at a local level means new rules will fit local needs. The supercommunity is a recipe, not a blueprint, which must be adjusted according to the ingredients you have available and the tastes of the people you are cooking for. Or you could see it as the genetic code for a society with greater wellness, that each community exposes to local influences in order to express its own reality.

It is particularly important for all of us to have some basic understanding of economics, since it is so often the basis on which powerful people make decisions. Economics is commonly defined as the study of resources in times of scarcity. It certainly produced fascinating evidence for the scarcity of common sense among economists during the twentieth century. Neoclassical economists claim that market prices not only define the value of products and services but automatically regulate their demand and supply in the interests of society. This idea might be closer to reality if their notion of a market didn't relegate to the sidelines everything that is important to the people who actually inhabit society.

In the world view of a mainstream economist, human concerns are externalities, imperfections and frictions that cause market failures, so they should be competed or regulated away. The notion that markets consist of impersonal transactions aimed solely at maximizing profit is not only at odds with what we know of human society throughout history, makes no allowance for how businesses make use of shared community capitals, and leads to more general ways of thinking that affect the way individuals deal with the world around them. In the economic theory of family, for example, people marry in order to reduce living expenses and insurance costs, and children behave well in order to maximize total family income.[340] This theory changed government policies, and policies change people's behaviour. It may be that people are more likely now to use such calculations in making life-changing decisions about their partners, children, and parents.

Stories about the way the world works are parables. They have a powerful impact, leading people to re-evaluate things they have done in past and behave differently going forward. When personal freedom and hence social stability was threatened by oligarchic wealth accumulation in the Bronze Age, a ruler would cancel all household debts and renew society. The proclamation that set out details of such measures declared that the ruler was acting in the name of the gods to restore justice and truth in the land, and was typically accompanied by a general public ceremony celebrating social renewal. At times when the ruler's power was threatened by private interests, the story underpinning such a proclamation was vital in making its measures a reality.

This book tells a story about supercommunity, and like a parable it's a story that aims to change ideas and behaviours. As in a village marketplace, the commercial deals in a supercommunity are relationships rather than transactions, and the outcomes of such deals are multi-faceted. When you buy or sell at local level, you don't just exchange goods or services for money, but join a network of people who know each other and take responsibility for their actions. If you made a plea for help to the people who run social enterprises, volunteer in the community, or take action to support others locally in some other way, they would not respond like a profiteering corporation, but rather with warmth, compassion, and positive energy — and it may well be that they have already put products and services in place that you can adopt without needing to make such a plea. By their actions, they are telling a different story about how the world works, an old story called do as you would be done by — and the oldest stories live on for a reason.

If this book has left you feeling inspired to help create change in your own community, or communities, then it has succeeded. As a first step, you might like to visit the website **www.supercommunities.info**, which brings together information about social businesses of all types from across the world with demonstration Web apps for digital hubs and stakeitbacks along with other techniques and tools for building supercommunities.

You may also be interested to read the further exploration and developments of this book's ideas in my blog at **www.harrison-broninski.info**, on which you are welcome to comment. For example, the blog discusses next generation internet technologies that could be brought into being to empower supercommunities.

The aspiration of this book is that it contributes to a global movement, initiative, or some other form of collaborative effort to create communities that are not only better places to live now but also better placed for whatever is coming our way in the future. Policy makers, elected representatives, and civil servants can help establish the social structures necessary for supercommunities. Business people and technology innovators can help provide techniques and tools. You, I, and everybody else will need to do the heavy lifting – which should be a hugely rewarding experience. I look forward to meeting you along the way.

Supercommunities in a nutshell

Preface: By 2050, almost half the world's population, in both developed and developing economies, will be living on some form of knife edge. To address this, we must create more cohesive and caring communities.

Introduction: To become antifragile, communities need to develop local modifications of the market economy based on social enterprise, in which participants aim not only to make profit but also to benefit people and the planet.

In order to prevent inequality that led to social breakdown, early societies protected individuals from unmanageable debt. Human rights go further in some ways now but no longer include debt protection.

The economic shock of the 1970s led to commercial interests determining government policies. The rules of society are now shaped by businesses, whose access to a global workforce means they can disregard social concerns.

Increasing freedom from taxation and regulation combined with privatization of national resources mean that the largest economies in the world are now corporations, leaving states deeply in debt with no way out.

Throughout history the rise of oligarchic wealth destroyed societies. Now, corporate power dominates political decisions, so privatization continues although the resulting public services are expensive and poor quality.

The rise of corporate power is creating human misery,

exacerbated ever further as inequality grows unchecked. Debts are escalating out of control at both household and state level.

We can create a better society without extremism by building supercommunities, which adopt emergent behaviours to become antifragile whether or not new sources of value provide economic growth.

Wellness: Wellness is not the same as absence of illness, and is not a purely medical concept but more holistic. Definitions vary, and attempting to standardize wellness may lead to undesirable intervention into private life.

Positive psychology explores how becoming self-activated can help you flourish. PsyCap captures the importance of Hope, (Self-)Efficacy, Resilience, and Optimism in overcoming challenges and achieving goals.

Some people cannot increase their wellness without access to, and help in using, practical as well as psychological resources - the poor in particular, since early disadvantage lowers your ability to thrive unaided.

People who consume many government services generate massive cost to society. They are stigmatized as criminal or lazy but typically have long-standing health conditions that generate further wellness issues.

Using a wellness wheel to show how practical life issues are interconnected enables people to work through their personal challenges and set achievable goals for each one. This is the first step towards PsyCap.

Community: Social cohesion and engagement are at a historically low ebb. Restoring the trusting, reciprocal relationships that characterize community will release forms of value that help remedy major social challenges.

Communities take varied forms and can be fluid. It is belonging that matters. The human brain evolved through social behaviour, since reciprocal altruism delivers powerful benefits that are otherwise unavailable.

The strength of your community connections outweighs everything else when it comes to wellness. This is because community connection enables, or the lack of it disables, everything on your wellness wheel.

A community can help marginalized people increase their wellness at low total cost by providing social rather than medical resources to help them thrive. However, some people need more than a social prescription.

The holistic support needed for wellness can be provided at low cost via a personal support network – a group of people who help you make your wellness plan, then provide help and encouragement as you implement it.

Collaboration: Taking on a role is not about tasks but about accepting responsibilities for achieving goals. You need to know about other roles in the team, and ensure that it includes a mixture of thinkers, doers, socializers, and leaders.

Communication coordinates behaviour as well as transferring information. To work well with others, have conversations for Context, Possibility, Disclosure, then Action and communicate about one thing at a time.

In order to engage with their work, people need recognition and appreciation. Praise should be personalized, heartfelt, and timely. Volunteering has huge benefits, most of which accrue to the volunteers themselves.

To achieve great impact for low effort, make interventions local and personal, focus on outcomes not outputs, and ensure that organisations work together. Depending on the scale, use Agile techniques or value maps.

To notice events and respond, use Research-Evaluate-Analyze-Constrain-Task (REACT). To conduct Research, use Access-Identify-Memorize (AIM). Separate leadership into Strategic, Executive, and Management Control.

Ownership: Building a strong community requires years of civic engagement at grass roots, which must be multi-faceted and inclusive. It can be sustained or destroyed by municipal efforts towards regeneration.

Ownership takes many forms. Useful ways to think about it are stewardship and stakeholding. Opening up control over activity typically increases its success, both economically and by more holistic measures.

Community capitals are enablers of community assets and can be separated into natural, human, and industrial. Community members can map assets in an online database, and plan their maintenance using visual models.

Local economies can build social cohesion and access specialist finance via social trading, which has ethical as well as commercial aims. Social traders must act cooperatively. They think differently about opportunity cost.

Some social traders cannot access traditional community finance or impact investment. They can access global capital markets at low cost via stakeitbacks – a new way to fund good things, see the impact, and get a return.

Measurement: To ensure that outputs lead to desirable outcomes, benefits must be managed. This can be hindered by cognitive biases of various types, and helped by application of REACT and AIM to create virtuous loops.

A community that aims to become antifragile needs its members to assess their own progress towards wellness. This can be enabled by providing diverse but standardized self-assessment tools in a digital hub.

Assessing wellness of the community as a whole means identifying gaps and overlaps in provision of resources that support individual wellness. Data from wellness plans can be aggregated with data from other sources.

Transformation: Communities that use autopoiesis to become antifragile must tell their stories to inspire others. Community wealth building, grass roots regeneration, and social prescribing are a starting point but not yet fully holistic.

To ensure that all community stakeholders play a positive part in change, it is vital to be inclusive, ask open-ended questions that generate action, and use facilitation techniques to manage meetings effectively.

Engaging with community can be emotionally and spiritually draining. It can also be massively restorative, bring new and rewarding relationships, help you develop personally, and make you feel better about your life.

Afterword: Business will not save us from inequality, climate change, and new global crises. Government policies may help eventually, but when is unclear. Communities need to act now. The first step is to develop local social trading.

Further reading

If you would like to read more about some of the ideas mentioned in this book, here are some places to start.

1. Ridley, M. (1996). The Origins of Virtue.
2. Putnam, R. D. (2000) Bowling Alone. The collapse and revival of American community.
3. Harvey, D. (2005). A brief history of neoliberalism.
4. Wilkinson, R., Pickett, K. (2009). The Spirit Level — Why Equality is Better for Everyone.
5. Graeber, D. (2011). Debt: The first 5,000 years.
6. Taleb, N. N. (2012). Antifragile: Things that gain from disorder.
7. Chang, H.-J. (2012). 23 things they don't tell you about capitalism
8. Piketty, T., Goldhammer, A. (2013). Capital in the twenty-first century.
9. Jones, O. (2015). The establishment: And how they get away with it.
10. Klein, N. (2015). This changes everything: Capitalism vs. the climate.
11. Harari, Y. N. (2016). Homo Deus: A Brief History of Tomorrow.
12. Mazzucato, M. (2016). Value of everything: Making and taking in the global economy.
13. Varoufakis, Y. (2017). And the weak suffer what they must? Europe, austerity and the threat to global stability.

14. Bullough, O. (2018). Moneyland: The inside story of the crooks and kleptocrats who rule the world.

15. Hanna, T. M. (2018). Our common wealth: The return of public ownership in the United States.

16. Kelly, M., Howard, T. (2019). The making of a democratic economy: Building prosperity for the many, not just the few.

17. Krznaric, R. (2020). The Good Ancestor: How to think long-term in a short-term world.

18. Bregman, R. (2020). Humankind: A hopeful history.

References

[1] www.worldbank.org/en/news/press-release/2018/09/19/decline-of-global-extreme-poverty-continues-but-has-slowed-world-bank, last updated 2 October 2019

[2] ourworldindata.org/grapher/declining-global-poverty-share-1820-2015?time=1820..2015

[3] ophi.org.uk/resources/infographics-2

[4] Organisation for Economic Co-operation and Development (2018), "States of Fragility 2018"

[5] The Guardian (20 January 2020). UK benevolent funds hand out £216m as hardship grows.

[6] Joseph Rowntree Foundation (15 February 2017). Just about managing: Four million more people living on inadequate incomes in modern Britain.

[7] United Nations Department of Economic and Social Affairs, Population Division. World Population Prospects 2019.

[8] Royal Society of Arts (2015). Community Capital — The Value of Connected Communities.

[9] Spiegel, A.D (1997). Hammurabi's Managed Health Care — Circa 1700 B.C.

[10] Hudson, M. (2018). ... And forgive them their debts: Lending, foreclosure and redemption from Bronze Age finance to the Jubilee Year.

[11] Westbrook R. (2003), ed., "A history of ancient Near Eastern law", Leiden: Brill.

[12] Lauren, P. G. (January 01, 2013). The Foundations of Justice and Human Rights in Early Legal Texts and Thought. The Oxford Handbook of International Human Rights Law, 163-193.

[13] Fuller, E.W. (2019). Was Keynes a socialist? Cambridge Journal of Economics, Volume 43, Issue 6, November 2019, Pages 1653-1682

[14] Roosevelt, F.D. (1938), Fireside Chat on Present Economic Conditions and Measures Being Taken to Improve Them. April 14, 1938.

[15] Johnson, L.B (1964), State of the Union address on 8 January 1964 (War on Poverty Speech).

[16] United Nations, Geneva (1996), "Fact Sheet No.2 (Rev.1), The International Bill of Human Rights", www.ohchr.org/Documents/Publications/FactSheet2Rev.1en.pdf

[17] Hayek, F. A. (1944). The road to serfdom.

[18] Mazzucato, M. (2018). The value of everything — making and taking in the global economy.

[19] U.S. Department of State, Office of the Historian. Report by the Policy Planning Staff, PPS/23, February 24, 1948.

[20] U.S. Department of State, Office of the Historian. OPEC Oil Embargo 1973-1974.

[21] Friedman, M. (1962). Capitalism and freedom. Chicago: University of Chicago.

[22] Agreement establishing the World Trade Organization, (1995). World Trade Organization.

[23] Rothschild, E. (1995). Social Security and Laissez Faire in Eighteenth-Century Political Economy. Population and Development Review, 21(4), 711-744. doi:10.2307/2137772

[24] Viner, J. (1927). Adam Smith and Laissez Faire, Journal of Political Economy, Vol. 35, No. 2 (Apr., 1927), pp. 198-232, The University of Chicago Press

[25] Smith, A. (1776). Wealth of Nations.

[26] Chang, H.-J. (2012). 23 things they don't tell you about capitalism.

27 Mackenney, R. (2010). 'In Place of Strife' - The Guilds and the Law in Renaissance Venice.

28 Hetzel, R.L. (2016), What Remains of Monetarism after the Great Recession?

29 Lee, T.B. (2014). Why printing more money could have stopped the Great Recession.

30 Graeber, D (2011). Debt: The First 5,000 Years.

31 Chohan, U. W. (2020). Modern Monetary Theory (MMT): A General Introduction.

32 Smith, A. (1776). Wealth of Nations.

33 Wray, L. R. (2000). The Neo-Chartalist Approach to Money.

34 Mazzucato, M. (2018). The value of everything — making and taking in the global economy.

35 Megginson, W. L., and Netter, J. M. (2001), From State to Market: A Survey of Empirical Studies on Privatization. Journal of Economic Literature 39 (2): 321-89.

36 Privatization Barometer (2016), "The Privatization Barometer Report 2015/16", www.privatizationbarometer.com/PUB/NL/5/9/PB_AR2015-2016.pdf

37 Devereux, M. P., & Sorensen, P. B. (January 01, 2006). The Corporate Income Tax: international trends and options for fundamental reform. Economic Papers European Commission Directorate General for Economic and Financial Affairs, 264.).

38 Deutsche Bank Research (2020). An inflection point in global corporate tax?

39 Babic, M., Fichtner, J., & Heemskerk, E. M. (January 01, 2017). States versus Corporations: Rethinking the Power of Business in International Politics. The International Spectator: Italian Journal of Interna-

tional Affairs, 52, 4, 20-43.

[40] Bureau of the Fiscal Service, U.S. Department of the Treasury. Monthly Treasury Statement, Receipts and Outlays of the United States Government for Fiscal Year 2020 through November 30, 2019 and Other Periods.

[41] A one-dollar bill is 0.0043 inches thick (0.000000067866 miles), so a stack of 1,000,000,000,000 one-dollar bills would be 67,866 miles high.

[42] US Congressional Budget Office (January 2020). The Budget and Economic Outlook: 2020 to 2030.

[43] Reinhart, C. M., Rogoff, K. S. (2011). This time is different: Eight centuries of financial folly.

[44] Deutsche Bank Research (2020). Ibid.

[45] Deutsche Bank Research (2020). Ibid.

[46] Financial Times (4 December 2019). Countries vow to press ahead with digital taxes despite US threat.

[47] Megginson et al, ibid.

[48] Megginson et al, ibid.

[49] Lambooy, T., 2014. Legal Aspects of Corporate Social Responsibility. Utrecht Journal of International and European Law, 30(78), pp.1-6. DOI: http://doi.org/10.5334/ujiel.bz

[50] Friedman, M. (1970). The Social Responsibility of Business is to Increase its Profits.

[51] Jensen, M. C., Meckling, W. H. (1976). Theory of the firm: managerial behavior, agency costs and ownership structure.

[52] Mazzucato, M. (2018). The value of everything — making and taking in the global economy.

[53] Fang, L. (2014). Where Have All the Lobbyists Gone? The Nation.

54 Jones, O. (2015). The establishment: And how they get away with it. London: Penguin Books.

55 Collaborate and the Institute for Government (2014). Beyond big contracts: commissioning public services for better outcomes.

56 Mazzucato, M. (2017). Value of everything: Making and taking in the global economy.

57 Guardian, 24 July 2012. London 2012 Olympics: G4S failures prompt further military deployment.

58 Guardian, 1 June 2011. The rise and fall of Southern Cross.

59 Guardian, 18 September 2013. Abandoned NHS IT system has cost £10bn so far.

60 Institute of Government (2019). Performance Tracker 2019 — A data-driven analysis of the performance of public services.

61 Joseph Rowntree Foundation (2018). UK Poverty 2018.

62 Trussell Trust (2019). State of Hunger — A study of poverty and food insecurity in the UK.

63 Guardian, January 2020, www.theguardian.com/society/2020/jan/02/levels-child-criminal-exploitation-almost-back-to-victorian-times

64 Guardian, May 2019, www.theguardian.com/commentisfree/2019/may/14/mental-health-services-crisis-patients-vulnerable-off-rolled

65 Homeless Link (2018). Rough sleeping statistics for England 2018.

66 World Health Organization (2019). Fact sheet — Mental disorders, 28 November 2019.

67 UN-Habitat project, 2019, unhabitat.org/topic/housing

68 World Meteorological Organization (2019). Press Release, 22 September 2019.

[69] Intergovernmental Panel on Climate Change (2019). IPCC Special Report on Climate Change, Desertification, Land Degradation, Sustainable Land Management, Food Security, and Greenhouse gas fluxes in Terrestrial Ecosystems — Summary for Policymakers.

[70] Piketty, T., & Goldhammer, A. (2013). Capital in the twenty-first century, Chapter 10, Inequality of Capital Ownership.

[71] Piketty, T., & Goldhammer, A., ibid. Chapter Eleven, Merit and Inheritance in the Long Run.

[72] Piketty, T., & Goldhammer, A., ibid. Chapter Twelve, Global Inequality of Wealth in the Twenty-First Century.

[73] "A World Without Fear", TEDx talk by Brother David Steindl-Rast, www.ted.com/talks/brother_david_steindl_rast_a_world_without_fear

[74] King, M. A. (2016). End of alchemy: Money, banking, and the future of the global economy.

[75] Wilkinson, R., and Pickett, K. (2010). The Spirit Level — Why Equality is Better for Everyone, Penguin.

[76] U.S. Bureau of Labor Statistics (November 22, 2019). Employed full time: Median usual weekly real earnings: Wage and salary workers: 16 years and over: Men [LES1252881900Q].

[77] Woolf S.H., et al. (2019). Life Expectancy and Mortality Rates in the United States, 1959-2017.

[78] Wilkinson, R., and Pickett, K. (2010), ibid.

[79] Public Trust in Government: 1958-2019 (11 April 2019), Pew Research Center for the People and the Pres

[80] International Monetary Fund (2012). Dealing with Household Debt.

[81] Institute of International Finance (13 January 2020). Global Debt Monitor: Sustainability Matters.

[82] Jubilee Debt Campaign (2020). Countries in crisis.

[83] Graeber, D (2011). Debt: The First 5,000 Years.

[84] Luke 4:14-30

[85] Hudson, M. (2018). ... And forgive them their debts: Lending, foreclosure and redemption from Bronze Age finance to the Jubilee Year.

[86] Varoufakis, Y. (2017). And the weak suffer what they must? Europe, austerity and the threat to global stability.

[87] Reinhart, C. M., Rogoff, K. S. (2011). This time is different: Eight centuries of financial folly.

[88] King, M. A. (2016). End of alchemy: Money, banking, and the future of the global economy.

[89] Harrison-Broninski, K. (2005). Human Interactions.

[90] Mazzucato, M. (2017). Value of everything: Making and taking in the global economy.

[91] Lakatos, I. (1976). Proofs and refutations: The logic of math. discovery. Ed. by John Worrall and Elie Zahar. Cambridge: Cambridge Univ. Pr.

[92] Taleb, N. N. (2007). The black swan: The impact of the highly improbable.

[93] Taleb, N. N. (2012). Antifragile: Things that gain from disorder.

[94] rcc.harvard.edu/knowledge-technology-and-complexity-economic-growth

[95] Dumenil, G., Levy, D. (2004). The Economics of US Imperialism at the Turn of the 21st Century. Review of International Political Economy, 11, 4, 657-676.

[96] Bureau of Economic Analysis (20 December 2019). Gross Domestic Product, 3rd quarter 2019 (third estimate); Corporate Profits, 3rd quarter 2019 (revised estimate).

[97] Piketty, ibid.

[98] Bender, M. H. (2001). An economic comparison of traditional and conventional agricultural systems at a county level.

[99] Rydberg, T., & Jansen, J. (2002). Comparison of horse and tractor traction using energy analysis.

[100] Saha, S.K. (2014). Comparative study of Bullock driven tractors.

[101] Harari, Y. N. (2016). Homo deus.

[102] Krznaric, R. (2020). The Good Ancestor: How to think long-term in a short-term world.

[103] www.nhs.uk/news/medical-practice/homeopathy-remains-on-nhs/

[104] House of Commons (8 February 2010). Science and Technology Committee — Fourth Report — Evidence Check 2: Homeopathy

[105] U.S. Food & Drug Administration (15 December 2017). Don't Get Burned: Stay Away from Ear Candles.

[106] Daily Mail (16 March 2019). A very upper crust cult: Run by a wealthy old Etonian in deepest Somerset, it claims you can burp out bad spirits and disabled children were evil in a past life. Ridiculous? Tell that to the husband who lost his wife to its clutches.

[107] World Health Organization (1958). The first ten years of the World Health Organization.

[108] Gray, S., Pilkington, P., Pencheon, D., Jewell, T. (2006). Public health in the UK: success or failure? Journal of the Royal Society of Medicine, 99(3), 107-111. doi:10.1258/jrsm.99.3.107

[109] Royal College of Psychiatrists (November 2015). Medically unexplained symptoms.

[110] Mental Health Foundation (2005). Up and running? Exercise therapy and the treatment of mild or moderate depression in primary care.

[111] The Guardian (5 July 2016). Antidepressant prescriptions in England double in a decade.

112 Our campaigns, Public Health England, <u>campaignre-</u>
<u>sources.phe.gov.uk/resources/campaigns</u>

113 Swarbrick, M. (2006). A Wellness Approach. Psychiatric Rehabilitation Journal, 29(4), 311-314

114 Cohen, S. (1983). The Mental Hygiene Movement, the Development
of Personality and the School: The Medicalization of American Education, History of Education Quarterly 23.2, Summer 1983.

115 Guthrie, R.V. (1998). Even the Rat was White.

116 Paul Lombardo, P. (University of Virginia). Eugenic Sterilization
Laws. <u>www.eugenicsarchive.org/html/eugenics/essay8text.html</u>

117 Grekul, J., Krahn, H., & Odynak, D. (2004). Sterilizing the 'feeble-
minded': eugenics in Alberta, Canada, 1929-1972. Journal of Historical Sociology, 17, 358-384.

118 Tydén, Mattias (2002). Från politik till praktik: de svenska steriliс-
eringslagarna 1935-1975. Stockholm studies in history, 0491-0842; 63.
Stockholm: Almqvist & Wiksell International. pp. 69-70. ISBN 978-
91-22-01958-9.

119 The Guardian (18 March 2019). Victims of forced sterilisation in
Japan to receive compensation and apology.

120 Dawkins, R. (20 November 2006). From the Afterword
(<u>www.heraldscotland.com/news/12760676.from-the-afterword</u>)

121 Mukherjee, S. (2017). The gene: An intimate history.

122 Maslow, A.H. (1943). Theory of human motivation.

123 Maslow, A.H. (1970). Motivation and personality.

124 Maslow, A.H. (1971). Farther Reaches of Human Nature.

125 Hoffman, E. (1988). The Right to be Human: A Biography of Abraham Maslow.

126 Hoffman, E. (1988), ibid.

[127] Maslow, A.H. (1962). Toward a Psychology of Being.

[128] Seligman, M.E.P. (1975). Helplessness: On Depression, Development, and Death.

[129] Seligman, M.E.P. (2004). TED talk: The new era of positive psychology.

[130] Seligman, M.E.P. (2011). Flourish.

[131] Bolier L., et al. (2013). Positive psychology interventions: a meta-analysis of randomized controlled studies". BMC Public Health. 13 (119).

[132] Newman, A., Ucbasaran, D., Zhu, F., & Hirst, G. (2014). Psychological capital: A review and synthesis.

[133] Hallam, S. (2015). The power of music: A research synthesis of the impact of actively making music on the intellectual, social and personal development of children and young people.

[134] Levitin, D. J. (2006). This is your brain on music: Understanding a human obsession.

[135] Savage, J., Barnard, D. (2019). The State of Play — A Review of Music Education in England 2019

[136] Goodman, A., Gregg, P. (2010). Poorer children's educational attainment: how important are attitudes and behaviour?

[137] Deckers, T., Falk, A., Kosse, F., Pinger, P., & Schildberg-Hörisch, H. (2017). Socio-Economic Status and Inequalities in Children's IQ and Economic Preferences.

[138] Nunns, A. (2013). Fostering social mobility as a contribution to social cohesion.

[139] Bowles, S., Gintis, H., Osborne, M. (Eds.) (2006). Unequal Chances: Family Background and Economic Success.

[140] Joseph Rowntree Foundation (15 February 2017). Just about managing: Four million more people living on inadequate incomes in mod-

ern Britain.

141 Charlesworth, A., Watt, T. (2019). The real cost of a fair adult social care system.

142 Cameron, D. (15 December 2011). Speech on troubled families, Sandwell Christian Centre, Oldbury.

143 Casey, L. (2012). Listening to Troubled Families. Department for Communities and Local Government

144 Portes, J; Bewley, H. (2016). National Evaluation of the Troubled Families Programme — Final Synthesis Report.

145 The Guardian (18 October 2016). The troubled families programme was bound to fail — and ministers knew it.

146 Ministry of Housing, Communities and Local Government (March 2019). National evaluation of the Troubled Families Programme 2015-2020: Findings.

147 Owen Jones (2016). Chavs: the demonization of the working class.

148 The Independent (19 April 2011). Secret memos expose link between oil firms and invasion of Iraq.

149 BBC (16 September 2004). Excerpts: Annan interview.

150 The Iraq Inquiry — Statement by Sir John Chilcot: 6 July 2016.

151 www.unrefugees.org/emergencies/iraq

152 www.iicsa.org.uk/investigations/all

153 Feldblum, C. R., Lipnic, V. A. (2016). Select Task Force on the Study of Harassment in the Workplace: Report of co-chairs Chai R. Feldblum & Victoria A. Lipnic.

154 Le Défenseur des Droits (January 2014). Enquête sur le harcèlement sexuel au travail.

155 The Guardian (27 March 2019). Life expectancy gap widens between rich and poor women.

[156] Gusmano, M.K., Rodwin, V.G. (13 February 2006). The Elderly and Social Isolation — Testimony to Committee on Aging, NYC Council.

[157] Tanskanen, J., Anttila, T. (2016). A Prospective Study of Social Isolation, Loneliness, and Mortality in Finland.

[158] Green, M. (1984). The wheel as a cult-symbol in the Romano-Celtic world: With special reference to Gaul and Britain.

[159] Putnam, R. D. (2000) Bowling Alone. The collapse and revival of American community.

[160] Mill, J.S. (1861). Considerations on Representative Government.

[161] Holt-Lunstad, J. et al (2010). Social Relationships and Mortality Risk: A Meta-Analytic Review.

[162] Cacioppo, J. (2014). Rewarding Social Connections Promote Successful Aging.

[163] www.createstreets.com

[164] Golding, L. (1932). Magnolia Street.

[165] Deacon, T. (1997). The symbolic species: The co-evolution of language and the human brain.

[166] Ridley, M. (1993). The Red Queen: Sex and the Evolution of Human Nature.

[167] British Phonographic Industry (April 2019). All About the Music 2019.

[168] Citi GPS: Global Perspectives & Solutions (August 2018). Putting the Band Back Together — Remastering the World of Music.

[169] Levitin, D. J. (2006). This is your brain on music: Understanding a human obsession.

[170] Ridley, M. (1996). The Origins of Virtue.

[171] Hardin, G. (13 December 1968). The Tragedy of the Commons.

172 Lloyd, W.F. (1833). Two Lectures on Population.

173 Ostrom, E. (1990). Governing the commons: The evolution of institutions for collective action.

174 Ridley, M. (1996). The Origins of Virtue.

175 Putnam, R. D. (2000) Bowling Alone. The collapse and revival of American community.

176 Dunbar, R. I. M. (1992). Neocortex size as a constraint on group size in primates.

177 Dunbar, R.I.M. (1998). Grooming, gossip, and the evolution of language.

178 Louis de Bernières (2004). Birds without wings.

179 The Guardian (3 April 2013). Manchester police to record attacks on goths, emos and punks as hate crimes.

180 Watchtower Online Library, retrieved 4 February 2020. Extracurricular Activities — School and Jehovah's Witnesses.

181 Martínez-Ariño, J., Teinturier, S. (2019). Faith-Based Schools in Contexts of Religious Diversity: An Introduction.

182 Ferrara, C.A. (2017). Transmitting Faith in the Republic: Muslim Schooling in Modern Plural France.

183 Reichard, J.D. (2016). "Religionless" Religious Private Schools? Secularizing for the Common Good through Tuition Voucher Programs.

184 Hirsch, S., McAndrew, M., Amiraux, V. (2015). Grandir dans la communauté juive à Montréal. Approches éducatives de quatre écoles juives.

185 Gravel, S. (2015). Impartiality of Teachers in Quebec's Non-Denominational Ethics and Religious Culture Program.

186 BBC News (19 September 2013). Viewpoints: What should be done

about integration?

[187] Royal Society of Arts (October 2015). Community Capital — The Value of Connected Communities

[188] LGA Media Office (Press release, 9 May 2013). Government cuts risk 'failing communities'.

[189] Civil Exchange (January 2015). Whose Society? The Final Big Society Audit.

[190] The Guardian (19 July 2010). Ed Miliband, quoted in Politics live blog.

[191] Financial Times (6 October 2010). Cameron's speech strongest on Big Society.

[192] Hardman, I. (2019). Why we get the wrong politicians.

[193] Haass, R. (December 2018). Europe in Disarray. Council on Foreign Relations.

[194] U.S. Department of the Interior U.S. Geological Survey (2013). Groundwater Depletion in the United States (1900-2008).

[195] USA Today (28 May 2012). Venezuela's PDVSA oil company is bloated, 'falling apart'.

[196] BBC News (5 September 2017). How Macquarie bank left Thames Water with extra £2bn debt.

[197] Morris, Z. S., Wooding, S., & Grant, J. (2012). The answer is 17 years, what is the question: understanding time lags in translational research.

[198] Royal Society of Arts (October 2015). Community Capital — The Value of Connected Communities

[199] Harrison-Broninski, K. (2005). Human interactions: The heart and soul of business process management: how people really work and how they can be helped to work better.

[200] www.england.nhs.uk/news/?filter-category=new-care-models

201 Niche Health and Social Care Consulting (March 2019). Evaluation of New Care Models in Mental Health.

202 Elliott, R. (2017). The economics of intensive care: the decision-maker's perspective.

203 www.healthconnectionsmendip.org/groups-we-run

204 Brown, M. (2018). Tackling loneliness and isolation reduces health bill.

205 Somerset Live (21 January 2019). These are the 'most deprived' neighbourhoods in Somerset.

206 Ministry of Housing, Communities & Local Government (30 September 2015). National Statistics File 7: all ranks, deciles and scores for the indices of deprivation, and population denominators

207 www.healthconnectionsmendip.org/resource-centre

208 Polley, M., Bertotti, M., Kimberlee, R., Pilkington, K., Refsum, C. (June 2017). A review of the evidence assessing impact of social prescribing on healthcare demand and cost implications.

209 University of Westminster (2018). Making sense of social prescribing.

210 Torjesen, I. (2016) Social Prescribing could help alleviate pressure on GPs.

211 The Low Commission (2015). The role of advice services in health outcomes: evidence review and mapping study.

212 World Health Organisation (2015). WHO global strategy on people-centred and integrated health services — Interim Report.

213 The Health Policy Partnership (2015). The state of play in person-centred care: A pragmatic review of how person-centred care is defined, applied and measured.

214 NHS England (2014). Multi-disciplinary Team Handbook.

[215] American Psychological Association (2006). Stress Weakens the Immune System.

[216] SafeLives (2014). Frequently asked questions — Multi-Agency Risk Assessment Conferences (MARAC).

[217] Robinson, A. (2013). A Risk-Led Approach to Domestic Violence: The MARAC Model in the UK.

[218] Wittgenstein, L. (1953). Philosophical Investigations.

[219] Warboys, B. (1995). The IPSE 2.5 Project: Process Modelling as the basis for a Support Environment.

[220] Standish Group (1994). Chaos Report 1994.

[221] Standish Group (2015). Chaos Report 2015.

[222] The New York Times (5 June 1992). 'Fifth Generation' Became Japan's Lost Generation.

[223] Ould, M.A., Roberts, C. (1986). Modelling iteration in the software process.

[224] Egeland, B. (2017). 5 Key Reasons Why Some Projects Succeed and Some Don't.

[225] Belbin, R.M. (2010). Management Teams — Why They Succeed or Fail.

[226] Maturana, H. R., and Varela, F. J. (1980). Autopoiesis and Cognition: The Realization of the Living.

[227] Margulis L, Lovelock J.E. (1989). Gaia and geognosis.

[228] Maturana, H. R., and Varela, F. J. (1987). The Tree of Knowledge.

[229] Winograd, T., Flores, F. (1986): Understanding Computers and Cognition: A New Foundation for Design.

[230] Clancey, W. J. (1987). Review of Winograd and Flores' understanding computers and cognition: A favorable interpretation.

231 Suchman, L. A. (1987). Speech Acts and Voices: Response to Winograd et al.

232 Medina-Mora, R., Winograd, T., Flores R., Flores, F. (1993). The action workflow approach to workflow management technology.

233 CBC News (21 June 2013). Prairie dogs' language decoded by scientists.

234 Putnam, R. D. (2000) Bowling Alone. The collapse and revival of American community.

235 Statista Research Department (2017). Most important employment factors when choosing jobs worldwide 2014.

236 Thibault, L. A., Schweyer, A., Whillans, A. (2017). Winning the War for Talent: Modern Motivational Methods for Attracting and Retaining Employees.

237 International Labour Organization (December 2019). Unemployment, total (% of total labor force).

238 Kahn, W.A. (1990). Psychological Conditions of Personal Engagement and Disengagement at Work.

239 Judge, T. A., Piccolo, R. F., Podsakoff, N. P., Shaw, J. C., Rich, B. L. (2010). The relationship between pay and job satisfaction: A meta-analysis of the literature.

240 Thibault, L. A., Schweyer, A., Whillans, A. (2017). Winning the War for Talent: Modern Motivational Methods for Attracting and Retaining Employees.

241 Achor, S. (2016). The Benefits of Peer-to-Peer Praise at Work.

242 O.C. Tanner Institute (2019). 2020 Global Culture Report.

243 World Health Organisation (28 May 2019). Burn-out an "occupational phenomenon": International Classification of Diseases.

244 Thibault, L. A., Schweyer, A., Whillans, A. (2017). Winning the War for Talent: Modern Motivational Methods for Attracting and Retain-

ing Employees.

[245] Thibault, L. A., Schweyer, A., Whillans, A. (2017). Winning the War for Talent: Modern Motivational Methods for Attracting and Retaining Employees.

[246] Volunteering England (2008). Volunteering and health: what impact does it have?

[247] www.timebanking.org/what-is-timebanking/what-is-timebanking

[248] International Labour Office (2011). Manual on the measurement of volunteer work.

[249] UN General Assembly (2001). Resolution on recommendations on support for volunteering, A/RES/56/38. Fifty-sixth session, New York, 2001.

[250] UN General Assembly (2005). Resolution on the Follow-up to the implementation of the International Year of Volunteers, A/RES/60/134. Sixtieth session, New York, 2005.

[251] www.probonoeconomics.com/about

[252] Haldane, A. (9 September 2014). In giving, how much do we receive? A Pro Bono Economics lecture to the Society of Business Economists, London.

[253] HM Treasury (4 September 2019). Policy paper — Spending Round 2019.

[254] Volunteering England (2008). Volunteering and health: what impact does it have?

[255] Knight, G., for Policy Exchange (2014). The Estate We're In — Lessons from the Front Line.

[256] Drucker, P. F. (2007). The essential Drucker: Selections from the management works.

[257] www.wardleypedia.org

[258] Shewhart, W.A. (1931). Economic Control of Quality of Manufac-

tured Product.

259 Moen, R. (2009). Foundation and History of the PDSA Cycle.

260 Boyd, J.R. (1987). Organic Design for Command and Control.

261 Watkins, A. (1925). Old straight track.

262 Defoe, D. (1724-1726). Vision of Britain, Letter 4, Part 2: Somerset and Wiltshire

263 www.intbau.org

264 The Prince's Foundation (2019). The Value of Community — An Evidence Informed Development Model.

265 Hanna, T. M. (2018). Our common wealth: The return of public ownership in the United States.

266 Schumacher, E.F. (1973). Small Is Beautiful: A Study of Economics As If People Mattered.

267 Legatum Institute (2017). Public opinion in the post-Brexit era: Economic attitudes in modern Britain.

268 Chang, H.-J. (2007). State-Owned Enterprise Reform.

269 Bel, G., Warner, M. (2008). Does Privatization of Solid Waste and Water Services Reduce Costs? A Review of Empirical Studies.

270 Flores-Macias, F., Musacchio A. (2009). The Return of State-Owned Enterprises.

271 Organisation for Economic Co-operation and Development (May 2014). Economic Surveys: Germany 2014.

272 www.communityhospitals.org.uk/defining-community-hospitals.html

273 Hanna, T. M. (2018). Our common wealth: The return of public ownership in the United States.

274 The Guardian (1 November 2018). Preston named as most improved city in UK.

[275] cles.org.uk/what-is-community-wealth-building/the-principles-of-community-wealth-building

[276] Chang, H.-J. (2012). 23 things they don't tell you about capitalism.

[277] Transnational Institute (2017). Reclaiming public services: How Cities and Citizens are Turning Back Privatisation.

[278] Wilkinson, R., Pickett, K. (2009). The Spirit Level — Why Equality is Better for Everyone.

[279] www.csdila.unimelb.edu.au/sis/Sustainability_Theories/Four_capital_model.html

[280] www.forumforthefuture.org/the-five-capitals

[281] www.sfu.ca/sustainabledevelopment/about-us.html

[282] www.rivervalley.k-state.edu/docs/Seven_Community_Capitals.pdf

[283] www.sustainablemeasures.com/Training/Indicators/Capital.html

[284] mycommunity.org.uk/resources/mapping-local-community-assets-online

[285] www.ottawaheart.ca/patients-visitors/tools-and-resources/find-wellness-resources-your-community

[286] Simmons, B. (2018). Community Engagement: Guidelines for Excellence.

[287] healthconnectionsmendip.org/category/arthritis

[288] www.towndigitalhub.info

[289] Locality, Local Government Association, National Association for Local Councils (2016). Making the most of assets – A guide for council officers and members.

[290] www.grassington.uk.com/grassington-hub/4564463593

[291] www.cilip.org.uk/news/421868/What-the-future-holds--the-

student-view.htm

292 https://insightmaker.com/article/186379/Fishing-economy

293 Forrester, J.W. (1971). World Dynamics.

294 Meadows, D. H. (1972). Limits to growth.

295 Meadows, D.H. (2008). Thinking in Systems.

296 Ridley, M. (1996). The Origins of Virtue.

297 www.socialechoes.info

298 www.socialenterprisemark.org.uk

299 en.wikipedia.org/wiki/B_Corporation_(certification)

300 Chang, H.-J. (2012). 23 things they don't tell you about capitalism.

301 Ruck, D. J., Bentley, R. A., & Lawson, D. J. (January 01, 2018). Religious change preceded economic change in the 20th century. Science Advances, 4, 7.)

302 Mishneh Torah, Hilkhot matanot aniyim ("Laws about Giving to Poor People"), Chapter 10:7–14.

303 bin Nordin, M.Z.F., binti Mustaffa, C.S. (2013) An Analysis of Waqaf and Zakat Information in Friday Sermons, Journal of Middle Eastern and Islamic Studies (in Asia), 7:2, 96-120.

304 Smietana, B., Churchgoers Say They Tithe, But Not Always to the Church, lifewayresearch.com, USA, 10 May 2018

305 Canon 222, Code of Canon Law, http://www.vatican.va/archive/cod-iuris-canonici/eng/documents/cic_lib2-cann208-329_en.html

306 Ricardo, D. (1817). On the Principles of Political Economy and Taxation.

307 King, M. A. (2016). End of alchemy: Money, banking, and the future of the global economy.

[308] Hudson, M. (2018). ... And forgive them their debts: Lending, foreclosure and redemption from Bronze Age finance to the Jubilee Year.

[309] Middleton, G. D. (2012). Nothing Lasts Forever: Environmental Discourses on the Collapse of Past Societies. Journal of Archaeological Research. 20 (3): 257–307.

[310] Drews, R. (1993). The End of the Bronze Age: Changes in Warfare and the Catastrophe ca. 1200 B.C.

[311] Story, L., Dash, E. (30 July 2009). Bankers Reaped Lavish Bonuses During Bailouts.

[312] Mazzucato, M. (2016). Value of everything: Making and taking in the global economy.

[313] Edelman (2017). 2017 Edelman Trust Barometer.

[314] Freeman, R. E., Harrison, J. S., Wicks, A. C., Parmar, B. L., & Colle, S. (2014). Stakeholder theory: The state of the art.

[315] Community Economic Development (2015). Guide to community finance.

[316] Securities Industry and Financial Markets Association (2019). SIFMA Capital Markets Fact Book 2019.

[317] Wharton University of Pennsylvania (28 October 2019). Untapped Opportunities: How Is Impact Investing Poised to Grow?

[318] Global Impact Investing Network (2019). Sizing the Impact Investing Market.

[319] Jones, M. (15 October 2019). For ESG investors, the newest challenge is separating fact from 'greenwashing'.

[320] Social Finance (2016). Social Impact Bonds – The Early Years.

[321] Brookings Institution Global Impact Bond Database. Brookings Impact Bonds Snapshot – January 1, 2019.

[322] Boggild-Jones, I., Gustafsson-Wright E. (2 January 2019). A global

snapshot: Impact bonds in 2018.

323 Townsend, B. (2017). From SRI to ESG: The Origins of Socially Responsible and Sustainable Investing.

324 Edmiston, D., Nicholls, A. (2017). Social Impact Bonds: The Role of Private Capital in Outcome-Based Commissioning.

325 Edmiston, D., Nicholls, A. (2017). Social Impact Bonds: The Role of Private Capital in Outcome-Based Commissioning.

326 Roy, M.J., McHugh, N., Sinclair, S. (2018). A Critical Reflection on Social Impact Bonds.

327 www.stakeitback.com

328 UK Financial Services and Markets Act 2000 (Regulated Activities) Order 2001, No. 544, PART III (Specified Investments)

329 Financial Conduct Authority (July 2019). Guidance on Cryptoassets – Feedback and Final Guidance to CP 19/3 (Policy Statement PS19/22).

330 The Economist (2019). The World in 2020.

331 www.supercommunities.info

332 Hastie, R., & Dawes, R. M. (2001). Rational choice in an uncertain world: The psychology of judgement and decision making.

333 Block, P. (2018). Community.

334 Weisbord, M.R., Janoff, S. (2007). Don't Just Do Something, Stand There! Ten Principles for Leading Meetings That Matter.

335 Cox, A. D., Cox, D., & Anderson, R. D. (January 01, 2005). Reassessing the pleasures of store shopping. Journal of Business Research, 58, 3, 250-259.

336 "Research: Ads increasingly pull heartstrings", 27 October 2020, https://advanced-television.com/2020/10/27/research-ads-having-more-emotional-negative-impact

[337] Bainbridge, D. (2009). Teenagers: A Natural History.

[338] Kelley, W.M. (20 May 1962). If You're Woke You Dig It.

[339] Mazzucato, M. (2016). Value of everything: Making and taking in the global economy.

[340] Becker, G.S. (1981). A Treatise on the Family.

Index

About the Author

You can reach the author through his website: www.harrison-broninski.info

KEITH HARRISON-BRONINSKI wrote "Human Interactions" (Meghan-Kiffer Press, 2005), described as "the overarching framework for 21st century business technology". Using the principles for cross-boundary collaboration that he developed, Keith has given conference keynotes worldwide, contributed to other books and research, and led award-winning social enterprises for healthcare innovation, wellness, and community finance. His current focus is helping build stronger communities across the world through social trading.

Keith has also released six jazz, classical, and traditional folk albums.

Figure 53: Author, February 2021

Watch for forthcoming titles.

Meghan-Kiffer Press
Tampa, Florida, USA
www.mkpress.com
Innovation at the Intersection of Business and Technology

Printed in Great Britain
by Amazon

56945887R00237